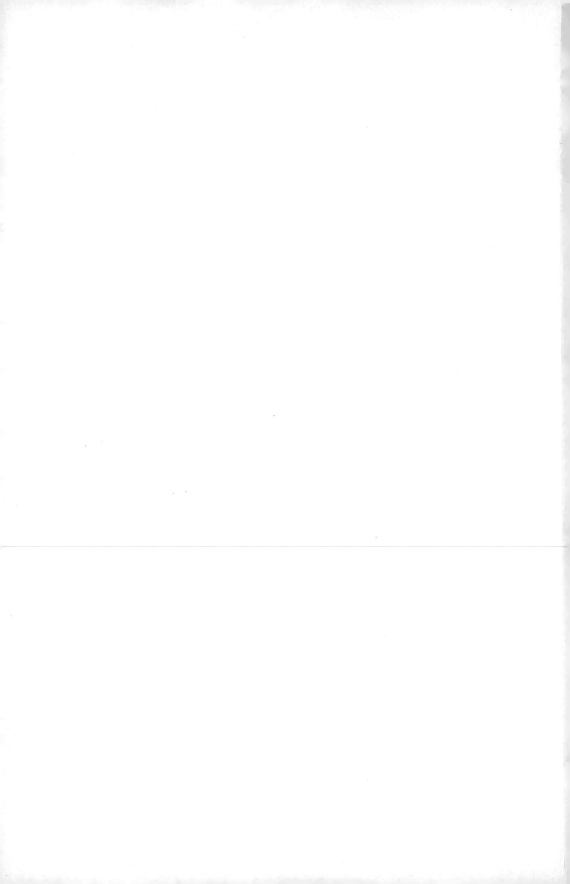

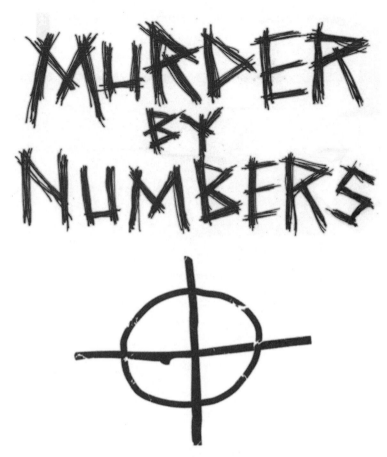

MURDER BY NUMBERS

FASCINATING FIGURES BEHIND
THE WORLD'S WORST CRIMES

JAMES MOORE

The
History
Press

First published 2018

The History Press
The Mill, Brimscombe Port
Stroud, Gloucestershire, GL5 2QG
www.thehistorypress.co.uk

British Library Cataloguing in Publication Data.
A catalogue record for this book is available from the British Library.

ISBN 978 0 7509 8145 3

Typesetting and origination by The History Press
Printed and bound in Great Britain by TJ International Ltd

CONTENTS

ACKNOWLEDGEMENTS

Numerous people gave their help and support to make this book possible, but I'd particularly like to thank Tamsin Moore, Laurie Moore, Alex Moore, Philippa Moore, Geoffrey Moore, Sam Moore, Dr Lana Matile Moore, Dr Tom Moore, Dr Claire Nesbitt, Jan Hebditch, Daniel Simister, Sarah Sarkhel, Jim Addison, Samm Taylor, Judi James, Peter Spurgeon, Fran Bowden, Martin Phillips, Robert Smith and Mark Beynon.

James Moore
Gloucestershire, 2017

INTRODUCTION

Sherlock Holmes was obsessed by numbers. 'It is a simple calculation enough,' he said, while explaining one of his conclusions in *A Study in Scarlet*, the first of Arthur Conan Doyle's works to feature the great fictional detective. In the story, Holmes works out the height of a man from measuring the length of his stride and the writing on a wall, while estimating his age from the size of a puddle over which he has jumped. Numbers run through his adventures from the mysterious 'five orange pips' to the bizarre smashing of the 'six busts of Napoleon'. Even the number of the address at which Holmes lived, 221B Baker Street, has become world famous. His most notorious foe, Moriarty, was a master mathematician.

Agatha Christie, who gave us Miss Marple and Hercule Poirot, loved numbers too. Her most acclaimed novel, *And Then There Were None*, revolves around the number ten in a tale that chillingly parallels the fate of those in the nursery rhyme 'Ten Little Indians'. In 2015 a group of scientists even collected data on methods, motives and locations from twenty-six of Christie's works and were able to come up with a formula enabling readers to identify who the culprit is before the author herself reveals the killer. Among the fascinating findings was that if the setting was a country house there was a 75 per cent chance the murderer would be female.

Numbers also provide the key to real-life crimes, especially murders. This book examines in thrilling, and often graphic, detail how numbers provide the backdrop to some of the most fascinating cases from history.

Motives for murder may often involve sex or revenge, but money is often at the root of homicide, and whether the numbers involved are small or large, they can be both shocking and revealing – often giving police vital leads too.

From the moment a murder is committed, numbers are at the heart of any investigation. In forensics, medical examiners aim to identify the time of death, looking at factors such as body temperature and rigor mortis. They determine the number of wounds on a victim and perhaps their length and depth, as well as taking the physical measurements of the corpse and estimating the person's age. All these are recorded in digits.

In murders involving firearms, ballistics experts may seek to identify the calibre of a weapon used or calculate the angle of trajectory at which a bullet struck its victim. They use mathematical formulas to calculate the twist of the barrel and might even weigh ammunition, looking for vital information.

Toxicology tests can reveal how much poison is in a body, while measuring hairs or fibres found at a murder scene can be highly revealing, as can figures relating to the distribution of blood. Even shoe size or, for that matter, the age of pollen on an item of footwear, can reveal an important number. So can the length of time insects have been at work on a body. DNA evidence can provide startling statistics when it comes to determining whether an individual should be ruled in or out of an enquiry.

Detectives also pore over numbers as they try and crack cases, studying the measurements taken at a crime scene, for instance, to get a picture of what happened. They'll log timings of a victim's or suspect's movements too. They may seek to discover the number of victims linked to a single killer or note the typical height or age of victims when analysing a murderer's modus operandi. Knowing the murderer's own age and build could be equally crucial to tracking them down.

Numbers found on cars, weapons, clothes, tickets or phones can often provide the important breakthroughs in investigations. Then there are the numbers that reveal the scale of police enquiries – interviews conducted, calls logged, fingerprint records checked and so on.

The influence of numbers does not end when the investigation is wrapped up. Numbers continue to be vital when it comes to proving a case in court, with juries asked, for example, to weigh up probabilities expressed in numbers as they make their deliberations about whether the accused is guilty. Even where someone has been condemned to death, their executioners may have had to make careful calculations to ensure a swift and 'humane' death.

Sometimes, the startling figures in murder stories relate to how long it has taken for a body to come to light or the length of time it has taken to find the culprit. Often, despite the best efforts of investigators, cases continue to go unsolved, leaving behind only the stark and intriguing numbers involved.

Certain murderers have even been obsessed with particular numbers, while other cases are bound up with mysterious numerological associations. Occasionally, numbers reveal disturbing and puzzling coincidences between crimes.

Murder by Numbers looks at some of the fascinating statistics behind the phenomenon of murder, including its incidence as well as the nature of killers and their victims. It has been estimated that the number of people who have ever lived is around 108 billion. No one knows exactly how many of those have been murdered, but according to the World Health Organisation, in modern times a person is murdered every sixty seconds. This book covers hundreds of specific murders from across the centuries – a selection that affirms Sherlock Holmes' sage observation that when it comes to crime, 'There is nothing new under the sun, it has all been done before.'

According to the Bible, the world's first murderer was Cain, the son of Adam and Eve, who slew his own brother Abel in cold blood:

> Now Cain said to his brother Abel, 'Let's go out to the field.' While they were in the field, Cain attacked his brother Abel and killed him.
>
> Genesis 4:8

The story goes that Cain, a farmer, and Abel, a shepherd, both made sacrifices to God, but that the Almighty favoured Abel's. A furious Cain then murdered his brother.

Science, however, has highlighted other early victims of intentional slaughter going right back to our ancient ancestors. In 1991 a mummified body was found in melting ice high in the Italian Alps. It was originally thought to have been of a dead mountaineer. On closer examination by experts, the corpse turned out to be more than 5,000 years old. Dubbed 'Ötzi the Iceman', this Bronze Age body was remarkably well preserved, allowing numerous tests to be undertaken. Initially it was thought that Ötzi might have frozen to death, but thanks to a CT scan it emerged that he had an arrow wound in his left shoulder. Further analysis showed that the victim had also suffered a blow to the head and appeared to have suffered defensive injuries to his hands.

Whether Ötzi died from the head injury or bled to death, he had clearly met a violent end at the hands of another. But his was by no means the first homicide. Archaeologists have found evidence of the slaying of a Neanderthal male who lived around 50,000 years ago. Known as 'Shanidar-3', the victim had a cut on one of his left ribs that suggests that he was intentionally killed with a spear. An even earlier murder victim appears to have been found buried deep in Spain's Atapuerca Mountains at a location known as the 'pit of bones'. This cavern is located down a 43ft chimney only accessible after scrambling through a cave system. Over a twenty-year period, painstaking excavations have so far unearthed the remains of twenty-eight skeletons at the site belonging to the species *Homo heidelbergensis*, an early human ancestor pre-dating the Neanderthals.

One skull, belonging to a young adult and dating back some 430,000 years, was carefully reassembled from fifty-two separate pieces. Cranium 17 turned out to be of particular fascination when it was found to have two gaping holes above the left eye socket. Scientists applied modern forensic techniques, including 3D imaging and a CT scan, to the skull and compared the fractures to modern cases of injury. They determined that the wounds had occurred before death but that they did not seem to have been the result of a fall. Nor did they show any signs of healing. The holes were a similar shape and seemed to have been inflicted with a blunt instrument striking at different angles. These multiple blows suggested violence administered face-to-face. Either strike, perhaps by a wooden spear or stone hand-axe, would probably have been fatal. The conclusion was that the victim was intentionally hit twice over the head before being purposely plunged down the hole. This, the earliest case of homicide so far identified, suggests that murder was a behaviour associated with our earliest origins.

Recognition that the crime was something abhorrent goes a long way back too. The earliest-known recorded law against murder comes from the Sumerian Code of Ur-Nammu, set down on clay tablets sometime between 2100 and 2050 BC. It states that 'If a man commits a murder, that man must be killed.' The earliest recorded murder trial comes from another clay tablet dating to just a little later, 1850 BC. It was recovered from the same region of modern-day Iraq and reveals that three men, from the city of Nippur, were accused of murdering a temple official. They told his wife that her husband was dead, but perhaps under pressure, she stayed quiet about the crime. Somehow the killing came to light. The case was first brought before King Ur-Ninurta, who sent the three culprits and the woman for trial in front of the Citizens Assembly in Nippur. There was much debate as to whether the woman was guilty as an accessory. In the end, however, it was only the three men who were found guilty of murder and executed. Symbolically, their punishment was carried out in front of a chair belonging to the dead man.

One of the first murder victims we can name is the pharaoh Rameses III, whose throat was cut by an assassin in 1155 BC. Before long, cases of serial killers were being recorded too. Roman writer Pliny the Elder recorded that, in 56 BC, Calpurnius Bestia was accused of murdering a string of wives by rubbing the poison aconite into their genitalia. In the same era, in what is modern-day Sri Lanka, Queen Anula of Anuradhapura poisoned several

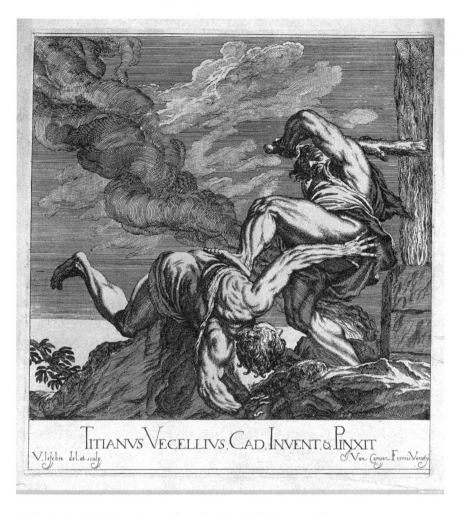

Cain and Abel. (Courtesy of Wellcome Library, London)

husbands who weren't to her liking, and was eventually burned alive for her crimes. A man from Yemen, Zu Shenatir, is known to have raped a series of young boys in the fifth century AD, after luring them to his house with promises of food and money. He then threw them to their deaths out of a window. Shenatir's killing spree ended when one boy, named Zerash, managed to stab him before avoiding the same fate.

2 ... missing bodies, in the case of the 'Princes in the Tower'

During July 1674 workmen were demolishing a ruinous turret and staircase at the Tower of London. In the rubble, at the foot of some old stairs once used as a private entrance for the royal chapel, they found an intriguing wooden chest. Inside were two skeletons, seemingly of two young boys. One would have stood about 4ft 10in tall; the other, 4ft 6in. Still clinging to the bones were traces of aristocratic velvet. Word soon went round that these were the remains of murdered royalty.

Following the death of Edward IV in 1483, Richard, Duke of Gloucester, had seized the throne of England, while his nephews, the 12-year-old Edward V and 9-year-old Richard, Duke of York, were thrown in the Tower of London, never to be seen again. After Richard III himself was killed at the Battle of Bosworth in 1485, his successor, Henry VII, let it be known that the princes had been killed on Richard's orders. Indeed, Tudor writer Thomas More said that one of Richard's men, Sir James Tyrrell, had confessed to carrying out the crime before his execution for treason in 1502. More had even given a clue as to the whereabouts of the bodies, stating that they were buried at the foot of a set of stairs under some stones. Now, it appeared, they had turned up after nearly 200 years.

Physicians who examined the skeletons on behalf of Charles II pronounced that they were indeed the princes, and the king ordered that the bodies be interred in a marble urn at the Henry VII Lady Chapel in Westminster Abbey. But that wasn't the end of the story. In 1933, under pressure from those who believed Richard III was innocent of the murder, the authorities agreed that the bodies could be disinterred and examined. Two medical experts found that the bones matched the ages of the princes at the time of their disappearance and that the velvet found with them was from the correct period. They also found evidence that the older individual had been suffering from an infection of the jaw (Edward was known to be unwell) and even that he might have been suffocated. They could not, however, establish the gender of the bodies, and subsequent analysis of the findings in the 1950s led to scepticism about their conclusions. By this time the bodies had been reinterred, and despite a more recent campaign for the bones to undergo DNA testing, both the Church of England and the Queen have refused

The Princes in the Tower. (Courtesy of Wellcome Library, London)

permission for further forensic analysis, leaving their identity – and the exact fate of the boys – a much-debated mystery.

The disappearance of the princes remains the ultimate cold case. But it is not the only instance where murder has been assumed, and a culprit accused, without a body. Indeed, there have been many convictions in the absence of a corpse. In the United States there have been more than 250 trials without a body, dating as far back as 1843 when several crew members of the ship *Sarah Lavinia* were found guilty of throwing shipmate Walter Nicoll overboard.

In Britain, however, one infamous seventeenth-century scandal meant that the presence of a cadaver would effectively become an essential prerequisite in order to prosecute murder for three centuries. On 16 August 1660, 70-year-old estate manager William Harrison set out from his home in Chipping Campden, Gloucestershire, to collect rents at a nearby village. When Harrison failed to return home that night, his wife sent servant John Perry to look for him. It seemed there was no trace of Harrison, apart from some bloodstained clothes found on a nearby road. When suspicion fell on Perry himself, he suddenly accused his own brother and mother of murdering Harrison for money. A year later all three were found guilty and hanged for the crime. Yet, in 1662 Harrison sensationally turned up alive, claiming to have been abducted and sold into slavery.

The 'Campden Wonder', as it became known, led to the adoption of a 'no body rule', but that began to change in the twentieth century. A landmark case in 1954 concerned decorated Polish soldier Michael Onufrejczyk, who had decided to stay in Britain after the Second World War and run a farm. He took on fellow Pole Stanislaw Sykut as a business partner. But when the pair fell out over money, Sykut mysteriously vanished from the property. Onufrejczyk maintained that Sykut had returned to Poland. Suspicious, police found 2,000 tiny bloodstains at the farm, but no body. Nevertheless, amid rumours that Sykut had been slain and fed to the farm pigs, Onufrejczyk was charged with the killing and convicted of murder, going on to serve a life sentence.

The ensuing decades have seen many more convictions in cases without a corpse, but there have continued to be some notable miscarriages of justice too. In 1982 Lindy Chamberlain was convicted of murdering her 9-week-old daughter Azaria in the Australian Outback despite her pleas that a dingo had taken the baby. In 1987 she was given a pardon after some of Azaria's bloodied clothing was found near a dingo's den. Those who believe Richard III did not slay the princes in the tower are still hopeful that new evidence might emerge to clear the monarch of murder.

3 ... times that murderer John Lee was unsuccessfully hanged

Many people have got away with murder over the centuries, but some evaded the death penalty even after being caught and convicted. In the past a killer could be given a reprieve if their execution failed, with the event usually deemed to be a sign of divine intervention. There was, for instance, the case of Maggie Dickson, hanged in Edinburgh for infanticide in 1724. She was left dangling from the end of a rope for thirty minutes, but for some reason had survived the ordeal. Maggie was later found to be alive, after knocking was heard from inside her coffin. She was given a full pardon.

Like all forms of capital punishment, hanging is, of course, an expert business, and even by the nineteenth century professional executioners could get things badly wrong. James Berry hanged 131 people during his time as an official public executioner and helped refine the so-called 'long drop' method, where the height and weight of the condemned individual were taken into account in order to establish how much slack would be needed in the rope to break their neck. This was deemed a 'cleaner' end than death by strangulation, which was often the result of a hanging. However, the long drop technique was still in its infancy. In November 1885, Berry oversaw the hanging of wife murderer Robert Goodale at Norwich, but the calculations were flawed and the culprit was decapitated by the rope.

It was a very different problem that had led to the botched execution of convicted murderer John Lee earlier the same year, with Berry again overseeing proceedings. Lee, 20, had been found guilty of slitting the throat of his employer, Emma Keyse, at her home in Babbacombe, Devon – albeit on flimsy evidence. He was due to be hanged on 23 February at Exeter Prison, and Berry duly tested his equipment beforehand, including the trapdoor through which Lee was set to plunge. As was traditional, Lee emerged from his cell at 8 a.m. that day and was led to the gallows. A belt was tied around his ankles, a hood put over his head, then the rope placed around his neck. Asked if he had any last words, Lee said calmly, 'No, drop away.' Berry duly pulled the lever. Nothing happened. Lee was led away and the mechanism tested again. It worked perfectly. Lee was brought back and the lever was pulled a second time. Again, nothing happened. With both Lee and Berry now frantic, the whole exercise was repeated a third time, only to end without a hanging. The whole execution was temporarily called off. The home secretary, Sir William Harcourt, became involved and soon decided to commute Lee's sentence to life. He would serve twenty-two years in jail.

Lee was dubbed 'the man they couldn't hang'. Yet Lee's case was not the first. Australian Joseph Samuel, convicted of murdering policeman Joseph Luker in 1803, was hanged near Sydney three times, but on each occasion the rope unravelled or snapped. The country's governor intervened and also decided that the guilty man should serve life imprisonment instead of being executed a fourth time.

A different kind of escape from the noose occurred in the case of Reginald Woolmington. A jury at the Bristol Assizes had taken just 69 minutes to find the 21-year-old guilty of murder, and he was sentenced to death on 14 February 1935. He had been convicted of killing his 17-year-old estranged wife, Violet, in what appeared to be a crime of passion. Violet had left Woolmington, running away to her mother's home, but Reginald was desperate to get her back. Reginald went to Violet's mother's house in Milborne Port, Somerset, and when Violet refused to return with him she was shot through the heart. Woolmington was quickly arrested, charged and even told police, 'I done it.'

The farm labourer had admitted that he'd brought a shotgun to the house, but he maintained that he had not intended to shoot Violet and had actually meant to kill himself with it if she could not be persuaded to renew their relationship. The gun, Woolmington said, had gone off by mistake, killing the woman he loved. The judge who condemned him to death had directed the jury that it was the job of Woolmington's defence to demonstrate that the shooting was accidental. But, after the verdict, an appeal was brought and the case eventually came before the House of Lords. It found that 'No matter what the charge or where the trial, the principle that the prosecution must prove the guilt of the prisoner is part of the common law of England.' Woolmington was acquitted in what would become a defining moment in English law regarding the presumption of innocence in cases of murder.

4 ... assassins who murdered Thomas Becket

Thomas Becket was not the only person to be savagely murdered in a cathedral. In 1478 Giuliano de' Medici, co-ruler of Renaissance Florence, was stabbed to death during High Mass inside the city's *duomo* as part of a failed conspiracy to overthrow him and his brother. But it is Becket's death, in Canterbury Cathedral, on the evening of 29 December 1170, that is much better known today. At the time it sent shock waves through medieval Europe, and his murder remains the most notorious of the period.

'Will no one rid me of this turbulent priest?' Henry II's famous frustrated plea came after the king of England had finally lost all patience with Becket, his former friend. Henry had ascended to the throne at just 21, in 1154, and soon appointed Becket as chancellor – effectively his right-hand man – on the advice of the then Archbishop of Canterbury, Theobald. Becket, the son of a London merchant, had been Theobald's own clerk and shown himself to be highly competent. Henry was initially delighted with the choice. Becket reliably carried out the king's bidding and the pair spent time carousing and hunting together.

It was only when Henry made a reluctant Becket take up the position of Archbishop of Canterbury, in 1162, that the trouble began. Becket had never been a priest, but once in England's most senior ecclesiastical post he promptly resigned as chancellor, became increasingly devout and a strident defender of Church power. Rather than helping Henry control the institution as the monarch had hoped, Becket became a thorn in his side. The pair clashed over issues such as the right of clergy to be tried by the Church's own courts, and Becket incurred the king's wrath by excommunicating one of his senior barons. When Henry tried to put Becket on trial, the Archbishop fled abroad.

In December 1170, the two factions reached an accommodation, but when Becket returned to England to resume his position he immediately excommunicated three bishops appointed by Henry. The king, in Normandy at the time, was irate. He may not have used the exact words of the much-repeated line above, but contemporary chroniclers recorded that he spoke angrily of being 'treated with such shameful contempt by a low-born clerk' and asked why no one had 'avenged' him.

Depiction of the Thomas Becket murder. (Courtesy of Wellcome Library, London)

It might not have been meant as a call to action, but four impressionable knights who were present certainly got that idea. William de Tracy, Reginald fitz Urse, Hugh de Morville and Richard le Breton rushed to England determined to teach Becket a lesson. At Canterbury Cathedral they confronted the archbishop, trying to take him prisoner. He refused, saying, 'I am prepared to die for Christ and for His Church.'

First they tried to drag Becket outside, but he clung to a pillar in the north-west transept of the cathedral. The first to strike him was de Tracy, who gave Becket a glancing blow to the head with his sword. As de Morville held back onlookers, the other three knights rained down more blows on their victim. A final blow by le Breton smote off the top of the archbishop's head – his brains spilling out as he collapsed on to the stone floor. It was delivered with such force that the weapon shattered into pieces.

The killers fled. When Henry heard what they'd done, he is said to have been filled with remorse, admitting that his 'incautious words' might have been to blame. There was widespread shock and anger at Becket's murder, and he became seen by worshippers all over the continent as a martyr. His tomb in Canterbury was soon a place of pilgrimage. In 1173 Becket was canonised by Pope Alexander III. In such a climate Henry was forced to do public penance at Becket's tomb by walking to it barefoot in a smock whilst being whipped.

So what of the four actual culprits? For a year they holed up in Knaresborough Castle in Yorkshire. Henry did not have them arrested but neither did he lift a finger to help them. When they were excommunicated by the pope, all four travelled to Rome in a bid to gain forgiveness. The pope exiled them to the Holy Land for fourteen years. No one is sure of their fate after that. Some said they died in Flanders as hermits. There were many other stories, but it's likely that they died within a few years, while still in the Middle East. Twenty years after Becket's murder, chronicler Roger Howden claimed to have found their graves in Jerusalem inscribed with the epitaph: 'Here lie those wretches who martyred Blessed Thomas, Archbishop of Canterbury.'

5 ... feet long – the bath that convicted serial killer George Smith

On 9 July 1912, Bessie Mundy bought a 5ft cast-iron bath for £1, 17s, 6d, successfully haggling the price down from £2. Little did she know that, within days, it would become the instrument of her murder.

Bessie's 'husband' was picture restorer Henry Williams. She possessed a large inheritance, and had originally married Henry two years earlier in Weymouth. It wasn't his real name. He was in fact George Smith, a 40-year-old serial bigamist with a history of conning women into marrying him and then absconding with their cash and belongings. After disappearing for eighteen months with some of her money, Williams resurfaced. The pair reconciled and took up lodgings in Herne Bay, Kent. Smith had discovered that to get his hands on Bessie's full £2,500 fortune, held in a trust, she would have to make a will in his favour, and this was duly arranged on 8 July.

Over the next few days Smith twice took Bessie, 33, to a doctor. She had complained of headaches, but Smith told Dr Frank French that she had been suffering from 'fits'. French could find little wrong, prescribing sedatives. Then, on the morning of 13 July, a note from Smith was delivered to French with some dramatic news – his wife was dead, having apparently drowned in the bath while he was out. French rushed over and found Bessie submerged in the new tub, still clutching a bar of soap. He found no evidence of a struggle and put her death down to an epileptic fit. Within a few months Smith inherited all her money. The bath was returned to the ironmonger for a full refund.

By November 1913, Smith had married another woman, 25-year-old nurse Alice Burnham. A month later the couple went on honeymoon to Blackpool where they stayed in a boarding house. Again Smith took her to the doctor with headaches. Three days later, on 12 December, he apparently went upstairs and discovered that his wife had died in the bath. An inquest found that Alice had drowned after fainting. Smith collected £500 in life insurance.

No connection between the two deaths was made until January 1915, when the police were contacted by Alice's father who, from newspaper reports, had noticed the similarity between his daughter's death and a third, that of 38-year-old Margaret Lloyd of Highgate, London. She had died in similar circumstances, in her bath, having been found by her husband, John Lloyd, just one day after their marriage on 18 December 1914.

Police intercepted Lloyd at a solicitor's office where he was due to discuss Margaret's £700 life insurance policy, and it soon became clear that he and George Smith were one and the same. He was arrested. Further enquiries by Detective Inspector Arthur Neil made the connection with Bessie's death in Kent.

Renowned pathologist Bernard Spilsbury was called in to help determine how the women had drowned. Spilsbury had established his reputation with the 1910 Dr Crippen case (see page 20). His work had also brought arsenic poisoner Frederick Seddon to justice in 1912. The 'Brides in the Bath' case would cement Spilsbury's fame.

The bodies of all three women were now exhumed. Spilsbury could find no signs of violence or poison. He asked for the bathtubs in which the women had died to be sent up to London for examination. Spilsbury considered whether the women might have died from epileptic fits. He considered the shape and measurements of the baths. Bessie's was just 5ft long – considerably shorter than her height, at 5ft 7in. The tub tapered at the foot end and at the time of her death it had just 9in of water in it. If she had really died from drowning as a result of an epileptic fit, Spilsbury figured that the stiffening and extension of her legs would have pushed her head up out of the water, not underneath it. However, towards the end of a fit the muscles relax, in which case why had she still been holding the bar of soap when Dr French found her?

Experiments using an experienced female swimmer were conducted and Spilsbury concluded that the only way to have drowned the victims, without signs of a struggle, was to have suddenly pulled them under the surface of the water by the ankles. When this was done with the swimmer in question, water had rushed into her nostrils and mouth. She became unconscious and had to be revived.

At Smith's trial in June 1915 the bath itself was brought into the courtroom so that Spilsbury could demonstrate his theories. It was enough to convince the jury of the defendant's guilt and Smith was convicted and hanged that August.

6 ... crucial letters in the telegraph that caught a killer

'Have strong suspicions that Crippen, London cellar murderer and accomplice are among saloon passengers. Moustache taken off, growing beard. Accomplice dressed as a boy. Voice, manner and build undoubtedly a girl.'

This message, sent at 3 p.m. on 22 July 1910, via the new wonder of the Marconi wireless telegraph machine, came from Captain Kendall, skipper of the SS *Montrose*. He had become convinced that aboard his ship, which was making its way across the Atlantic to Canada, were Dr Hawley Harvey Crippen and his lover, Ethel Le Neve. The couple were wanted for the murder of Crippen's wife, Cora, who had suddenly vanished that February. Crippen had claimed that his adulterous wife, a musical hall singer, had left him and subsequently died of natural causes in America. But Cora's friends raised their concerns with police after seeing Le Neve wearing Mrs Crippen's clothes and jewellery. Police interviewed Dr Crippen and searched his London home but could find nothing. Rashly, Crippen and Le Neve then fled the country, prompting detectives to search the house again. This time, under the basement floor, they found a dismembered human torso, with traces of poison, and put out urgent arrest warrants for the runaway pair, whom they now believed responsible for Cora's murder. Recognising his fugitive passengers from a newspaper report, Kendall's prompt alert gave police the chance to board a faster ship across the ocean and intercept Crippen and Le Neve as they arrived in Quebec. Crippen, who maintained his innocence to the end, was convicted of murdering Cora and hanged on 23 November at Pentonville Prison. Le Neve, charged as an accessory, was acquitted.

Crippen's capture was made possible through the new 'ship to shore' telegraph, but this was not the first time similar technology had been used to catch a killer. In fact a pioneering electric telegraph system had proved crucial in a murder case more than half a century earlier.

On 1 January 1845, a Mrs Ashley of Salt Hill, Slough, was alerted by screaming from the adjoining cottage. Going next door, she found her neighbour Sarah Hart lying on the floor, frothing at the mouth. Mrs Ashley had also seen a man in a distinctive Quaker-style coat disappearing down the road. Sarah had been poisoned with prussic acid, added to her glass of

DR. CRIPPEN AND MISS LE NEVE.

Crippen on trial. (Courtesy of Wellcome Library, London)

beer. She died almost immediately. The alarm was raised and a Reverend Champnes raced to the local station, suspecting that the killer, dressed in the distinctive clothes of a Quaker, would try and make his getaway by rail. Sure enough, Champnes arrived just in time to see the man boarding the 7.42 p.m. train to London. Champnes informed the station master, who seized the opportunity to use the new electric telegraph machine at his disposal. The new equipment, patented by two English scientists in 1837, involved needles that pointed to different letters on a board. Introduced primarily as a means of improving safety on the railway, it would now be used to alert police that a suspected murderer was on the way to the capital. A message was sent stating that the man in question would be arriving on a train to Paddington in the second first-class carriage. However, the machine was unable to transmit the word Q and so the message read that the suspect was in the garb of a 'KWAKER'. After being asked to repeat the message several times by the London operator, it was eventually understood that these six letters were in fact meant to read 'Quaker'. Armed with this description, local police successfully identified the suspect, wearing his long brown coat, as he left the train. He was followed and later arrested.

He was John Tawell, a man who had already cheated the noose once in 1814 after being found in possession of forged notes from a Quaker-owned bank. The Society of Friends, of which he would become a member, had interceded then to get him the lesser sentence of being transported to Australia, where he had gone on to become a wealthy businessman. Tawell later returned to England with his family. However, he had then begun an affair with Sarah Hart, a nurse, fathering two illegitimate children by her. When Tawell's wife died, rather than marrying Sarah, he had wed a Quaker widow. Worrying that his secret family might be exposed, Tawell decided to poison his mistress. At Tawell's trial in Aylesbury, Buckinghamshire, his laughable defence was that Sarah had not been poisoned at all but had died after eating too many pips from apples, which contain tiny amounts of cyanide. Tawell was swiftly convicted and hanged.

There seems little doubt that Tawell was guilty and had been brought to justice speedily thanks to advances in science. Ironically, however, new techniques would cast doubt on Crippen's conviction more than 100 years after he went to the gallows. DNA tests on skin samples presented at the original trial, conducted at Michigan State University in 2007, apparently showed that the body found by police at Crippen's home was male.

7... pounds – how much serial killers Burke and Hare were paid for their first body

In the Greyfriars Kirkyard in Edinburgh there are two graves covered in strange ironwork cages, dating back to the early 1800s. Known as mortsafes, these devices were once widespread throughout cemeteries. They afforded some protection against grave robbers aiming to steal bodies of the recently deceased in order to sell them on for dissection in what was, by the start of the nineteenth century, a lucrative business. Body-snatching has been with us for centuries, with physicians keen to get their hands on fresh corpses to identify how human anatomy works but often thwarted by the legal and religious restrictions of their times. In Britain, the Murder Act of 1752 allowed for the remains of hanged killers to be given over for dissection, but with the burgeoning of medical science, there were still simply not enough dead criminals to keep up with the growth in demand from surgeons. By the turn of the century body-snatching had become rife, with many in the medical profession prepared to pay tidy sums for cadavers to so-called 'resurrectionists' without asking many questions about their provenance.

Two of the first people to hit upon the idea that murder might provide a better resource of bodies than pilfering them from churchyards were Helen Torrence and Jean Waldie. In the same year as the Murder Act came into force, they went to the gallows in Edinburgh having smothered 9-year-old John Dallas and sold his body to a doctor for 2s. It would take another eighty years before William Burke and William Hare would turn this deadly concept into a fully fledged business.

In November 1827 the Irish-born pair were hard up and living at a boarding house run by Hare's wife, Margaret, in the city's West Port. When an elderly lodger called Donald died of natural causes still owing rent, they came up with a plan to make up for the shortfall. Stuffing his real coffin with bark, Burke and Hare put the old soldier's body into a tea-chest and hauled it round to the back door of Dr Robert Knox, a distinguished anatomy lecturer. He paid them £7 10s for the body – more than they could hope to earn in months.

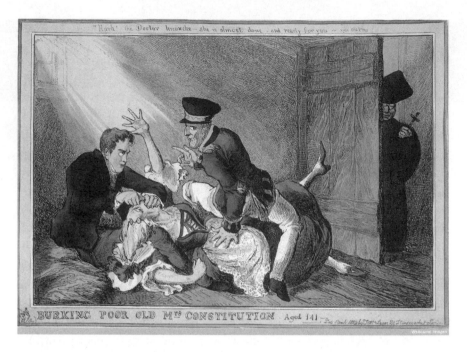

Burke and Hare. (Courtesy of Wellcome Library, London)

This, thought Burke and Hare, was easy money and, as Edinburgh was then one of the leading centres for the study of anatomy, the demand for corpses was huge. Knox himself sometimes conducted dissections for students twice a day. It was then that the duo had a brainwave about how to get more bodies: by preying on the sort of individuals unlikely to be missed! Thus in early 1928 Burke and Hare targeted their first victim, another lodger at Hare's wife's boarding house. They got the man, named Joseph, drunk and smothered him until he expired. This time Knox paid £10 for the body, which would become Burke and Hare's standard fee as they delivered a string of corpses to the eager anatomist over the next few months. Fifteen more people, drawn from the city's underclasses, would perish at the hands of Burke and Hare, including prostitutes, a salt pedlar and even a relative of Burke's partner, Helen McDougal. The usual method of murder was first to ply the victim with alcohol, then sit on their chest while covering their nose and mouth. This technique, henceforth known as 'burking', had the added benefit of leaving the bodies virtually pristine, something the anatomists preferred.

There's no doubt that by the time Burke and Hare killed a well-known local character, 'Daft' Jamie Wilson, Knox knew what they were doing – his medical students recognised the corpse – but he turned a blind eye, allowing the killing to continue.

Burke and Hare were finally caught in November 1828, when the corpse of one victim, Margaret Docherty, was found under a bed by two suspicious lodgers. However, while they were alerting the authorities, the victim's body was spirited away to Knox. With no bodies now in a fit state to prove that Burke and Hare had actually murdered them, the police struggled to put together a case. Eventually Hare ratted on his associate in exchange for his freedom. Burke was convicted and hanged on 28 January 1829. Knox escaped punishment.

The case of Burke and Hare did not appear to put off others trying the same ruse. In 1831 the so-called London Burkers, John Bishop and Thomas Williams, went to the gallows at Newgate after trying to sell the body of a 14-year-old boy they'd killed to surgeons. In the same year Elizabeth Ross was hanged for killing Catherine Walsh and selling her body on.

Ironically, all of them, including Burke, would end up on the dissecting table themselves, as provided for by the law. The following year, legislation was brought in making it easier for anatomists to procure bodies legitimately.

8 ... steps at the heart of a Tudor murder mystery

Suicide or murder? It's sometimes hard to tell. What appears to have been a case of someone taking their own life can later turn out to be a homicide. On the morning of 18 June 1982, the body of a man was found hanging from scaffolding underneath Blackfriars Bridge in London. His clothes were stuffed with bricks and $15,000 in three currencies. Police quickly discovered that the dead man was an Italian, Roberto Calvi, the ex-chairman of the Banco Ambrosiano, an institution that was closely linked to the Vatican and had just gone bust, owing the Mafia millions. An inquest initially ruled that the disgraced 62-year-old had committed suicide, but a year later a new inquest recorded an open verdict in light of the suspicious circumstances. In 2005 five men were prosecuted in Italy for murdering Calvi and were acquitted, though it's now generally accepted that there were powerful factions at play who had an interest in seeing 'God's Banker' silenced.

In other cases what seems a straightforward unlawful killing can turn out to be a suicide after all. In 1721 Catherine Shaw was found in the Edinburgh flat where she lived, lying in a pool of blood, a knife by her side. A constable had broken in after a neighbour, Mr Morrison, had heard Catherine arguing with her father William about her love life. Morrison swore that he had overheard Catherine say, 'Cruel father, thou art the cause of my death!' through the thin partition wall, followed by the sound of Shaw leaving the property. Then, hearing desperate groans, Morrison had rushed to get help. Catherine lived long enough to be asked if she'd been attacked by her father. She appeared to give a slight nod. William's fate was sealed when he returned with blood on his shirt, which he said was the result of cutting himself shaving. He was, however, found guilty of murder and hanged that November. A few months later the authorities were left red-faced when Catherine's suicide note turned up – it had slipped down the back of the mantelpiece in the room where she was found dying.

History is littered with other examples of mysterious deaths that may have been tragic suicides or possibly something more sinister. For example, was the artist Van Gogh really stupid enough to shoot himself in the stomach, leading to an agonising twenty-nine-hour death? Did actress Marilyn Monroe take an overdose or was she the victim of a murder and a clever cover-up?

One of the most intriguing such cases was the puzzling death of Amy Robsart, which captivated Elizabethan England. By 1560 Amy was estranged from her husband Robert Dudley, who had become close to Queen Elizabeth I. When her body was found at the bottom of some stairs at her home, Cumnor Place, in Oxfordshire, on 8 September, there were whispers that the 28-year-old had not simply fallen, breaking her neck, as the official inquest concluded. Lord Robert's steward, Thomas Blount, alluded to suicide when he wrote to his master suggesting that Amy may not have been in her right mind. Others suggested that Amy might have been murdered, with Dudley the chief suspect. The idea was that with his wife out of the way, Dudley would be free to marry the queen.

Dudley, however, seems to have been genuinely shocked when informed of Amy's death, and if he did hope to advance his cause at court via murder, then he was to be sorely disappointed. The queen was forced to distance herself from Dudley, who was left permanently tainted by the rumours. Both the queen and Dudley seem too shrewd not to have known the likely fallout caused by any association with such a scandalous scheme.

So what happened? If Amy had planned suicide then throwing herself down a flight of stairs that 'by reporte was but eight steppes' seems an unusual method to choose. If she did have a death wish, why had she just written to her tailor ordering alterations to a gown? Some have proposed that Amy may have been unwell with breast cancer and that this caused her to fall. But the evidence is scant and, while it is possible to break your neck falling down a few steps, the timing of her death seems rather convenient. There were two wounds on Amy's head. These were consistent with the accident scenario but also with the notion that she was subjected to violence.

It seems very possible that foul play was involved. Perhaps Amy died on the orders of William Cecil, Elizabeth's manipulative chief adviser who was vehemently opposed to a union between Dudley and the queen. Alternatively it could have been the work of Dudley's over-zealous retainer, Sir Richard Verney, or some other unknown figure with their own motive. Some 400 years later we are little closer to knowing the truth.

9... inches of pipe in the case of Lord Lucan

In past times English peers of the realm could expect to get away with murder, or perhaps receive a lesser conviction for slaying their fellow man. They might, for instance, receive a pardon from the king, especially if they were an ally. From the fourteenth century (until 1948) peers had the right to be tried by fellow members of the House of Lords. But their colleagues in ermine were often reluctant to bring in a guilty verdict for murder, frequently opting for acquittal or an alternative conviction for manslaughter instead.

Some were not so lucky. In 1541, after a man was killed in a late-night poaching prank in Sussex, Lord Dacre was expecting a royal pardon for his part in the affair. Instead, under heavy direction from the irate Henry VIII, his peers found him guilty of murder. Dacre, 26, was hanged at Tyburn, London, like a 'common criminal'. In April 1760, 40-year-old Earl Ferrers was found guilty by his peers of murdering his steward, John Johnson. An inebriated

Ferrers had shot Johnson at his mansion during a business meeting. He also went to the gallows at Tyburn.

While Earl Ferrers was the last member of the House of Lords to be convicted as a murderer, he was not the last to be branded as such by a court. More than two centuries later, an inquest jury concluded that Lord Lucan, 39, was responsible for a much more duplicitous killing. However, thanks to Lucan's now notorious disappearance, he would never face a criminal trial on the charge. In fact, the controversial episode would itself lead to a change in the law, meaning that inquest juries could no longer name murderers.

By the time of the events of 7 November 1974, Lucan was deeply in debt from gambling and estranged from his wife, Veronica, having fought a fierce custody battle over their children. At 9.50 p.m. Lady Lucan burst into a pub near the family home in No. 46 Lower Belgrave Street, London, crying, 'I've just escaped from being murdered … he's murdered my nanny.'

In the basement of the house, police found the dead body of the nanny, Sandra Rivett, in a sack. She had been beaten over the head with a blunt instrument. Lady Lucan had been assaulted too, after going to find Sandra, who was supposed to have been making tea. She stated that her attacker was Lucan and that after grappling together they had ended up in a heap, exhausted. He had then admitted to killing Sandra. Lucan had apparently mistaken the 29-year-old in the darkened room for his real target, his wife, who was of a similar build. He knew that Sandra usually had Thursday nights off, but not that on this occasion she had changed the day. A little later Lady Lucan managed to trick her husband and flee out of the house to the pub.

In the hallway, police found a 'grossly distorted' 9in section of lead pipe, which had surgical tape attached. On it were found a mixture of Group A blood (Lady Lucan's type) and Group B blood (Sandra's). It was quickly judged to be the weapon that had been used to kill Sandra and attack Lady Lucan.

There was no sign of Lord 'Lucky' Lucan, now the prime suspect. Later that evening he'd called his mother to report a 'catastrophe'. He claimed to have been driving past the house and to have seen Veronica tussling in the basement with an intruder and run inside to help, though there was no sign of forced entry and doubt whether he could have seen into the basement from that angle. The last known sighting of Lucan was by friend Susan Maxwell-Scott at her house in Sussex, where he turned up at 11.30 p.m. Here he wrote letters to a friend, maintaining his innocence and saying that Lady Lucan had accused him of hiring a hitman to kill her.

On 10 November police discovered a borrowed Ford Corsair that Lucan had been driving on the night of the 7th, in the port of Newhaven. In the boot was another 16in piece of piping, wrapped in surgical tape. No blood samples could be retrieved from it and there was no direct evidence that it was part of the same piece of pipe that had been found at No. 46, but other places in the car turned up a mixture of Group A and Group B blood. Two of the recovered letters Lucan had written also contained the tell-tale blood types. A third had been penned on a sheet of paper from a notepad that was found in the Ford.

On the weight of the evidence, the inquest, held in June 1975, found that Lord Lucan had killed Sandra, but no further trace of the wanted man was ever found. There has been continuing speculation that Lucan survived, perhaps fleeing to Africa, but there have been no substantiated sightings. He was declared legally dead in 1999.

10... age of James Bulger's killers

In August 1748 a 10-year-old boy appeared at the Assizes in Bury St Edmunds, Suffolk. He was on trial for murder. William York was alleged to have killed 5-year-old Susan Mayhew, a fellow pauper, on the morning of 13 May. The pair used to share a bed at the home of a couple who were looking after them in the village of Eyke. The man and woman went out to work one morning and came back to find Susan gone. William denied knowing where she was. A search was made and the man of the house noticed that a pile of dung nearby had been newly turned over. Examining the manure, he was horrified to find the girl's dead body 'cut and mangled in a most barbarous and horrid manner'.

William at first denied knowing anything, but he later admitted he had been to blame, confessing that, following an argument, he had slit Susan's wrists with a knife, then slashed at her body with a bill-hook before burying her in the dung heap. He'd then filled a pail of water, washed the murder weapons and his clothes, then calmly sat down to breakfast. William showed no remorse for the murder, and when asked why he'd done it, he could only answer that Susan would often soil the bed.

William was found guilty and sentenced to death, but his execution was postponed pending further consultation among senior judges. Most of them were of the opinion that William ought to be hanged, despite his youth, in case children should believe they could murder with impunity. However, the execution was repeatedly deferred. William was kept in prison until 1757 when he was granted a pardon on the condition that he joined the navy.

It would not have been that unusual if William had gone to the gallows. At the time, the age of criminal responsibility was 7 and children as young as 9 are known to have been executed for all manner of crimes including rape, arson and even housebreaking. It wasn't until 1908, that 16 became the minimum age for hanging in Britain. John Bell, 14, was the last child under 16 to be hanged, in 1831, for killing another boy, Richard Taylor, for the sake of 9s.

Throughout the next 150 years there continued to be many cases involving child killers. Among the most notorious was that of 14-year-old American Jesse Pomeroy, from Boston, who narrowly avoided the gallows in 1875 after a sickening murder spree which included the death of Horace Millen, 4, and Katie Curran, 10. He spent the rest of his life in prison. Then there was British girl Mary Bell who, aged 10, strangled 4-year-old Martin Brown and then Brian Howe, 3, in 1968, solely 'for the pleasure and excitement of killing'. Convicted of manslaughter on grounds of diminished responsibility, she was detained before being released in 1980 with a new identity.

Mary Bell's case did nothing to diminish the shock and revulsion felt across the nation when the killers of 2-year-old Jamie Bulger were unmasked in 1993. That February the toddler's dead body had been found on railway tracks in Walton, Liverpool. He'd been tortured and battered with bricks and an iron bar, suffering forty-two separate injuries. Police uncovered footage from CCTV cameras of Jamie being led away from a shopping centre in nearby Bootle by two young lads. This led police to Robert Thompson and Jon Venables, who had been playing truant from school that day and could be linked to the crime scene via DNA evidence.

When it emerged that Bulger's killers were only 10, police officers and the public alike were stunned that two such young children could be so cruel. In 1963, 10 had become the age of criminal responsibility, and Venables and Thompson were given a full adult trial at Preston Crown Court, in which experts testified that they were able to tell right from wrong. Found guilty of murder, the pair would go on to be freed on licence eight years later. The case caused much controversy and debate about what had driven the boys to commit such a heinous crime as well as what should be done with them once convicted.

Despite the concern that the nature of modern society might in some way be to blame, there was actually a chilling parallel with a little-known case from 1861 in Stockport, Cheshire. On 12 April, 2-year-old George Burgess had been found nearly naked, lying dead in a brook. He had been beaten to death with sticks. Just as in the Bulger case, a number of witnesses had seen two boys wandering off with the toddler but had not intervened. James Bradley and Peter Barratt admitted killing Burgess, referring to the dead child only as 'it'. They were found guilty of manslaughter at the Chester Assizes and sentenced to spend a month in jail and five years in a reform institution. Bradley and Barratt were both only 8 years old.

11 ... cast number of a set of teeth that would convict a strangler

Teeth have been used for centuries to identify corpses and, when murders are committed, dental records can contribute not only in establishing who the victims are but sometimes in helping track down the killers. The use of dentistry in criminal cases is known as forensic odontology. One of the first high-profile cases where it proved relevant involved Harvard academic Dr George Parkman who was murdered in 1849. His killer, chemistry professor John Webster, went to the gallows after Parkman's remains were identified thanks to his distinctive false teeth. They had been recovered and linked to Webster despite his attempts to destroy Parkman's body by cremation.

In some cases, bite marks on victims have provided police with crucial evidence. In 1948 Robert Gorringe quickly became the chief suspect in the murder of his wife, Phyllis, after an argument. Marks on her breast were matched with a cast of Gorringe's teeth. He was convicted, but a similar case, almost two decades later, would prove more difficult to solve. Again the victim, 15-year-old Linda Peacock, was left with a bite mark on her right breast. She had gone missing on 6 August 1967, after an evening out near her home in Biggar, Scotland. The next day her bloodied body was discovered lying in a local graveyard. She had been hit over the head and strangled, though not raped.

Police called in forensic dental expert Dr Warren Harvey, who determined that the bite mark she'd suffered was inflicted by a uniquely malformed set of teeth. If the police could find someone with a matching set, they would also have found Linda's killer. Detectives were soon focusing their attention on Loaningdale School, an institution for young offenders, located a short walk from the murder scene. A total of twenty-nine individuals from Loaningdale were asked to give dental impressions of their teeth and each cast was given a number. Painstakingly, Dr Harvey then compared them to photos of the marks on the deceased and conducted other experiments using acrylic models based on the casts. Slowly his team whittled down the suspect casts to five, then one – cast number 11. With its strangely pitted canines, a very rare defect, it was a perfect fit to the unusual marks found on Linda.

Number 11 belonged to 17-year-old Gordon Hay, known to be a petty thief but not for violent behaviour. He also had an alibi. Official records showed that he'd been inside his school dormitory on the evening of the 6th, when Linda's murder had occurred. Then came another breakthrough. Some of Hay's fellow inmates volunteered that on the evening in question he had actually slipped out for an hour or so. At his trial the prosecution alleged that Hay had probably tried to get Linda to have sex with him but that she had refused. Yet it seemed he had gone prepared to assault her. He had used a boathook, brought back from a summer camp, to hit Linda over the head and used a dressing gown cord as a ligature with which to strangle her. It was, however, the bite mark evidence that was the key to the guilty verdict, which was delivered on Hay at Edinburgh's High Court in February 1968.

Bite mark evidence would also prove important in the case against serial killer Ted Bundy, responsible for the rape and murder of thirty women in 1970s America. One of his victims was 20-year-old Lisa Levy, whom he brutally attacked and killed in 1978, leaving her with a vicious bite mark on her left buttock among other injuries. When Bundy was finally caught, he was ordered to give dental impressions. These would be used in his 1979 trial to show that they matched the mark left on Lisa. Bundy would eventually go to the electric chair in January 1989.

Incredibly, the bite mark left by a killer doesn't even need to be on his victim to provide police with important evidence. On 23 October 1983, Basil and Avril Laitner celebrated the marriage of their daughter Suzanne with a wedding reception at their home in Sheffield. Just hours later an intruder broke into the house and ended up stabbing both of them to death along with their son Richard, then raping their other daughter Nicola, 18. But the perpetrator could not resist taking a swig of champagne from a leftover bottle and a bite out of a piece of cheese before fleeing the scene. When Arthur Hutchinson was tracked down via his prints on the bottle, the bite mark on the cheese was matched to his teeth and helped secure his conviction for the murders.

12 ... O.J. Simpson's shoe size

'I would have never worn those ugly-ass shoes.' So said the former American football star and actor O.J. Simpson in a pre-trial deposition. This emphatic statement wasn't made in advance of the notorious eight-month trial in 1994–95 that eventually saw him acquitted of the murders of ex-wife Nicole Brown Simpson and waiter Ron Goldman. It came as Simpson testified for a civil trial brought against him in 1997 by the victims' families. During these proceedings, their attorney, Daniel Petrocelli, focused on one of the pieces of evidence that had been submitted by the prosecution at the original trial, but had been overshadowed at the time by other elements of the case – in particular, the infamous 'gloves that didn't fit'. This time a new development had made the luxury footwear the crux of whether the families would get a measure of justice for the horrific slayings.

At 12.10 a.m. on 13 June 1994, a neighbour came across the bodies of Nicole and Ron outside her Los Angeles apartment. Brown, 35, was lying by the doorstep. She had been stabbed multiple times in the head and neck. The wounds were so savage that she was almost decapitated. The corpse of Ron, who had been returning a pair of glasses left at a restaurant, was found next to a fence nearby. The 25-year-old had been stabbed several times in the torso.

Police swooped on O.J. Simpson's home but found that he had recently departed on a flight to Chicago. The 47-year-old was eventually taken into custody on 17 June after a televised chase along the city's freeways watched by 95 million Americans. He was charged with both murders.

Simpson declared, 'I'm absolutely, 100 per cent, not guilty.' No murder weapon had been found, yet at his trial a wealth of other evidence seemed to have been gathered against him. He had no credible alibi for the time of the murder and a white Ford Bronco, like the one Simpson drove, was seen in the vicinity around the time the killings had taken place, roughly 10.15 p.m. Drops of Simpson's blood were found at the murder scene while Nicole's blood was found on a pair of his socks and both her and Ron's blood were alleged to have been found in the Bronco. A bloodied leather glove was found at the murder scene and another at Simpson's home. They matched. DNA from Simpson and both victims were found on these.

Bloody shoe imprints had also been found at the scene. They came from a size 12 shoe, which happened to be Simpson's size too. A Federal Bureau of Investigation (FBI) footwear expert, William Bodziak, was able to identify that the prints had been made by a pair of Bruno Magli Lorenzo lace-ups. Only 299 pairs of the expensive Italian shoes had ever been sold in the United States.

The defence team argued that Simpson had never worn such a pair of shoes and had been wearing Reeboks that day. Indeed, there was nothing to prove Simpson had owned a pair of what were apparently the killer's footwear. And, amid accusations of racism and contamination of evidence, Simpson's lawyers orchestrated events so that he tried on the bloodied gloves. They had been kept in cold storage and had undergone a series of tests – but nothing could detract from the visual impact of the fact that they appeared to be too small for his hands. After a trial that had kept millions agog on TV, Simpson was dramatically found not guilty of the murders on 3 October 1995.

Quizzed about the shoes for the civil trial, O.J. Simpson said that he would never buy a pair as they weren't his taste. Yet this time Petrocelli had a trump card – a photo, taken by a freelance photographer at a Buffalo Bills football game in September 1993, which had been unearthed after the criminal trial had ended. It showed Simpson wearing a pair of shoes that Bodziak testified showed eighteen distinctive features that matched the Bruno Magli Lorenzo style. A stunned Simpson said that he must have borrowed them. His defence team reckoned the image had been doctored. So Petrocelli produced more images of Simpson wearing the shoes. Here, it appeared, was 'the smoking gun' that the first trial had lacked.

On 4 February 1997, the new jury found Simpson 'responsible for the death of Nicole and Ron and ordered him to pay $33.5 million in damages to the families. Little of it was ever paid, but in 2008 Simpson was convicted for other crimes, including armed robbery, and jailed.

13... in the murders of Jack the Ripper

The origins of the superstition that the number 13 is unlucky lie in stories of death and murder. Triskaidekaphobia, as fear of the figure is called, is thought to date back to a Norse myth that tells the story of twelve gods having a dinner party at Valhalla, the Viking version of heaven. The tale goes that when a thirteenth guest, the mischievous and uninvited god Loki, arrived he managed to trick Hodur, the blind god of darkness, into shooting and killing Balder the Beautiful, the god of joy, with a mistletoe-tipped arrow. The whole earth was said to have been plunged into mourning.

Whatever the truth behind its ominous association, 13 has certainly been considered a dark combination of digits for centuries. Chillingly, there are several links between the number and the most infamous killer in the history of murder, Jack the Ripper, believed to have brutally butchered at least five women during the late nineteenth century.

By the time the mutilated body of Mary Jane Kelly was discovered on 9 November 1888, the police were desperate to catch a serial killer reckoned to have already slain at least four prostitutes in London's East End: Mary Ann Nichols, Annie Chapman, Elizabeth Stride and Catherine Eddowes.

On the night of her death, several witnesses had seen Mary Jane Kelly in the company of mystery men. At 2 a.m. she had been spied going home with a man in a dark astrakhan coat by a labourer It was about 10.45 a.m., that morning when Thomas Bowyer, an employee of Mary's landlord, went to knock on the door of her single-room lodging in Spitalfields. When he got no response, he peered through the cracked window and was confronted by a bloody scene. Mary's abdomen had been removed, her breasts cut off and her face gashed beyond recognition. Her heart was also missing.

When the alarm was raised, police were soon at Mary's address in Miller's Court, behind Dorset Street. Few of the officers at the scene that day would probably have paid any attention to the significance of the room number. It was 13. A chilling coincidence? Or was the Ripper secretly enjoying this freakish link with the ill-fated figure, even goading his pursuers by choosing this address as the only home in which he would commit one of his ghastly crimes?

Despite all their best efforts, the police failed to identify the Ripper, and some claim that Mary Jane Kelly was the last murder in his horrific killing spree. But it was not the last Ripper murder according to the police's official Whitechapel murders file, which contained details of four subsequent cases. There was the slaying of prostitute Rose Mylett in December 1888, Alice McKenzie in July 1889 and an unidentified woman killed in September 1889, in the case of the Pinchin Street torso. The last murder in the file was that of Frances Coles, another prostitute, who was found dead in February 1891. The date was not auspicious – it was 'Friday the 13th'.

'Friday the 13th' has historically been seen as especially forbidding, its omens traced to the Bible. Judas, the disciple who betrayed Jesus for thirty pieces of silver, condemning him to be crucified, was the thirteenth guest at the Last Supper which occurred the night before Christ's death on Good Friday. In another link, Cain is believed to have killed his brother Abel on a Friday. There is even scientific research to back up the unlucky nature of Friday the 13th. In a 1993 study, reported in the *British Medical Journal*, it was found that the incidence of traffic accidents is significantly higher on this date.

Frances' demise certainly added to the disquiet that surrounds Friday the 13th. It was at about 2.15 a.m. in the morning that PC Ernest Thompson stumbled across her body in a passageway underneath a railway arch. Her throat had been cut and she was dying. The constable reported having heard the footsteps of someone running away moments before his gruesome discovery. James Sadler, a man who had been seen drinking with Coles the previous evening, was arrested and put on trial, but the case against him was dismissed for lack of evidence.

Whether Sadler was the Ripper, or indeed if it was the Ripper who had killed Coles, is still much debated. Whatever the truth, adding a certain spice to the link between the world's most infamous killer and the ill-famed digit is his moniker itself. For the number of letters in 'Jack the Ripper' just happens to be thirteen.

Interestingly, the number 13 crops up in a number of other well-known murderous episodes. There was the murder of Kitty Genovese on Friday, 13 March 1964 in a New York street, which became notorious as it was alleged that countless passers-by did nothing to help. David McGreavy killed three children on Friday, 13 April 1973 in Worcester, impaling their bodies on railings, all apparently because he could not stop one of them, a baby, from crying while babysitting. Then there is the death toll of another serial killer who, like the Ripper, preyed on prostitutes. Peter Sutcliffe, dubbed the Yorkshire Ripper, is known to have killed thirteen women.

14... percentage of homicides perpetrated by women

Murder is a predominantly male crime. One study, by Arthur Kellermann and James Mercy, analysing data from the Federal Bureau of Investigation Uniform Crime Reports, is indicative. Looking at 215,273 homicides recorded between 1976 and 1987, they found that just 14.7 per cent were committed by women, despite that gender making up at least 50 per cent of the population. Another study of US statistics found that men are nine times more likely to murder than women. Elsewhere the figure for female murderers may even be lower. In the UK, between 2002 and 2012, just 6.1 per cent of convicted murderers were women.

Perhaps it is because the 'murderess' is a rarity that cases involving women who kill have, since ancient times, garnered more than their fair share of attention. Sexism has no doubt underpinned the shock that the so-called 'fairer sex' could commit such atrocities, as well as the notion that when they do kill, women are likely somehow to favour underhand methods. For example, since Roman times, when the infamous trio of poisoners Canidia, Martina and Locusta were at work, poison has often been considered a woman's weapon. In truth, while poison is popular with female killers, figures show that the average poisoner is still more likely to be male.

It would be wrong to suggest that there aren't differences when it comes to men and women who murder. Women are, for instance, more likely to murder a significant other, while men more often kill strangers. High-profile cases have included Ruth Ellis, who shot her lover outside a London pub in 1955; Linda Calvey, who blasted lover Ronnie Cook to death with a shotgun in 1990; and Tracie Andrews, who stabbed her fiancé forty-two times with a penknife six years later, trying to pretend he had been killed in a road rage incident.

However, there have been plenty of women who have had other motivations for murder than doing away with a partner. Take 24-year-old Charlotte Corday, who was driven by the prevailing political climate of the French Revolution to assassinate Jacobin leader Jean-Paul Marat in 1793. Corday took matters into her own hands when she stabbed Marat in the chest with a 6in knife on 13 July 1793, as he lay in his bath. Four days later she went to the guillotine.

Women make up only a slightly higher proportion of serial killers than they do of more run-of-the-mill murderers. Criminal historian Peter Vronsky, for example, puts the figure in the United States at 16 per cent over the last 200 years. Many female serial killers have also committed their crimes in association with a male counterpart, such as Myra Hindley and Rosemary West. Yet, where they act alone, female serial killers are very unlikely to sexually assault, torture or mutilate their victims. In fact, Vronksy's analysis put the proportion of those who have had financial gain as their chief motivation for multiple killings at nearly three-quarters.

Examples of those spurred on by the chance to make a profit certainly abound. In nineteenth-century Britain, Mary Ann Cotton murdered perhaps twenty-one adults and children who became inconvenient to her, mostly poisoning them with arsenic. These included three out of four husbands, and each time she was able to cash in on an insurance policy.

In America the physically formidable and equally acquisitive Belle Gunness killed children, husbands and suitors to get her hands on insurance payouts, cash and valuables. It's thought that between 1900 and 1908 Gunness may have killed as many as forty people, who all disappeared in mysterious circumstances, many of them at her farm in Indiana. Gunness was skilful at avoiding detection. At one point she managed to persuade the authorities that one of her husbands had died when a sausage grinder fell off a shelf and hit him on the head, even though her daughter told schoolmates that she had hit him with a cleaver.

In 1908 the farm burned down and the police discovered remains of multiple bodies buried at the property. It was never conclusively proven that the corpse of a woman discovered in the ruins was Gunness, with many believing that she had been behind the fire, faking her own death to disappear successfully with her ill-gotten loot.

Sometimes a female serial killer comes along who appears to break many of the supposed norms. Aileen Wuornos was one of this select group, unusually using a gun to kill all of her seven male victims, who were shot in Florida over a period of several months during 1989–90. Also marking Wuornos out was the fact that all of her victims were previously unknown to her. Wuornos would later claim that she killed the men in self-defence, but she would end up convicted of murder and executed by lethal injection on 9 October 2002.

15... men, the baffling weight used in the murder of Edward II

In 1940 Leon Trotsky was assassinated with an ice axe; murderess Christina Edmunds put strychnine poison in chocolate creams; and in 2008, a Canadian man was battered to death with a toilet lid. Throughout history, anything and everything seems to have been used as a murder weapon. Perhaps the most infamous of all, however, is the instrument supposedly used to kill Edward II in 1327. The manner of Edward's untimely end is one of those little snippets of history we think we all know. But did the tragic sovereign really die from having a red-hot poker thrust up his behind?

Edward's reign was not a happy one. He came to power in 1307 on the death of his father, the formidable Edward I, who had ruled with skill and military acumen. Edward II, on the other hand, soon fell out with many of his barons, thanks partly to the political influence handed to 'favourites' such as Piers Gaveston, with whom he may have had a sexual relationship. Edward also suffered a heavy defeat at the hands of the Scots at the Battle of Bannockburn in 1314. Years of famine followed. Then, in 1326, Edward II's own French wife, Queen Isabella, raised an army against him with the help of her lover, the exiled noble Roger Mortimer. Edward's support crumbled and he was soon deposed.

Edward was imprisoned at Kenilworth Castle in Warwickshire while de facto rulers Isabella and Mortimer set about entrenching their position. The barons agreed to put Edward and Isabella's 14-year-old son, Prince Edward, on the throne and his father was persuaded to abdicate. The new king, Edward III, was crowned in February 1327. But there was still the problem of what to do with the old monarch. Fearing he might be rescued, his captors moved Edward to a location deemed safer, Berkeley Castle in Gloucestershire. Here, in the care of Sir Thomas Gurney, Sir John Maltravers and man-at-arms William Ockley, he was allegedly mistreated, being locked in a small room and half-starved.

By openly executing Edward, Isabella and Mortimer might have risked public wrath, but did they order his secret murder? Exactly what happened is much disputed. The traditional story is that he was killed on the night of 21 September by his jailors, who pinned him down and inserted a red-hot implement into his back passage.

This version of events comes mainly from several accounts written a few years later. The most florid is by chronicler Geoffrey le Baker, who wrote that Edward's captors:

> …suddenly seized him as he lay on his bed and smothered and suffocated him with great, heavy mattresses, in weight more than that of fifteen strong men. Then, with a plumber's soldering, made red-hot, and thrust through the tube leading to the secret parts of his bowels, they burnt out his inner parts and then his breath of life.

They took care, le Baker tells us, that no wound should be discernible on the royal body. He adds that Edward's cries of anguish were so loud that they could be heard outside the castle walls.

Was such an elaborately gruesome death necessary or even likely? Other fourteenth-century sources handle Edward's death differently. One agrees that a hot spit was put into his fundament but suggests that a table was used to pin Edward down. Elsewhere it's reported merely that he was 'vilely murdered' or that he was 'strangled'. Some records state that Edward passed away from natural causes. Le Baker's description certainly seems overblown and the logic that the killers did not want to leave a mark on Edward's body is spurious. They could, of course, have simply smothered him and left it at that. However, if the history of murder tells us anything, it's that in a fit of blood-lust human beings can perpetrate terribly cruel acts. It's not inconceivable that Edward's killers decided to add an extra form of punishment for what they saw as Edward's sin of sodomy, perhaps going beyond their brief from Mortimer.

There is even disagreement among historians as to whether Edward did die at Berkeley at all. Some suggest that he might have escaped and survived abroad. If he did perish in September 1327, the timing seems highly suspicious, it being advantageous to the new regime to have Edward, a potential figure of opposition, quickly neutralised.

Edward III certainly believed that his father was murdered and it was officially announced as such in November 1330, following his full seizure of power from Isabella and Mortimer. Gurney fled abroad, Ockley disappeared and Mortimer was hanged at Tyburn on 29 November 1330. He was 43, the same age as his alleged victim.

16... traits of a psychopath

Psychopaths have no doubt been with us since the beginning of human existence, but it was in 1941 that American psychiatrist Hervey Cleckley produced a ground-breaking list of the characteristics that actually define the personality disorder. His book, *The Mask of Sanity*, listed the traits he had identified as follows: superficial charm and good intelligence; absence of delusions and other signs of irrational thinking; absence of nervousness or neurotic manifestations; unreliability; untruthfulness and insincerity; lack of remorse and shame; inadequately motivated antisocial behaviour; poor judgement and failure to learn by experience; pathologic egocentricity and incapacity for love; general poverty in major affective reactions; specific loss of insight; unresponsiveness in general interpersonal relations; fantastic and uninviting behaviour with alcohol and sometimes without; suicide threats rarely carried out; sex life impersonal, trivial and poorly integrated; and failure to follow any life plan.

Later Canadian psychologist Robert Hare would update this to twenty items, including other traits such as pathological lying, conning or manipulative behaviour and a grandiose sense of self-worth. He created the PCL-R, a checklist commonly used to test psychopathy. From the research it's clear that key to the nature of a psychopath is a lack of empathy, emotion and guilt, combined with an ability to appear outwardly normal, even pleasant. Along with recklessness, arrogance and a propensity for deceit and manipulation, it is a toxic mix. The criminologist David Wilson described psychopaths as operating in a 'different moral universe'.

Psychopathy is a risk factor for criminal behaviour and violence. Studies suggest that around 20 per cent of all prisoners behind bars show psychopathic tendencies. Of course, possessing psychopathic traits doesn't mean an individual will become a criminal, never mind a murderer; nor does it mean that every killer is a psychopath. Psychopaths are not regarded as insane – they know the difference between right and wrong. But when psychopaths do turn to murder, they can become some of the most dangerous of all killers.

Many of the world's worst serial killers have been psychopaths, exhibiting characteristic traits. Ted Bundy, who killed at least thirty people, described

Ted Bundy. (Courtesy of State Library & Archives of Florida)

himself 'the most cold-hearted son of a bitch you'll ever meet' and admitted that he felt no guilt. Charming and intelligent, he was also very manipulative, sometimes pretending to be injured by wearing his leg in a fake cast or dressing up as a police officer to gain the sympathy and trust of his victims.

Dennis Rader, the infamous 'BTK' killer (Bind, Torture and Kill), was another example. He managed to maintain his position as a family man, church-goer and Scout leader, holding down steady jobs as he killed ten people over a seventeen-year period. It was his arrogant, grandstanding behaviour – in tune with the psychopathic profile – that led to his downfall. He taunted the police through the media and was finally caught when computer experts were able to trace him through information he'd left on a floppy disk that he'd sent to a TV station.

In Britain, Joanna Dennehy, who killed three men in 2013 and dumped their bodies in ditches near Peterborough with the help of accomplices, was identified as having psychopathic tendencies. She showed no emotion about the crimes she had committed – and had stabbed her victims in the heart. Dennehy was also a perpetual liar and controlling, boasting, 'I want to have my fun.' Just before she was caught, Dennehy went on a reckless rampage in the town of Hereford, stabbing more male victims.

Showboating to the last, the 30-year-old shocked a court by pleading guilty to the murders, just before her trial commenced. Ordered to spend the rest of her life behind bars for the crimes, she told a psychiatrist, 'I killed to see how I would feel, to see if I was as cold as I thought I was. Then it got more-ish.'

Though there are many theories, no one has yet been able to determine whether psychopaths are 'born' or 'made', or a bit of both. While the nature or nurture argument will no doubt rumble on, it's estimated that between 1 and 2 per cent of the world's adult population are psychopaths, meaning that all of us probably know one.

Ironically, the real-life killer who inspired the novel and film *Psycho* was not a psychopath. Ed Gein, from Wisconsin, who murdered two women in 1957, was also a grave-robber who collected female body parts. Obsessed with his mother, he even made a gruesome 'woman suit' from some of these trophies that he would dress in. A court determined that he was psychotic – meaning that he had lost touch with reality. Gein was confined to a psychiatric hospital where he died, aged 77, in 1984.

17... lash marks that led police to the notorious Neville Heath

'Find that whip and you've found your man,' forensic pathologist Keith Simpson told detectives investigating the horrific and perplexing death of a young woman in the summer of 1946. The mutilated body of 32-year-old actress Margery Gardner had been found on the afternoon of Friday, 21 June in room No. 4 at the Pembridge Court Hotel in London's Notting Hill. Staff, who had been unable to get a reply, had forced their way in. It was quickly clear that Margery had been the victim of a sadistic attack. She was lying on her back with her ankles tied together. There were bite marks on her breasts and a savage tear to her vagina. On her back, buttocks and face were seventeen brutal lash marks. After Simpson had carefully examined the corpse, he concluded that Margery had died from suffocation in the early hours of that night, but not before suffering many of her brutal injuries. Looking at the whip marks more closely, he identified a distinctive diamond-shaped weave, consistent with the design of a leather riding crop. It was missing and finding it, he believed, was the key to convicting Margery's killer.

There was no sign, however, of the man calling himself Lieutenant-Colonel Heath who had booked into the hotel with Margery on 20 June. But a few days later police received a letter signed by an 'NGC Heath', stating that he had lent his hotel keys to Gardner so she could have a tryst with another man, only to come back to find her body. He indicated that her real killer was not him but a man called Jack. By this time the police had put out a description of Neville Heath, a dashing, 6ft 29-year-old wanted in questioning with the Notting Hill murder. But, crucially, a photograph was not included when this was printed in the newspapers. So when Heath, who was actually both a court-martialled captain in the South African Air Force and a petty criminal, booked into the Tollard Royal Hotel in Bournemouth, under the alias of Group Captain Rupert Brook, he was able to avoid suspicion.

On 5 July the local police were called by the manager of the nearby Norfolk Hotel to report that a guest, Doreen Marshall, had been missing for two days after going to the Tollard on a dinner date. He also rang the manager there, who knew that Doreen had joined Heath, still posing as Brook, for dinner. He advised Heath to get in touch with the authorities, which he did, phoning the police and going down to the station, where he confirmed that he'd taken supper with Doreen. 'Brook' admitted that he'd walked her half way back to the Norfolk, but said that he'd left her alive.

By this stage there was a wanted poster of Neville Heath pinned up at the station and Detective Constable Suter noticed the resemblance of the image to the man in front of him. When confronted, Heath denied it was him. But Suter detained him while he made further enquiries. Meanwhile Heath asked for his jacket to be brought to him from his hotel. Officers obliged but took the opportunity to search it. Inside they found a train ticket that had belonged to Doreen Marshall, but most significantly there was a left-luggage ticket, no. 0800, from Bournemouth West Station. The ticket was submitted at the station and in return the police retrieved a leather suitcase. Inside, along with some other objects bearing the name 'Heath', was a bloodied riding whip with a distinctive diamond-weave pattern.

It wasn't until the following day that Doreen Marshall's naked decomposing body was discovered in undergrowth by a woman walking her dog. The 21-year-old's ankles and wrists had been tied together. She had been bludgeoned over the head and her throat slashed. Among her many other wounds it was noted that one of her nipples had been bitten off and her vagina had been mutilated, in a similar way to that of Margery Gardner.

Presented with the contents of the suitcase, Heath admitted his real identity and was charged with just one murder – that of Margery. The whip would be a crucial part of the evidence against him, with Simpson confirming that it was the same one that had been used to attack her. At his Old Bailey trial Heath pleaded not guilty, with his defence claiming insanity. But prison doctors gave evidence that, while he was undoubtedly a psychopath and a pervert, Heath was not mad. He was found guilty and hanged on 16 October 1946.

18... pieces of bones in the case of the 'Acid Bath Murderer'

Interviewed by police in connection with the disappearance of 69-year-old widow Olive Durand-Deacon in February 1949, John George Haigh told them, 'I have destroyed her with acid. Every trace has gone. How can you prove murder if there is no body?' Haigh was not quite correct that a body was always essential to achieve a murder conviction. Yet that would be immaterial in Haigh's case because, in fact, he had not obliterated every remnant of his victim as he had thought.

A convicted fraudster, Haigh had befriended Olive, a fellow guest at the Onslow Court Hotel in Kensington, London, telling her that he was an inventor and offering to show her his workshop in Crawley, West Sussex. He duly took her to the secluded storeroom on 18 February 1949. There he shot Olive in the back of the head with a .38 calibre Webley revolver, then stripped the woman of her fur coat and jewellery, before plunging her corpse into a 40-gallon drum filled with acid, leaving her body to turn to sludge. Haigh had Olive's coat cleaned and sold both this and the jewellery.

When Olive's disappearance was noticed by another guest at Onslow Court, police began investigating Haigh's background, discovering his criminal past. Meanwhile, they were contacted by a jeweller in Horsham who had recognised the description of the items Mrs Durand-Deacon had been wearing and told them that a man matching Haigh's description had come in to sell them. When officers searched Haigh's storeroom, they found the gun and mysterious drums full of acid. There was also a dry cleaner's receipt for the fur coat.

At the station Haigh confessed to doing away with Mrs Durand-Deacon and would go on to admit that there were other victims. After meeting former employer William Donald McSwann in a local pub, in September 1944, Haigh had lured the man back to No. 79 Gloucester Road, Kensington. Later he'd hit McSwann over the head with a table leg and shoved him into a barrel of sulphuric acid, dissolving the body and even drinking some of his victim's blood. Haigh told McSwann's parents that their son had gone away to avoid conscription, and in a bid to get hold of their assets he persuaded them to visit him the following year. Donald and Amy McSwann were dispatched in identical fashion and Haigh got his hands on £8,000. In February 1946, after making the acquaintance of a Dr Archibald Henderson, Haigh stole his gun and shot him with it during a visit to the storeroom, putting his body in one of the drums of acid. He then went to fetch Henderson's wife, Rosalie, telling her that her husband was sick, before disposing of her in the same gruesome way. Again Haigh profited by selling their possessions.

When pathologists conducted a thorough search of the Crawley storeroom and the yard outside, they found three gallstones, 28lbs of fat and eighteen fragments of bone. These showed signs of osteoarthritis, a condition from which Olive was known to suffer. Along with these remains was a set of dentures, which had also survived the effects of the sulphuric acid. These were successfully identified by Olive's dentist as belonging to her. A plaster cast of a partially dissolved left foot found at the scene was made and found to fit perfectly into one of Olive's shoes. It was all enough to find Haigh, 40, guilty of her murder when his case came to trial at Lewes Assizes in July 1949. His claim to be insane was found wanting, and the 'Acid Bath Murderer' was hanged.

Careful piecing together of bone fragments has often been key to making a case of murder, as in the tale of the Wigwam Murder in 1942. On 7 October that year, two soldiers on a routine exercise spotted an arm sticking out of the earth on Hankley Common in Surrey. It was soon discovered that it belonged to the badly decomposed body of 19-year-old Joan Wolfe, who had been buried in a shallow grave. After piecing together thirty-eight fragments of her shattered skull, forensic experts were able to say that she had been stabbed with an unusual hook-pointed knife, then hit over the head with a heavy object. Joan had been living rough and dating Canadian serviceman August Sangret, who had helped build her wigwam-style shelter. A letter was found near the body in which Wolfe told Sangret she was pregnant. Despite his denial of the killing, a knife matching the wounds was found in a wastepipe at Sangret's barracks. He was subsequently hanged for Joan's murder, following a trial in which a reconstructed skull was introduced as evidence for the first time in British legal history.

19... months before Rasputin's murderous prediction came true

At just after 2 a.m. on 17 July 1918, the former Tsar of Russia, Nicholas II, along with his wife and five children were ushered into a small storeroom at a 'house of special purpose' in Ekaterinburg, deep in the Ural Mountains, where they were being held as prisoners. They were then curtly informed that, in their absence, they had been sentenced to death. Over the next twenty minutes, in a frenzy of inaccurate gunfire and wild slashing of bayonets, the royal family were all brutally butchered by their guards. After a botched attempt to throw their bodies down a mineshaft, they were hurriedly buried in a shallow pit by the side of a road.

It was a gruesome end for the House of Romanov which had ruled Russia since 1613. Down the years the family had suffered their fair share of assassinations. Tsar Paul I, for example, had been cut down with a sword in his own bedroom in 1801, while Tsar Alexander II had been blown up by a bomb in 1881. Somehow the dynasty had always staggered on. But following Russia's February Revolution in 1917, Nicholas had been forced to abdicate his throne, a victim of his own failure to embrace political reform and the disastrous performance of Russia's armed forces in the First World War. He had hoped to find asylum, but when the Bolsheviks seized power in October, and began a civil war, the family were deemed to pose too much of a political threat. It was decided that they should be executed.

There was another factor in the demise of the Romanovs and that was their association with the infamous mystic, Grigori Rasputin, which had begun in 1905. The tsar and his wife, Alexandra, turned to the eccentric holy man in the hope that he could 'cure' their son Alexei, who had been born with haemophilia. Many around the Romanovs were appalled by Rasputin's reputation for womanising and hard drinking, but the tsarina, especially, became devoted. When, in 1915, Nicholas went to the front to take personal command of his struggling army, Rasputin began to exert political power as an adviser to Alexandra, already disliked for her Anglo-German origins. The situation left many wanting to get rid of the 'mad monk'.

On 19 December 1916, the lifeless body of Rasputin was found in the frozen Neva River in St Petersburg. Rumour and myth have swirled around the manner of Rasputin's death ever since. What seems clear is that he attended a late supper meeting at the Moika Palace in St Petersburg on 16 December. It was the home of Prince Felix Yusupov, who was married to the tsar's niece. He'd asked Rasputin over to help cure his wife's headaches. Also present on the night were the tsar's cousin, Grand Duke Dmitri Pavlovich, as well as a right-wing politician, Vladimir Purishkevich. It was an invitation to murder, as the nobles felt that killing the 47-year-old was the only way to save the monarchy from ruin.

Legend has it that Rasputin was first given cakes and Madeira wine laced with enough cyanide 'to kill a horse'. His assassins were astonished when it appeared to have no effect. So Yusupov shot him in the chest. Still Rasputin refused to die, managing to run out of the house into the snowy courtyard, where he was shot again, in the kidneys. It was only a third bullet, fired into his forehead, that proved fatal. In the early hours of 17 December, Rasputin was tossed into an ice hole that had been dug into the nearby river. Some accounts say that Rasputin was still not dead and that he drowned. In fact, an official autopsy showed that there was no poison in his system or water in his lungs. There was little secret about who had killed Rasputin, but the perpetrators faced only banishment, not murder trials.

Just days before he was killed, Rasputin is alleged to have written a letter to the tsarina in which he predicted his own murder, stating that 'I shall leave this world by 1 January.' He continued to say that if he should be killed by common assassins then the royal family had nothing to fear and that the Romanov dynasty would continue to rule Russia for centuries. However, he prophesied that if the murder was carried out by the tsar's own relations then 'no one of your family, that is to say, none of your children or relations, will remain alive for more than two years'. The cold-blooded execution of the royal family occurred nineteen months later.

20... days before the *Mignonette*'s survivors resorted to cannibalism

I took out my knife … and I said to the boy, 'Richard, your time has come.' The boy said, 'What, me sir?' I said, 'Yes, my boy.' I then put my knife (into the side of his neck). The blood spurted out, and we caught it in the bailer and we drank the blood while it was warm; we then stripped the body, cut it open, and took out his liver and heart, and we ate the liver while it was still warm.

This was how 31-year-old Captain Thomas Dudley described how he'd killed his fellow shipmate Richard Parker, some twenty days into a terrible battle for survival in the middle of the Atlantic Ocean. Dudley went on to state that he and the other starving crew members had consumed their meal of human flesh like 'mad wolves'.

It was on 5 July 1884 that the *Mignonette*, a yacht sailing from England to Australia, via Cape Town, had been struck by a huge wave. The craft quickly sank, its four-man crew having only enough time to grab a couple of tins of turnips and scramble aboard a lifeboat.

Crammed aboard the 13ft craft were Dudley, Ned Brooks, Edwin Stephens and the 17-year-old cabin boy, Parker. They were 1,600 miles from land, with no drinking water. Over the next few weeks the survivors faced an extraordinary battle for survival. In the first few hours they managed to fight off a shark with their oars, but it was hunger and thirst that would pose the biggest challenge. By the eighteenth day supplies had run out. They had resorted to drinking their own urine, and by 20 July, Parker was seriously ill. Having gulped down seawater he languished in the bottom of the boat, delirious and suffering with diarrhoea.

At some point over the next few days, Dudley suggested to the other men that they draw lots to see which one of them should be sacrificed in order to save the others. Resorting to cannibalism in this way was not unprecedented among those adrift on the oceans without supplies. The unwritten 'custom of the sea' dated back to at least the seventeenth century. Usually it only involved eating those who were already dead, but sometimes lots would be drawn to see which member of the party would be purposely killed in order that the others might be saved by feasting on their remains.

In the eighteenth century, a Spaniard called Anthony Galatea was chosen to perish in this manner – shot and eaten aboard a ship called the *Dolphin*, which had been struck by famine. In 1765 aboard the *Peggy*, a black slave was the loser, his body rationed out for nine days to keep the starving crew alive. And in 1820 the American whaling ship the *Essex* was sunk by a sperm whale in the Pacific Ocean and survivors in lifeboats drew lots to see who would be shot to provide sustenance.

Ned Brooks did not want to draw lots. Dudley briefly dropped the idea. But on 24 July he suggested that Parker, who now seemed to be dying anyway, should be killed if no vessel arrived to rescue them by the next day. After all, Dudley argued, he and Stephens were family men – it was more important for them to survive. Brooks, however, continued to dissent. Parker wasn't consulted.

The next day, with no ship appearing, Dudley and Stephens agreed to do the deed. Dudley went over to Parker and plunged his blade into his companion's jugular vein, while Stephens held the teenager's legs. All three of the remaining men then ate his flesh. It was enough to sustain them until a passing ship sighted the lifeboat on 29 July. A month later, Dudley, Stephens and Brooks were delivered safely to Falmouth, Cornwall.

Back ashore, a relieved Dudley revealed what had happened to Parker, believing that he and Stephens had only done what was logical. The authorities disagreed. To the pair's astonishment they were promptly arrested for murder. No charges were pursued against Brooks. Public opinion was largely behind the men, as was Parker's brother.

The case was to determine, once and for all, the legal position in such instances. Could 'necessity' ever be used as justification for killing? It is worth noting, of course, that what made the case against the men stronger was that Parker had been given no say in his own demise. At the men's trial, which began that November, Judge Baron Huddleston would only allow the jury to state the facts of the case and bring in a 'special verdict' in which the men's fate would be decided not by their peers but by a higher court. Eventually a panel of five judges would confirm that 'necessity' was not a defence in a charge of murder, in case it became a 'legal cloak for unbridled passion and atrocious crime'. Dudley and Stephens were thus convicted and sentenced to death. However, partly because of public sympathy towards the men, this was commuted by the home secretary to six months behind bars.

23... the number of times Julius Caesar was stabbed

Some people believe that the number twenty-three has special, even mystical qualities. It was, for instance, the favourite number of John Forbes Nash, the Nobel Prize-winning economist. Devotees of the so-called 23 Enigma point to the way the number crops up with eerie regularity in important matters from the fact that each parent contributes twenty-three chromosomes to the start of human life, to its supposed link to a plethora of dramatic world events. For instance, the atomic bomb which obliterated the Japanese city of Hiroshima in 1945 was dropped at 8.15 a.m. and $8 + 15 = 23$. Another incident often quoted is the 9/11 terror attacks on America in 2001. Here, the digits of the date add up to twenty-three. Another important historical event that has been linked to the number is the assassination of Julius Caesar, who was stabbed twenty-three times. That this particular numerological association can be made at all is thanks to a landmark in the history of forensic science. For the Roman dictator's death was the subject of the first documented autopsy, which gave us precise details of how he was killed. The word 'forensic', incidentally, actually derives from the Latin *forum*, where criminal cases were often heard.

There was certainly a supernatural flavour to Caesar's murder. By 44 BC the Roman leader, famed for his military prowess, had become increasingly tyrannical. A conspiracy gradually grew against Caesar among a group of senators, each with their own motivation to see him overthrown, but with a united desire to 'save' the republic from his grasp. Amid rumours of plots, Caesar was advised by a soothsayer that the 'Ides of March', falling on the 15th of the month, looked like an ominous time. On that very morning Caesar was due to meet with the Senate at Pompey's theatre. His wife, Calpurnia, pleaded with Caesar not to attend. During the preceding night she'd had a nightmare in which he was killed. But Caesar ignored all the warnings. Having dismissed his bodyguards, he strode into the Senate, dressed in a dashing purple toga, and took his seat in a golden chair, before around 200–300 assembled senators.

His assassination had been carefully planned. First, two conspirators detained Marc Antony in conversation outside, for it was feared that the famous general might intervene during the imminent attack. Then, inside the Senate, a group went forward, gathering around Caesar's chair, ostensibly to pay their respects. Suddenly one grabbed Caesar by the toga and held him down, while Publius Servilius Casca pulled out a dagger from his own clothes to strike the first blow. He aimed for the neck, but instead plunged the knife into Caesar's breast. At this there was a rush of around twenty to sixty senators all pulling out daggers and lunging at Caesar's body. As blows rained down, Caesar only managed to cry, 'You too, my child' as he recognised former protégé Marcus Brutus as one of the assassins ('Et tu, Brute?' was a Shakespearean invention). Caesar then tumbled to the floor, dead.

Some hours after the murder, Caesar's bloodied body was picked up by three slaves and carried home. It was examined by the physician Antistius, who conducted a post-mortem. He found that Caesar had suffered twenty-three separate knife wounds. Remarkably, however, Antistius concluded that only one of the stab wounds had been fatal in itself – the second wound, to his chest, which had been delivered by Casca's brother Gaius.

The death of Caesar had unintended consequences for the assassins. It would actually spell the end of the republic, ushering in a chain of events that would see Caesar's appointed heir, Gaius Octavius, become the first Roman emperor, Augustus. The murderous history of Rome would continue unabated over the centuries that followed. Augustus' own death in AD 14 may have been hastened by his wife, Livia, who was intent on seeing her own son, Tiberius, become emperor. It was said that she murdered Augustus by putting belladonna juice into his favourite figs. In AD 37 Tiberius himself died, probably smothered by his grand-nephew Caligula, who then became emperor, only to be assassinated by members of his own guard. His successor,

Claudius, would succumb to poison at the hands of his wife. Many more emperors would be assassinated including Galba, Vitellius, Domitian, Commodus and, perhaps most wretchedly, Caracalla in AD 217. He was stabbed to death by an aggrieved soldier as he was urinating.

25... Menlove Gardens East – the address that never was

Many addresses have become synonymous with murder. No. 10 Rillington Place is forever associated with John Christie, the serial killer who strangled to death eight women there in the 1940s and 1950s. The very mention of No. 25 Cromwell Street sends a chill down the spine at the thought of the multiple bodies of victims buried in the cellar of this Gloucester house by serial killers Rose and Fred West. Yet one address is notorious because it never actually existed. The mystery surrounding '25 Menlove Gardens East' and the unsolved murder of Julia Wallace is so puzzling that crime writer Raymond Chandler branded it 'unbeatable'. Indeed, it has been called 'the perfect murder'.

In 1931 bookish insurance salesman William Herbert Wallace, 52, shared a house at No. 29 Wolverton Street, in Anfield, Liverpool, with his wife, Julia, who was seventeen years his elder and described as 'peculiar'. Wallace, plagued by kidney trouble, had led a pretty quiet life. When he was not working as a collections agent for the Prudential, he spent his time playing chess or playing the violin.

On the evening of 19 January, Wallace was due to play chess at a café in the city, but he had not yet arrived when, at 7.20 p.m., a phone call came through for him. A man giving his name as R.M. Qualtrough wanted to speak to Wallace about a potential business matter. The caller left a message with chess club captain Samuel Beattie, asking Wallace to meet him at No. 25 Menlove Gardens East in the Mossley Hill district of the city. They should rendezvous, said Qualtrough, at 7.30 p.m. the following evening. The message was duly passed on to Wallace when he arrived a little later.

Though he didn't know Qualtrough, the next night Wallace set out from his home on a tram for the address in question, hoping for some kind of commission. His story was that when he got to the area he found that, while there was a Menlove Gardens North, South and West, Menlove Gardens East did not exist. Wallace asked for help in a local shop and from a policeman on his beat, but no one could help him find the bogus address or knew a Mr Qualtrough. About forty-five minutes later he gave up and made his way back to Wolverton Street, arriving at 8.40 p.m.

There, according to Wallace, he found the front and back doors of his home locked. His neighbours, John and Florence Johnston, were just on their way out and an apparently bemused Wallace asked them if they had seen anything awry. Oddly, when he tried the back door again, in their presence, it opened. Wallace reappeared a few seconds later saying, 'Oh, come and see. She's been killed.'

Julia was lying face down on the floor of the front parlour. Her brains had been bashed in by eleven blows from a blunt object and there was blood spatter on the walls. According to Wallace, £4 of insurance collection money was missing from a tin, but other valuables had been left behind. Bizarrely, a partly burnt Macintosh was found underneath Julia's body.

Much police bungling followed in the case, with the time of Julia's death initially identified by the pathologist as 8 p.m., meaning Wallace couldn't have done it, then later as 6 p.m., meaning he could have killed her before setting off for Menlove Gardens.

Within two weeks, detectives had arrested Wallace and he was put on trial for Julia's murder. The prosecution case was that Wallace had pretended to be Qualtrough, making the call to the chess club himself in order to try and create an alibi. Indeed, the call had been traced to a kiosk just 400yds from the accused's home.

Yet Beattie had been sure that the call was not from Wallace and witnesses, including a milkboy, said they had seen Julia alive as late as 6.45 p.m. Wallace was known to have been on a tram twenty minutes later. Could Wallace really have had time to kill Julia, dispose of a murder weapon (possibly a missing fire poker), then go to the Menlove Gardens area and return in time to make it look as if an intruder had killed his wife – all without getting a speck of Julia's blood on his clothes? The police maintained that, if Wallace had sprinted, he could have managed it and that he had killed Julia naked apart from the mac.

Not helped by an emotionless demeanour, Wallace was found guilty on 25 April and sentenced to death. But the verdict was later sensationally thrown out by the Court of Appeal, which branded the evidence against him too circumstantial. Wallace would die, of natural causes, in 1933.

In the decades that have followed, one main alternative suspect has emerged, Richard Gordon Parry, a 22-year-old colleague of Wallace who was known to have stolen from the firm. Could he have been after Wallace's insurance collections and killed Julia when she let him inside the house? His alibi, that he was at a girlfriend's, has been challenged and, chillingly, a mechanic reported that when Parry had his car washed on the night of the murder, he had a bloodied glove with him. Whether the chess-loving Wallace, Parry or someone else was the culprit, the real killer had managed to execute the perfect criminal checkmate.

27... May – date of two murders with amazing coincidences

Minor coincidences crop up all the time when studying the history of murder. For example, on 9 July 1864 a banker called Thomas Briggs became the first man to be murdered on a train, a crime for which 24-year-old German tailor Franz Muller would later be convicted and executed. Briggs had been travelling on the 9.50 p.m. service from Fenchurch Street on the North London Railway and was robbed before being thrown out of the compartment. Both the first-class carriage number in which the killing had been committed and the age of the victim were 69.

Poisoner George Chapman, who became one of the suspects for the true identity of Jack the Ripper, had a relationship with a woman called Annie Chapman, which was also the name of a different woman known to have been murdered by the Ripper in 1888.

There are eerie parallels in the assassination of Abraham Lincoln and President John F. Kennedy, elected 100 years apart. Both were shot on a Friday, sitting next to their wives; both were succeeded by men with the same surname, Johnson, both born in '08. Both presidents' last names have seven letters and both of the assassins' full names have fifteen letters.

More recently, in October 2000, the murder of two women from Houston, Texas, both named Mary Morris, perplexed police officers. Both had been found dead in their cars within a four-day period. Initially it was thought a hitman might have eliminated the wrong target and made amends with the second killing. But police could find no evidence of this and put the two incidents down to happenstance.

All of these cases of criminal synchronicity might be explained by chance. Yet the coincidences in the murders of Mary Ashford and Barbara Forrest seem so unusually striking that if they hadn't happened 157 years apart, detectives would undoubtedly have been investigating the possibility that they were linked to the same killer.

Just after 6 a.m. on 27 May 1817, the body of Mary Ashford was found by a labourer in a water-filled pit near the village of Erdington. An examination indicated that the 20-year-old virgin had been sexually assaulted and drowned. The previous evening she had been to a dance at a local inn and been seen in the early hours of the 27th in the company of local farmer and builder Abraham Thornton. He was found to have bloodstained clothes and shoes that appeared to match the man-sized footprints found near the murder scene. Thornton was arrested and put on trial, with the prosecution alleging that he had raped Mary and that she had fainted. He had then thrown her, unconscious, into the pit, where she had drowned. Thornton admitted having sex with Mary and being with her until 4 a.m., but not to killing her.

The defence argued that it would have been difficult for Thornton to have had the time to kill Mary, if witnesses who saw him after that time, in different locations, were to be believed. The jury at Warwick Assizes found Thornton not guilty in just six minutes. When Mary's family took out a private prosecution against Thornton, which was heard at the Old Bailey, he used an archaic medieval law (abolished soon afterwards) allowing him to prove his innocence through 'trial by battle'. He literally threw down a glove to challenge Mary's brother William to combat. William did not accept and soon afterwards Thornton walked free.

In 1974 West Midlands police found themselves investigating a very similar case. Devoutly religious nurse Barbara Forrest was also 20. Like Mary she had spent a night out celebrating, in this case with her boyfriend. He left Barbara at a bus stop in the early hours of 27 May, but she had never made it home. Her semi-naked body was found in a park, covered with bracken in a ditch. As in the case of Mary, someone appeared to have tried to hide the body. The scene was just a few hundred yards from the spot where Mary Ashford's corpse had lain. Barbara had been strangled and raped.

A suspect was soon arrested. He was Michael Thornton, who worked at the same children's home as Barbara. He was said to have had blood on his trousers and a false alibi. Yet at his trial at Birmingham Crown Court, the judge ruled that the evidence against him was circumstantial and directed the jury to find him not guilty.

28... types of fibre that snared Atlanta serial killer Wayne Williams

In April 1912 the body of a 76-year-old millionaire, George Marsh, was found dumped by salt flats in Lynn, Massachusetts. He had been shot four times. The only clue detectives had to go on was a button, with some cloth attached, which was found near the body. They managed to match the cloth to a coat that belonged to a 31-year-old man, William Dorr. Using a microscope, scientists identified that the fibres of both had the same weave and texture. Dorr, who had aimed to kill Marsh to get an inheritance, would go to the electric chair in 1914.

The case was an early example of how textile trace evidence found at a crime scene could prove crucial to tracking down a murderer. Indeed, in the era of modern forensics, a case can literally hang by a thread. When a murder is committed, tiny fibres from carpets or clothes can be transferred to the victim or the culprit. Under the microscope these fibres all appear very different and tracing their origin can often point to perpetrators. Before the advent of DNA evidence this could prove pivotal in a murder investigation, as it did in a shocking case from 1968.

The body of Claire Josephs had been discovered on 7 February by her husband when he returned to their home in Bromley, in south-east London. Her throat had been slashed with a serrated knife. Given that there were no signs of forced entry, it appeared that Claire had known her killer. Police were soon focusing their investigation on a friend of the family, Roger Payne, who had previous convictions for attacks on women. They examined his clothes, which had been washed, but on closer inspection they were found to harbour sixty separate fibres that matched the cerise woollen dress Claire had been wearing on the day she'd been killed. A fibre from a red scarf similar to one owned by Payne was found under Claire's thumbnail too. Payne was sentenced to life imprisonment for her murder.

Multiple matches of fibre evidence can add weight to a prosecution case, as it did with Wayne Williams, believed to have been responsible for the deaths of as many as twenty-three young males, including many children, around Atlanta in Georgia from 1979 to 1981. As bodies mounted up, mostly strangled and dumped in woodland, police had no suspect. What they did have were lots of fibres collected from some of the corpses, particularly some unusual yellow-green carpet ones. This information was made public, and when more bodies began turning up, they did so in a local river. Was the killer trying to wash away the evidence?

Staking out a bridge in May 1981, police heard a suspicious splash in the darkness and stopped a man nearby driving a white Chevrolet. It turned out to be Williams, a 23-year-old black music-promoter. Within forty-eight hours the body of 27-year-old Nathaniel Cater had been washed up in the river and the police recovered more fibres. Williams was subsequently arrested for the murders of Cater and of another man, 21-year-old Jimmy Ray Payne, whose dead body had also been fished out of the river.

Without other damning evidence it would be the fibres that the prosecution team at Williams' trial would use to make a link between the accused and his victims. At Williams' parents' home, where he lived, police found a rare yellow-green carpet with fibres similar to those recovered from Carter's body. Tracking down the manufacturer, it was estimated that the odds of finding a home in Atlanta with the same shade of carpet as those found on the victims was 1 in 7,792. A violet-coloured fibre from a car carpet was found on Payne. There was a one 1 in 3,828 chance of the victim coming into contact with a car with this carpeting. There was only a 1 in 30 million chance of both occurrences. In all, twenty-eight different types of fibre found on twelve of the Atlanta victims were consistent with nineteen objects found in Williams' home and car.

It was enough to convince a jury, and in February 1982 Williams was sentenced to life imprisonment for the murder of Carter and Payne. There was some controversy about the use of statistics in the case and Williams was never charged with any of the other Atlanta killings. Yet DNA analysis of hairs found on the body of another victim, 11-year-old Patrick Baltazar, undertaken three decades later, found odds of 130 to 1 that the hairs didn't belong to Williams.

29... blows with a hatchet in the case of Lizzie Borden

Since 1980, a staggering 211,000 homicides have gone unsolved in the United States, but perhaps the nation's most famous murder case to remain unexplained goes back much further than that. In 1893 Lizzie Borden was sensationally acquitted of murdering her father, Andrew, and stepmother, Abby, but that did not stop a popular rhyme doing the rounds in the aftermath …

> Lizzie Borden took an axe
> And gave her mother forty whacks.
> When she saw what she had done,
> She gave her father forty-one.

In fact, between them, the two victims had suffered twenty-nine definite injuries, but the ditty certainly conveyed the brutality with which the blows had been inflicted. What made the case a cause célèbre was the idea that a respectable 32-year-old Sunday school teacher might have been responsible for killing her family members in such a gruesome manner, combined with the confusing mystery of what had actually happened on that fateful day.

Thursday, 4 August 1892, in Fall River, Massachusetts, was stiflingly hot. At 7 a.m., wealthy but frugal textile merchant Andrew Borden, 69, had joined his second wife, Abby, 64, at the breakfast table of their home at No. 92 Second Street. Also at the house was John Morse, maternal uncle to Andrew's two daughters, Emma, 42, who was out of town, and Lizzie, 32, who appeared a little later wearing a blue dress. Sometime after 9 a.m. Abby went upstairs to change the guest bed, while her husband and Morse left the house separately on errands. Bridget Sullivan, the live-in maid, began washing the downstairs windows.

At 10.30 a.m. Andrew returned home but couldn't open the door with his key. When Bridget went to let him in, she found that, unusually, an extra lock had been applied – she later testified that at this point she heard Lizzie laughing upstairs. Andrew went to take a nap on the sofa in the sitting room, and Bridget would testify that Lizzie went to tell him that Abby had been called out to a sick friend. Feeling unwell, Bridget then went to her room, via the back stairs, for a lie down.

At 11.10 a.m. Bridget heard Lizzie screaming that her father had been murdered and rushed down. His bloodied body was on the sofa, having suffered multiple injuries. When Bridget asked Lizzie where Abby was, she said she thought she might have come home. Going upstairs, the maid saw Abby prostrate on the floor of the guest bedroom. She too had been savagely attacked.

Police found no signs of forced entry – the doors had been locked. From the temperature of Abby's body, investigators determined that she had been killed first, between 9 and 10.30 a.m. She had suffered a blow to the side of her head with a hatchet-like weapon as she faced her attacker, then eighteen more on the back of her head. She had no defensive injuries, indicating the culprit might be someone she knew. Andrew, assaulted in his sleep around 11 a.m., had suffered ten horrific blows to the head and face – one had split his eyeball.

Lizzie claimed to have been in the loft of the outside barn and to have come to investigate when she heard her father groan. When an officer investigated, he noted that there were no footprints in the thick dust. In the locked cellar, police also found a hatchet head with a broken handle. In the days after the murders a neighbour who stayed over reported seeing Lizzie burning a blue dress – she explained this by saying it had got stained with paint.

At the inquest Lizzie gave contradictory evidence about her movements on the day of the killings. She also said that she'd removed her father's shoes when he went to have a nap – but police photographs showed them still on after death.

Lizzie was arrested and eventually brought to trial in June 1893. Her expensive lawyers managed to get Lizzie's contradictory inquest statements excluded. The prosecution also struggled to prove that the broken hatchet was the murder weapon – there was no blood on it. Their case was not helped by contradictory witness statements and police bungling. Officers had failed to cordon off the crime scene or properly examine Lizzie's clothing. The all-male jury let her go free.

Other candidates for the killer include John Morse, the maid and even a passing 'wild eyed' stranger. However, despite the lack of proof, the only credible suspect remains Lizzie Borden.

Spendthrift Lizzie certainly hated Andrew's miserly ways – the prosecution alleged that she feared Abby might inherit more than her fair share of her father's estate. Perhaps most crucially, evidence that Lizzie had tried to buy poison on the day before the murders was not heard at her trial.

Lizzie and her sister went on to inherit her father's fortune and moved into a larger house in a posher area. In 1897, she found herself in trouble with the law once again, accused of trying to shoplift a painting. The matter was settled out of court.

30...

milligrams of diamorphine – the fatal doses administered by Dr Harold Shipman

On 24 June 1998, a fit 81-year-old woman called Kathleen Grundy died suddenly at her home in Hyde, near Manchester, shortly after a visit from her GP, Harold Shipman. He signed her death certificate, citing 'old age' as the cause. Soon, however, her daughter, Angela Woodruff, smelled a rat. Kathleen's recently written will appeared to leave her entire £386,000 estate to Shipman. That August police ordered the exhumation of Kathleen's body. Toxicology tests showed a lethal dose of morphine in the ex-mayoress's body. Furthermore, police discovered Shipman's fingerprints on the will and linked it to his typewriter. Had the respected local doctor killed her?

Shipman, a seemingly kindly father of four, was popular with his patients, especially with the elderly, who appreciated his regular house visits. But there were hints that the 52-year-old was not all he seemed. In 1975 Shipman had been caught forging prescriptions of pethidine, for his own use, but would soon be allowed to continue working as a GP. Also, prior to Kathleen's death, concerns had been raised about Shipman's work. That spring, alerted by a funeral parlour, another local GP had contacted the coroner with worries about an unusually high death rate among Shipman's patients. Police took up the matter but did not find enough evidence to bring charges. But when local taxi driver John Shaw heard of Grundy's death, he got in touch with detectives to report fears he'd long harboured that more than twenty of his regular customers, all elderly women, might have been being killed by Shipman.

Morphine is a drug usually used for pain relief, but in large enough doses it can be fatal. Unlike many substances used by poisoners, it remains in the body for a long time. Knowing this, police decided to exhume more of Shipman's recently deceased patients. The body of each was examined by forensic experts and found to contain lethal amounts of morphine, with little evidence to justify the causes of death that Shipman had logged for them. For instance, Joan Melia, 73, who had died just twelve days before Kathleen, had not died of pneumonia as Shipman had said. It was becoming clear that Shipman was a serial killer.

Police discovered that he had been able to obtain large amounts of diamorphine (the medical name for heroin and twice as strong as ordinary morphine) by falsifying prescriptions, sometimes for patients who were already dead, or by ordering more than was needed for others. In this way he stockpiled the drug that he would use in his murderous enterprise. Over one six-year period Shipman obtained 24,000mg of diamorphine illicitly.

The doctor's typical method of murder was to go to a patient's home, then say he was going to take a blood sample. Instead he would inject them with 30mg of diamorphine – an easily lethal dose – directly into a vein and watch them die. He would often write the death certificate himself and alter the patient's medical history to fit in with the cause of death he had recorded. However, Shipman failed to account for the fact that his computer would log the times he had made these back-dated changes.

Shipman denied his guilt and would claim that his victims had been addicts who'd died from overdoses, but levels of morphine in victims' hair proved they were not habitual drug users.

In January 2000, Shipman was convicted of murdering fifteen people, including Kathleen Grundy, receiving a life sentence for each. However, police felt he might have been responsible for many more deaths. A government inquiry was launched looking into the fate of hundreds of Shipman's other former patients. It found that he had been murdering them for more than two decades, his first known victim being Eva Lyons, 70, killed in 1975 while Shipman was working in Todmorden, West Yorkshire. Although Shipman's typical victims had been elderly, his youngest was a 41-year-old man and there were suspicions about his part in the death of a 4-year-old too.

While Shipman's motive for killing Grundy may have had a financial bent, the only spur for his other murders appears to have simply been the thrill of exercising control over the last moments of his victims' lives.

The final report into Shipman's crimes ascribed 218 murders to him but estimated that he could be responsible for at least 250. Many believed the real total was much higher. The staggering death tally made Shipman Britain's worst serial killer. He hanged himself, in his cell at Wakefield Prison, in 2004.

35... road number in the case of serial killer Henry Lee Lucas

Roads often feature in murder cases. Sometimes this is because a body is found next to them, dumped by the killer, such as in the story of Melanie

Hall, the hospital worker whose remains were discovered in a bin bag next to the M5 motorway in Britain, in 2009. The 25-year-old had disappeared after a night out in 1996, and the case remains unsolved.

Incidences of road rage have sometimes led to murder. Kenneth Noye, for example, became known as the M25 killer after he stabbed to death another driver, 21-year-old Stephen Cameron, on a slipway of the motorway in Kent, also in 1996.

It was not the only case where the number of the road stuck to the crime. James Hanratty was hanged in 1962, having become known as the 'A6 killer'. In August 1961 he held up the car of scientist Michael Gregsten, 36, travelling with his lover, Valerie Stott, 22, in Buckinghamshire. Some hours later Hanratty shot Gregsten dead, before raping Stott and shooting her five times, though she survived. The murder occurred at a point on the A6 in Bedfordshire known as Deadman's Hill.

Perhaps the most baffling example of where a road was central to the crimes was the death of at least twenty-two motorists and hitchhikers killed along a 400-mile stretch of Interstate Highway 35 in Texas between 1976 and 1981. Particularly notable was that of an unidentified woman, whose strangled corpse was found on Halloween, 1979, dumped over the guardrail of the highway near Georgetown. She was naked apart from a pair of orange socks.

Police made little progress in identifying the killer, or killers, of these victims, until a man called Henry Lee Lucas began confessing to the murders. Lucas was from a troubled background and had killed his own mother, Viola, in Michigan, by stabbing her in the neck in 1960. However, he was released from prison in 1970 and became a drifter, hooking up with an associate, Ottis Toole. Lucas also befriended Toole's teenage niece, Frieda 'Becky' Powell, and they all hit the road together.

In 1983, when Lucas was arrested for a firearms offence, he suddenly confessed to killing Becky and an 82-year-old Texan woman, Kate Rich, for whom he'd worked. Police soon found what appeared to be the pair's remains, although forensic evidence never conclusively proved the identity of either.

Lucas' confessions didn't end there. In court he said he was responsible for about 100 other murders. Later the figure topped 350, with Toole supposedly helping in sixty-five. Many of his confessions related to the I-35, murders and in some cases he certainly seemed to possess suspiciously intimate knowledge of the killings. For instance, a young woman called Sandra Dubbs had been abducted in early October 1979, after her car had broken down on her way to a job interview in San Antonio. Her body was found near Austin, Texas. She had been stabbed thirty-five times. Lucas was able to lead police to the exact field where her mutilated corpse had been discovered. He also admitted to killing the 'orange socks' victim, saying that he had picked her up near Oklahoma. According to Lucas' account, when she'd refused sex, he had strangled the young woman and quickly dumped her body.

Lucas was eventually convicted of eleven murders, but he received the death sentence for only one, relating to the 'orange socks' case. From the outset there was unease about the sheer number of murders Lucas had put his name to, and he himself later withdrew the confessions. Indeed, one investigative journalist pointed out that Lucas would have had to travel 11,000 miles in one month to commit all the murders of which he was supposed to be guilty. It would also emerge that payroll records indicated that Lucas had actually been working as a roofer, hundreds of miles away in Florida, when the 'orange socks' murder had occurred.

On the basis of this evidence, Lucas' sentence was commuted to life imprisonment in 1999. It also transpired that sloppy police procedure had, on occasion, led to Lucas being allowed to read murder case files, enabling him to garner details of the killings to which he was confessing. It seems some detectives, eager to clear a backlog of unsolved homicides, had not been too diligent about verifying his claims. Lucas died in 2001 aged 64.

It's still unclear just how many murders Lucas committed, or if any of the spate of I-35 murders were definitely among them. Many believe that there was another, as yet unidentified serial killer criss-crossing the state.

37... British soldiers executed for murder in the First World War

At precisely 6.27 a.m. on 24 September 1918, less than two months before the end of the First World War, Second Lieutenant John Henry Paterson was executed by firing squad at Boulogne in France. Paterson, of the 1st battalion Essex Regiment, was a deserter. But he was also a murderer – and the only British officer to have been executed for the crime during the conflict.

Having served in the army since 1915 and been twice wounded, once in the neck on the Somme, by March 1918 Paterson had deserted from trenches near Ypres. After forged cheques were used by a man matching his description, military police were put on alert.

Sure enough on 3 July, two policemen spotted a man they thought could be Paterson walking down a road near Calais with a local woman. When confronted, Paterson eventually admitted who he was, but asked to be able to go inside a nearby house and have a farewell cup of tea with his companion before surrendering. Sergeant Collinson agreed and watched the back of the house, while Lance Corporal Stockton watched the front. An hour later Paterson emerged and shots were fired. Collinson was hit in the chest and later died of his wounds. Meanwhile, Paterson made his escape, but he was finally taken into custody by French police at Saint-Omer a fortnight later. At his trial Paterson maintained that he had just meant to scare Collinson and that his gun had gone off by accident. But his story was not believed, and the married former clerical worker was sentenced to death. Just what drove Paterson, who had been promoted through the ranks and had a good disciplinary record, to suddenly desert and then kill has never been properly explained.

A total of 346 soldiers of the British Empire were executed during the First World War, with most sentences handed out for desertion. A little-known fact is that during the years 1914–18 and the immediate aftermath of the conflict, thirty-seven servicemen also suffered the ultimate penalty after being found guilty of committing murder. Most of the incidents took place on the Western Front in France and Belgium, but ten of the murders took place in other theatres of war.

The majorty of cases involved the killing of comrades. Lance Corporal William Price, 41, and Private Richard Morgan, 32, of the 2nd Battalion Welsh Regiment had both served in the army for good portions of their lives. But on 20 January 1915, in freezing trenches near Bethune, they had apparently got drunk and shot their Sergeant Major, Hughie Hayes, amid rumours of victimisation by another man, a platoon sergeant. Morgan maintained it was all an accident, but he and Price were court-martialled and executed on 15 February.

Another inebriated man, Private Arthur Dale, faced a firing squad in an abattoir in March 1916, after being found guilty of killing a fellow solider. Many other cases involved alcohol and little evidence of premeditation.

One of the more unusual instances was that of Lance Sergeant Arthur Wickings of 9th Battalion Rifle Brigade, who had been serving in the trenches for three years and been wounded twice, before committing his crime whilst on leave. Wickings was convicted of strangling prostitute Henriette Tremerel, 52, in the port of Le Havre in December 1917. He pleaded not guilty at his trial and a motive was never identified. While witnesses had linked him to the scene of the crime and there were tell-tale scratches on his face, the evidence produced against Wickings was thin. He was, nevertheless, found guilty and put to death.

In 2006, after a long campaign, 306 of those executed by their own side during the war were given pardons by the government. Those who had committed murder and mutiny were not included. In reality, most of these wartime murderers would have been hanged if they had committed similar crimes on the Home Front and, at the time, their fate did not attract much sympathy back in Britain. But many of those put on trial for murder were provided with inadequate legal defence, and potentially mitigating factors were not taken into account. For example, on 11 February 1916, Private Thomas Moore shot Staff Sergeant James Pick dead. His mother had been in an asylum and Moore claimed to be 'out of his mind' at the time he had committed the act, but his psychological state was never examined and he was duly shot.

The British certainly took a hard line when it came to murders committed at the front, as did the French, who executed a total of over 600 of their own men during the conflict, with about 100 despatched for offences such as murder or espionage. The Americans executed twenty-four soldiers for murder, all of them black. The Germans, however, only appear to have enforced capital punishment for a handful of men.

40... minutes for a jury to wrongfully convict Timothy Evans

No one knows exactly how many men and women have been wrongfully executed for murder down the centuries, yet there's little doubt that many have, and continue to be, put to death for crimes they didn't commit. Indeed, a 2014 study by the University of Michigan identified that 4 per cent of those sentenced to death in the United States were not guilty, suggesting that 200 people then waiting on death row might be innocent. It also follows, of course, that many of the real culprits are still at large.

It did not take long for Welshman Timothy Evans to be found guilty of the murder of his 1-year-old daughter, Geraldine. At his trial, held in January 1950, the evidence was heard over just two days and the jury deliberated for a mere forty minutes before concluding that the man in the dock was guilty. By 9 March the 25-year-old lorry driver was dead, hanged by Britain's most famous executioner, Albert Pierrepoint (see page 172).

The dead bodies of Geraldine and Evans' wife, Beryl, whom he was also believed to have murdered, had been found concealed in a washroom at the back of No. 10 Rillington Place, in west London, where the family had been living in the top-floor flat. Evans, who had learning difficulties, had gone to the police in late 1949, telling them that he had killed his pregnant spouse and put her body down a drain. Initially officers couldn't find a corpse. Evans then told them that John Christie, who lived downstairs, had agreed to carry out an abortion on his wife but that the procedure had gone wrong and Beryl had died. A second search of the property had uncovered the bodies, and under police questioning Evans told them, 'Yes – I did it.'

Evans was put on trial for just one murder, his daughter's – but now he claimed that John Christie had killed both Geraldine and Beryl. At the trial, Christie denied involvement and testified that Evans and his wife had often argued. Apparently the model of respectability, it was Christie whom the jury believed, not Evans.

Three years would pass before Christie was unmasked as the real killer – and a serial killer at that. A new tenant at his flat discovered the dead bodies of three women concealed behind an alcove in the kitchen. Further investigation showed that Christie had strangled and sexually assaulted six women. He had even killed his own wife, Ethel. Christie confessed to the murders and was hanged on 15 July 1953, also by Albert Pierrepoint. It would later turn out that the police had fabricated Evans' confession. Indeed, at his trial, Christie confessed to killing Beryl and it's now generally accepted that he murdered Geraldine too.

Evans was given a posthumous pardon in 1966, a year after capital punishment was abolished in Britain. His case had been pivotal in changing attitudes towards the death penalty. Another was that of Derek Bentley, a 19-year-old man, said to have the mental age of 11, who was executed in 1953 for the murder of policeman Sidney Miles during a bungled burglary in Croydon, south London. His accomplice, Christopher Craig, had fired the fatal shot but was not hanged because he was only 16. Doubts were cast as to whether Bentley had really told Craig, 'Let him have it' before Miles was shot. It was later proven that certain police officers had lied under oath and that the judge had misdirected the jury. Bentley's murder conviction was quashed in 1998.

The scant attention paid to Bentley's mental faculties in his prosecution echoed the case of Joe Arridy, an American with an IQ of just 46, who was sentenced to death for the 1936 rape and murder of a 15-year-old girl in Pueblo, Colorado. Arridy spent much of his time on death row playing with a toy train, and the fact that he did not appear to understand that he was going to be executed didn't stop the authorities sending him to the gas chamber, aged 23, in 1939. He was posthumously pardoned in 2001, with evidence suggesting Arridy had not even been in Pueblo when the murder occurred.

Developments in forensic science have highlighted other miscarriages of justice decades after they occurred. Australian Colin Campbell Ross was hanged in 1922 for the murder of Alma Tirtschke, 12. Her naked body had been found in Gun Alley, Melbourne – she had been raped and strangled. The crux of the case against Ross, who owned a bar nearby, was that hair found on a blanket at his home came from the victim. But when a campaign saw the original exhibits undergo DNA testing in the 1990s, it was found that the hair did not belong to Alma. Ross also received a posthumous pardon.

44... Calibre Killer

Guns come in all shapes and sizes. As well as their make and what type of firearm they are, such as a rifle or revolver, another key to describing their differences is the calibre. This refers to the measurement of the diameter of the barrel, or the diameter of the ammunition that the gun fires. The figure is most often given in hundredths, or sometimes thousandths, of an inch. So a .22 calibre rifle has a barrel of twenty-two-hundredths of an inch. In everyday parlance the decimal point is often dropped, so a firearm with a barrel diameter of .45 of an inch is referred to as a '45 calibre'. The calibre is sometimes given in the metric measurement of millimetres too.

For example, Mark Chapman's 1980 murder of singer John Lennon in New York was perpetrated using a Charter Arms .38 calibre pistol, while

Ronnie Kray used a 9mm Mauser semiautomatic pistol to shoot rival gangster George Cornell in the head at the Blind Beggar pub in London in 1966.

In a criminal case, forensic ballistics experts examine bullets or their fragments and shell casings as well as wounds on victims to help them identify the relevant calibre. Sometimes even the weight of a deformed bullet can give a clue. In a murder case, knowing the calibre of gun that was used can be important evidence in linking a killer's weapon to the crime. The information may also give an indication of what kind of individual might be responsible. For instance, 9mm semi-automatic guns are often associated with career criminals. It was the firing of a single bullet, by a 9mm handgun – probably fitted with a silencer and pressed against the victim's head – that led some to believe TV presenter Jill Dando was killed by a professional hitman, when she was murdered on her London doorstep in 1999. The case remains unsolved.

Some calibres of gun become so synonymous with their users that they lend them a nickname, such as the '44 Calibre Killer', who terrorised 1970s New York. He first came to prominence after the indiscriminate shooting of two women who had been sitting in a car outside an apartment building in the Bronx in July 1976. The attack came without warning and left Donna Lauria, 18, dead and Jody Valenti, 19, badly injured. A bullet from a .44 Bulldog revolver was retrieved – this was a gun that was powerful but only accurate at close range.

The following months saw more random shootings. In October a couple in another parked car were also shot, as were two teenage girls walking home in the city. Although none of these incidents was fatal, one of the victims was left paraplegic. Then, in January 1977, Christine Freund, 26, and her fiancé John Diel, 30, were shot while sitting in their parked vehicle in Queens. Christine died from her injuries. That March, student Virginia Voskerichian, 19, was shot in the face and killed as she walked home. More .44 Bulldog bullets were found and analysis of their unique markings indicated that they'd been fired from the same gun. Police now believed a serial killer was on the loose.

Despite a huge manhunt, the police had sketchy descriptions to go on, and the activities of the 44 Calibre Killer – as the press now dubbed the perpetrator – continued. In April another couple, Alexander Esau, 20, and Valentina Suriani, 18, would both die from gunshot wounds as they sat in a car in the Bronx. On the seat of the car the killer had left behind a note vowing to continue killing and declaring cryptically, 'I am the "Son of Sam".'

In June two more youngsters were shot in their car, though they survived, while in July Stacy Moskowitz and Robert Violante, both 20, were kissing in a stationary car when the killer walked up and shot both of them. Stacy died a few hours later.

Ex-soldier David Berkowitz, 28, became a suspect through a parking ticket violation at the scene of the Moskowitz and Violante shooting. When police apprehended Berkowitz leaving his Yonkers apartment, a paper bag containing a .44 calibre Bulldog which matched that used in the shootings was found in his possession. Berkowitz soon confessed to the shootings and said that he had been ordered to carry out his crimes by a demonic dog owned by his neighbour, Sam Carr, hence the 'Son of Sam' moniker that he had used in the first note and others subsequently sent.

Despite his ravings, Berkowitz was found mentally fit to stand trial. He pleaded guilty to six murders and, on 12 June 1978, was sentenced to between twenty-five years and life in prison for each.

48... hours in the case of the 'Corpse in the Creek'

Establishing an approximate time of death is often vital in a murder case, not least to help police check a suspect's alibi. Modern forensic pathologists have a number of ways to estimate when a victim died. One method is taking the temperature of the body. A broad rule of thumb is a loss of 1 degree Centigrade for every hour after death until the body matches the environmental temperature. The degree of rigor mortis can also provide a clue. This refers to a natural process that occurs in the body after death, due to chemical changes, where the muscles stiffen and contract. Rigor comes on about two to six hours after mortality and typically disappears after thirty-six hours.

Rigor mortis was noted in Mary Jane Kelly, the most brutally mutilated of Jack the Ripper's victims, as her body was examined by a doctor carrying out a post-mortem on the afternoon of 9 November 1888. He was also able to use another well-known method of estimating a time of death – looking at the level of digestion of the food in her stomach. Dr Thomas Bond put the time of death at about 2 a.m.

The analysis of the stomach contents of the bodies of two young boys found in a pond at a Scottish quarry in 1913 would help solve their murder.

Pathologist Sir Sydney Smith found that, thanks to a particular set of environmental conditions, the fat in the bodies had been turned into a soap-like substance called adipocere, preserving them. Incredibly, he was able to ascertain that the boys had died about eighteen months earlier and had eaten a meal of broth an hour before they had died. Police tracked down a woman who had fed broth to William Higgins, 6, and his brother John, 4, just before the pair had last been seen in 1911. At the time their alcoholic father, also called John, said they had moved away. Higgins would be hanged for the murder of his sons.

There are other indicators of time of death, including the level of putrefaction in a corpse and the activity of insects on the body, as in the case of the murderous doctor Buck Ruxton (see page 85). However, it's hard to be exact as a range of factors such as sex, age, build and clothing can affect any of the processes which medical examiners observe. Indeed, some murderers have tried to disguise the time of death of their victims. Contract killer Richard Kuklinski, convicted of five murders in the 1980s, was nicknamed 'The Iceman' for his habit of freezing victims to slow down decomposition, then disposing of the bodies later, effectively masking when they had died. His duplicity was discovered when he failed to thaw out one of the bodies properly before dumping it, and a pathologist discovered ice crystals in the victim's heart.

In the so-called case of the 'Corpse in the Creek', it fell to Ellis Parker, one of America's most celebrated detectives, to notice the error made by two doctors who had given their opinion on the time of death. Bank employee David Paul, 59, was found dead by duck hunters on 16 October 1920, in a shallow grave amid some woods by Bread and Cheese Creek in Burlington County, New Jersey. He had disappeared eleven days earlier on his way from Camden to deliver around $80,000 in cheques and cash to a bank in Philadelphia.

Paul, found without the money, had been shot twice in the head. Examining doctors pronounced that, due to the state of decomposition, he could not have been dead more than forty-eight hours. Had Paul, who had a former conviction for mail theft, been part of a conspiracy to abscond with the cash and been killed by his accomplices? Or had he been kidnapped, then killed later? To local detective Parker, who knew Paul and identified his body, neither scenario seemed likely.

Curiously, the body was soaking wet but the ground around it dry. Parker identified marks showing it had been dragged out of the stream. Taking a sample of the water, he found that it contained high levels of tannic acid, produced by factories upstream. So did Paul's clothes. Everything indicated that the body had been dumped in the stream on the 5th and spent several days there, where it had been preserved, but that the killers had got nervous about it being found and returned to bury it. Using this information, Parker was able to establish that two suspected friends of Paul did not have sufficient alibis. When confronted with this new information, the pair confessed to the murder and stealing the money. Frank James and Raymond Schuck went to the electric chair on 20 August 1921.

50... micrograms of radioactive polonium-210 in a murder by teapot

While politically motivated assassinations might not be as commonplace in the British Isles as in some other countries, the nation has had its fair share of such incidents. There was the shooting of Prime Minister Spencer Perceval by John Bellingham in 1812 and, of course, the high-profile killings associated with the Troubles in Northern Ireland, such as the death of Lord Mountbatten, blown up on a boat in 1979. Nevertheless the assassination of Bulgarian dissident Georgi Markov was startling for the unique manner of his death. The 49-year-old was poisoned with deadly ricin, delivered from the tip of an umbrella, which had been jabbed into his leg as he waited for a bus on London's Waterloo Bridge in 1978. Although the culprits were never found, agents from behind the Iron Curtain were suspected. Surely, with the end of the Cold War, there would never again be a real-life murder on British soil that would so closely resemble the sort of plot normally found in the pages of spy-thrillers? On the contrary, the killing of Alexander Litvinenko, in 2006, would prove that, in the era of Vladimir Putin's Russia, even the most outlandish assassination scenario could become a horrifying reality on the streets of London.

When Litvinenko, a former Russian spy who had defected to Britain, arrived at a hospital in Barnet on 3 November, suffering with severe diarrhoea and vomiting, doctors vainly tried to establish what was wrong with him. The 44-year-old, who had been extremely critical of the Putin regime and had worked for MI6, believed he had been the victim of an assassination attempt and police were called in. Detectives began a series of lengthy interviews with Litvinenko, as his condition rapidly deteriorated.

Doctors initially considered thallium poisoning, but Litvinenko's symptoms didn't quite fit. Eventually a urine sample showed a faint trace of polonium-210, a rare radioactive isotope, 100 billion times more toxic than hydrogen cyanide. Ingested, it is deadly even in tiny amounts. Further tests on urine samples by scientists at the UK's Atomic Weapons Establishment confirmed that Litvinenko had received a fatal dose of polonium-210. Its use as a murder weapon was virtually unknown. Officials concluded that it had almost certainly originated in Russia, from the labs of Russia's FSB spy agency. Litvinenko was, according to one of the UK radiation experts, already a dead man. Sure enough, on the evening of 23 November, he died from heart failure.

The police were now treating Litvinenko's death as murder. Using the tapes of his interviews, they homed in on two main suspects, Russians Andrei Lugovoi and Dmitry Kovtun, whom Litvinenko said he had met at the Pine Bar of the Millennium Hotel in Grosvenor Square on the afternoon of 1 November 2006, ostensibly to discuss business opportunities. When Litvinenko had arrived at the bar, in a section carefully chosen to be out of the view of security cameras, there was already a teapot and several cups on the table. Lugovoi offered Litvinenko some of the tea and the latter proceeded to take just a few sips of the lukewarm liquid. It would, however, be enough to kill him. Once polonium-210 enters the bloodstream, its effects are nearly impossible to reverse. Neither Lugovoi nor Kovtun had drunk any of the tea in Litvinenko's presence.

When investigators took radiation readings at the hotel, the table where the party had sat measured 20,000 becquerels per square centimetre – clear evidence of contamination. Even though the teapot used to serve Litvinenko had been through a dishwasher several times, it was easily identifiable among the 100 tested – it measured 100,000 becquerels. Experts later concluded that at least 50 micrograms of polonium-210 had been put into the teapot, probably using a spray. Litvinenko was found to have 26.5 micrograms in his bloodstream. Just 1 microgram – the size of a speck of dust – would have been enough to kill him.

When Kovtun's room in the hotel, no. 382, was examined, there were even higher radiation readings. In a waste pipe of the bathroom sink there was a clump of sediment that measured an astonishing 390,000 becquerels. It was evidence that he had cackhandedly tried to dispose of the remaining polonium-210.

Indeed, the assassins had not been at all careful with the deadly substance they carried, leaving a radioactive trail across London during several trips. Police found traces of polonium-210 at a restaurant where Litvinenko had eaten with Lugovoi and Kovtun in October and also on planes the pair had used to fly into the UK. A hotel hand towel used by Lugovoi on an earlier trip gave a reading in excess of 17 million becquerels per square centimetre, making it dangerously radioactive. The findings indicated that the killers had tried to assassinate Litvinenko on at least two previous occasions before their successful attempt.

By the time the British police had accumulated this damning evidence, Lugovoi and Kovtun were back in Russia, and although the police were allowed to make visits to them for questioning, it was clear that the Kremlin was not going to allow their extradition. Both remained free. In January 2016 a public inquiry concluded that Lugovoi and Kovtun were 'probably' sent to murder Alexander Litvinenko on the orders of Russian president Vladimir Putin himself.

54... real age of the victim in the 'Tabernacle Street Horror'

When confronted with the body of an unknown murder victim, today's forensic scientists have an array of tools at their disposal to help them describe and identify the corpse. As well as fingerprints, DNA and dental records, forensic anthropologists can expertly analyse bones to help determine the age and sex of a victim. They can even pinpoint where the dead person may have originally lived. When a dismembered torso turned up in the River Thames in 2001, specialists were able to establish that it was of a 4- to 7-year-old boy, while trace minerals found in his bones suggested that he had actually come from a certain part of Nigeria. However, even with this information, police still struggled to prove exactly who he was.

In the nineteenth century, without modern, sophisticated techniques, identification of bodies was even harder. Inevitably, mistakes were made. In 1855 the body of a murdered man washed up under a bridge in Milwaukee. It was missing both legs and the head was almost severed by a gash to the throat.

However, the facial features were still largely intact. Police were dependent on the testimony of local people to help in identifying the corpse, and ten people affirmed that the dead man was John Dwire, who had recently vanished. They based these positive identifications on everything from a distinctive scar to missing teeth, as well as the colour of the victim's eyes and hair. Yet when an inquest was opened into Dwire's death, who should walk in during proceedings but Dwire himself to announce that he was alive and well. The real identity of the murdered man was never established.

Just four years earlier the inhabitants of Norwich, England, were horrified when body parts started turning up around the city. The first gruesome find, on 21 June 1851, was that of a severed hand lying in a road and then a solitary foot 300yds away. Over the next few days more grim discoveries were made around Norwich in fields, hedges and drains, including various pieces of flesh, a shin and thigh bone, a portion of pelvis and pieces of what appeared to be female breasts.

A surgeon and two other physicians were called in to examine the assembled remains and quickly determined that they were from one victim, a woman who had been hacked to pieces, somewhat inexpertly. The surgeons then agreed that, considering the delicacy of the skin and its 'well-filled understructure', this was an individual aged between 16 and 26 at the time of death.

Assuming that they had a savage murder on their hands, police publicised this information in the hope that it might encourage someone to come forward with details of a missing person, but to no avail. Given the supposed age of the mystery body, no one linked it with the sudden departure of 54-year-old Martha Sheward from her home in Tabernacle Street that June. Her husband, tailor William Sheward, had frequently argued with Martha, who was fifteen years his senior, so his story that she had left him and gone to London sounded credible to neighbours and relatives.

With no identity for the victim or any obvious suspect, police soon shelved their investigation. As the years passed, Sheward moved house, began new jobs as a pawnbroker and then a publican, and in 1862 remarried, describing himself a 'widower' on his marriage certificate. He even fathered four children. But he also became withdrawn and an alcoholic.

It was on 1 January 1869 that Sheward suddenly turned up in Walworth, London, where he walked into a police station and announced that he wanted to hand himself in for the murder of his first wife. He had made something of a pilgrimage, for it was in the capital that Sheward had first met and married Martha in 1836. Sheward admitted that, following an argument on 15 June, he'd slit Martha's throat with a razor, then cut up her body in their home before attempting to dispose of the evidence around the city. Although crude, Sheward's efforts had certainly been enough to disguise his crime. Finally, however, remorse had got the better of him.

Sheward was put on trial back in Norwich, where two of the original surgeons who'd made the pronouncement about Martha's age were questioned about their findings, which had now been discovered to be wildly inaccurate. They squirmed, eventually admitting that there had actually been 'nothing inconsistent' with the age of the deceased being 54. In his defence one blurted out, 'A woman is an extremely elastic subject.' Sheward was found guilty of Martha's murder and hanged on 20 April.

56... pounds of weight in the 'Tombstone Murder'

The Warwickshire town of Stratford-upon-Avon is celebrated as the birthplace of the playwright William Shakespeare, and the bard's grave is located at Holy Trinity church. But few know that the churchyard was also the scene of a chilling murder, which took place on 23 April, the date remembered as Shakespeare's birthday.

It was on the morning of Saturday, 24 April 1954 that the graveyard's gardener noticed a hat floating in the nearby River Avon and then a single brown shoe, a glove and a pair of glasses on the bank. Further along the riverbank were a handbag and purse. Police were called and soon pulled the body of a 4ft 11in woman from the water. She was quickly identified as 45-year-old midwife Olive May Bennett, who worked at a local maternity hospital. Suicide was suspected but a pathologist found bruising on Olive's neck – she had been strangled.

The gardener had also noticed something else strange. One of the tombstones had been wrenched from its position in the graveyard. A search was made of the river and the 56lb stone, dedicated to an Edward Adam, 63, was dragged out. It was so heavy that it took four officers to carry. The inscription read: 'In the midst of life we are in death.' Detectives surmised that the killer had tried to weigh down Olive's body using the object.

Olive, who had recently moved to the area, was described as a 'secretive woman' but seems to have undergone something of a change of character in the run-up to her death. Formerly rather quiet, she had begun smoking and drinking sherry heavily in the town's pubs.

The last confirmed sighting of Olive was after closing time at the town's Red Horse Hotel, where she had been drinking alone. Then, at about 11.30 p.m., a waiter had seen a woman matching Olive's diminutive description kissing a burly man in the churchyard. He was wearing a belted raincoat and had a shock of blonde hair. Olive had told colleagues that she had a particular boyfriend, but no one knew his identity.

The local force called in top Scotland Yard detectives. A re-enactment was staged and hundreds of people were questioned, but even a mysterious note that Olive had received from a man called Harry led nowhere. In 1962, police made a renewed appeal for information. Two women came forward to say that around the same time Olive was murdered they had been confronted by a man who had threatened to throw them in the river, but had not attacked them. Sadly, no further progress was made with the case. Olive's murder remained unsolved, and her ghost is said to haunt Holy Trinity's churchyard to this day.

Oddly, there had been another murder with a supernatural bent just 6 miles away in Warwickshire, nine years earlier. It occurred on another memorable date, St Valentine's Day, 1945. That evening the corpse of farm worker Charles Walton, 74, from Lower Quinton, was found in a field where he'd been working. His throat had been savagely slashed with a sickle. A pitchfork had been driven into either side of his neck, pinning him to the ground. Some said a cross was carved into his skin too.

Aptly, a Detective Tombs conducted the initial inquiry, but before long Chief Inspector Robert Fabian from Scotland Yard was called in. Already making a name for himself as one of Britain's greatest ever detectives, Fabian would go on to solve some high-profile cases. In 1947, for example, using a scrap of paper found in a raincoat, he tracked down the killers of motorcyclist Alec de Antiquis, who had been shot while trying to stop a London robbery.

However, in the Walton case, Fabian soon came up against something of a 'wall of silence' in the local community, as rumours flew round that the murder was linked to the occult. In 1875, Ann Tennant, 80, had been murdered in the same vicinity with a pitchfork by a James Heywood.

His motive had been that he believed her to be a witch. And, in an eerie coincidence, an old book of local folklore detailed how, in 1885, a boy called Charles Walton had seen a ghostly black dog on nearby Meon Hill, just before his sister had died.

Was Walton's murder part of some kind of ritual killing? While an Italian prisoner-of-war and the farm owner came under suspicion, this time Fabian failed to pin the crime on anybody. In his autobiography he related how, in the course of his enquiries, he had himself encountered a black dog on Meon Hill, then a small boy who had come running past. When he asked the child if he'd lost his dog, the boy went deathly pale and simply ran off.

60... second time-frame in the murder of Laetitia Toureaux

Some murders hold a rare fascination not so much for the question of 'who did it?', but 'how did they do it?' This has never been truer than in the intriguing case of a glamorous 29-year-old Italian woman, murdered on the Paris Métro in 1937. The exact circumstances of her killing remain so unfathomable that the crime ranks high on the list of those labelled 'impossible'.

On the evening of Sunday, 16 May 1937, Laetitia Toureaux was anything but inconspicuous. Having left a dance hall in one of the city's suburbs, she entered the Métro station at Porte de Charenton at 6.23 p.m., dressed in green with a white hat and gloves, furs and a distinctive parasol. Just four minutes later she was seen by witnesses stepping on to a first-class carriage on subway train no. 365. The carriage was in between other second-class carriages that were packed with passengers. According to those present, Laetitia was the only traveller who could be seen in her carriage as the train left the station to go through a tunnel to the next stop. It took just sixty seconds to pass through and the train duly arrived at the platform of Porte Dorée at 6.28 p.m.

As new passengers boarded the first-class carriage, from doors at either end, they were horrified to see a woman's body slump forward from her seat. A 9in stiletto-style blade was protruding from her neck. Laetitia tried to whisper something to the first police officer on the scene but, with blood now pulsing out of her wound, she didn't live long enough to name or describe her attacker. No one was seen leaving the carriage at the Porte Dorée, but witnesses who had been travelling in the second-class carriages swore they heard a scream just as the train pulled into the station.

An autopsy suggested that the blow to Laetitia's jugular vein had been delivered with such swiftness, force and accuracy that it must have been the work of a professional. The knife having been left in the wound also indicated the signature of a certain type of hitman. While there were some discrepancies in the statements of the witnesses who got on the train at the Porte Dorée, it was still puzzling that no one had seen the killer exit from the carriage. Adding to the conundrum was the fact that the doors between first-class and second-class carriages were locked – the killer could not simply have switched cars.

Laetitia was identified from documents on her person, and it was soon evident to detectives investigating her murder that she had been leading a complicated life. She was a widow who worked in a glue factory by day, but she spent much of her time in dance halls and had been dating an arms smuggler in La Cagoule, a fascist group working to overthrow the French government. In fact Laetitia had been leading a double life as an undercover informant working for the authorities. Her murder was almost certainly ordered by La Cagoule operatives after her cover was blown. Yet Laetitia's murder was carried out so expertly that police had little to go on and, despite hundreds of people being interviewed, no one was brought to book. Just how the murder was executed without anyone observing the culprit, in such a public location, remains truly perplexing.

The puzzle of Toureaux's murder echoes the so-called 'locked-room' genre of fictional murder mystery stories, featuring crimes so cleverly devised that they seem to have been impossible to commit. Yet truth *is* sometimes stranger than fiction, as exhibited by the story of New York laundryman Isidor Fink from New York. On 9 March 1929, a neighbour of Fink heard noises from the room where he was ironing. When a policeman went to investigate, he found that the room was bolted from the inside and the only access to it was through a high, tiny window. Using a child to wriggle through and open the door, the officer saw the dead body of Fink lying on the floor.

He had been shot twice in the chest and once in the left wrist. Investigators determined that the shots had been fired too far from the body for Fink to have committed suicide. There was no weapon and no evidence of a robbery. It was described by baffled detectives, who never found the killer, as an 'insoluble mystery'.

62... love letters that sent Edith Thompson to the gallows

Matters of the heart have been at the root of many a murder. Infidelity, in particular, is a powerful motive. Adulterous couples who have resorted to killing those who got in their way have, throughout history, been dealt with severely. One of the first such tales of sexual intrigue to capture the imagination of the public occurred in Tudor England. On 14 February 1551, the ex-mayor of Faversham, England, was murdered; his throat cut in the parlour of his own home in a plot orchestrated by his wife, Alice, and her lover, Thomas Morsby. Their crime was discovered when they attempted to dispose of the body but left a trail back to the house. Neither was shown any mercy by the authorities, with Morsby swiftly hanged and Alice burnt at the stake. Individuals who have murdered their love rivals have fared no better. When Mary Pearcey killed her lover's wife, Phoebe Hogg, in London during October 1890, she was tried, convicted and hanged before Christmas.

Yet a wronged wife or husband who has resorted to killing in revenge for an illicit liaison has often been met with a measure of legal tolerance. Throughout history and across different nations, adultery has been widely seen as a form of provocation for a so-called 'crime of passion'. In Roman times a man was legally allowed to kill his wife's lover in some circumstances, and even his married daughter and her lover if he caught them in the act.

In nineteenth-century America the idea that discovery of an infidelity could lead to a sudden 'loss of control' led to Congressman Daniel Sickles getting away with shooting Philip Barton Key in the street. Sickles had killed the lawyer in 1859 after discovering he was having an affair with his wife, but he claimed that being cuckolded had caused a bout of temporary insanity. He was acquitted.

No such leniency was shown to Edith Thompson, who was convicted of murdering her husband even though she, herself, had not wielded a weapon. Indeed, at the heart of the controversial case was whether she had incited her lover to do so, in order that she might be found guilty of a 'common purpose' and so suffer the same fate – being hanged for the crime.

Just after midnight, on 4 October 1922, Edith, a successful 28-year-old millinery manageress, and her shipping clerk husband, Percy Thompson, 32, were walking back to their home in Ilford, Essex, after a trip to the theatre. Suddenly a man leapt out of the bushes in front of them, wielding a knife, and stabbed Percy. Edith was knocked to the ground and neighbours reported hearing her screaming, 'Oh don't!' The attacker fled and Percy died of his wounds.

Within hours police had identified their chief suspect, Frederick Bywaters, a 20-year-old merchant seaman who had holidayed with the couple and lodged at their home in 1921. During this time Bywaters had begun a tempestuous affair with Edith. When Percy discovered what was going on, he threw Bywaters out, though the couple had continued to communicate.

After the murder, Bywaters was quickly apprehended and proved co-operative, leading police to the knife and admitting he'd killed Percy and had done so of his own volition, not just because he loved Edith but because he had witnessed Percy mistreating her.

In the course of their enquiries, police found sixty-two love letters that Edith had written to Bywaters. In these she not only expressed her devotion but also stated that she had, on occasion, tried to poison Percy and even sprinkled ground glass into his mashed potato. She'd also urged Percy to 'do something', sending him newspaper cuttings related to poisoning. This contrasted to what she'd told police after the attack: 'I never wanted him to do it.'

Both Bywaters and Thompson were charged with murder. The letters were produced in evidence at the trial that December, and Edith's failure to explain their contents would convince the jury that she was guilty of jointly planning the murder, even though she might not have known exactly when and where it would happen. Throughout the proceedings, Bywaters maintained that Edith was innocent – her letters were simply the product of an imaginative mind. Examination of Percy's body had found no evidence of poison or ingestion of glass. Nevertheless both of the accused were found guilty and sentenced to be hanged.

A million people signed a petition for clemency to be shown towards Edith, but the home secretary declined to intervene. The doomed lovers were hanged simultaneously, in separate prisons, at 9 a.m. on 9 January 1923. Edith was so hysterical that she had to be carried, barely conscious, to the gallows.

64... squares on Alexander Pichushkin's chessboard

Many serial killers keep souvenirs of their victims. Jeffrey Dahmer, for instance, dismembered many of the seventeen men he killed over thirteen years and kept body parts, including skulls and even genitals, as trophies. Indeed, the key to uncovering Dahmer's sickening crimes came in 1991 when one of his intended victims managed to escape from his apartment. An investigating police officer discovered gruesome photographs of mutilated men, which Dahmer had kept as mementoes, in his flat.

Some multiple murderers go further, keeping actual logs of their victims. One of the most notorious was Frenchman Henri Landru. By 1914 the sometime bric-a-brac dealer was 45, estranged from his wife and already a convicted swindler. With the outbreak of the First World War, he apparently saw an opportunity to ramp up his preferred method of fraud. Landru advertised in lonely hearts columns of Parisian newspapers, posing as a widower who would like to meet women who had lost their own partners, with a view to marriage. Balding, with a bushy red beard, Landru was an unlikely lothario but evidently had a good measure of charm and intelligence. With the carnage taking place on the Western Front, there was certainly no shortage of widows looking for companionship.

Exactly when and what made Landru turn to murder isn't clear, but using a string of aliases he was able to befriend and despatch a string of women for financial gain. His first known victim was Madame Jeanne-Marie Cuchet, 39. She moved into a rented villa with Landru, who was claiming to be an engineer called Monsieur Diard. But by January 1915 Jeanne-Marie, along with her son André, had disappeared. Somehow Landru had got his hands on 5,000 francs of Cuchet's cash, but he was soon in need of more. He would go on to lure nine other women to their deaths, each apparently vanishing without a trace, but only after Landru had carefully made sure their assets would fall into his hands. It was only when the sister of one of those missing, Célestine Buisson, tried to track down her sibling and identified the house where Landru was living, in Gambais, west of Paris, that police grudgingly agreed to launch a proper investigation.

A search of Landru's house revealed no corpses, but there was a notebook with cryptic jottings, apparently listing 283 women with whom he'd corresponded, including those known to have disappeared. Landru had also recorded the many noms de plume he'd used during his charades. Neighbours noted the evil-smelling smoke that had sometimes belched from his rented property's chimney. Examining the stove, police found fragments of bone and clothes. It was concluded that Landru had probably strangled and then burned his victims. He went to the guillotine on 25 February 1922.

More modern instances of killers who meticulously recorded their victims include Randy Kraft, convicted in 1989 of killing sixteen young men. He got the nickname of the 'Scorecard Killer' because, after his arrest, police found a list in his car containing sixty-one coded phrases. They were able to match these to the names of victims or the way in which they had been killed. Columbian Luis Alfredo Garavito, responsible for the deaths of more than 140 boys, also recorded his tally of death in a battered notebook, kept in his pocket.

More novel was the way in which Russian killer Alexander Pichushkin counted his killings. Preying on mainly the elderly and homeless in parks, he would get his victims drunk on vodka, then hit them over the head with a hammer before pushing their bodies down drains. The motivation for Pichushkin's murders seems to have been purely to exercise power over others, something he had been doing to his opponents in chess since he was a youth. Pichushkin was an expert player of the game and it was on a chessboard in his Moscow flat that he would log his victims, marking each square with the date every time he killed.

By 2006 police knew they were looking for a serial killer, and they finally got their break when the body of a woman turned up in a park. She'd left a note for her son, telling him that she was going for a walk with Pichushkin, 32, a co-worker in the same supermarket. When the authorities searched Pichushkin's flat, they found the chessboard on a table. Sixty-one squares had been filled in. Pichushkin later claimed that he had been aiming to fill in the whole board, possibly bidding to beat the body count of fellow Russian Andrei Chikatilo, nicknamed the 'Rostov Ripper', who had killed fifty-six women and children. In the end, police could only find evidence to link Pichushkin to forty-eight murders, for which he was convicted in 2007.

70... sickles in a thirteenth-century murder, solved by flies

Murders can often be solved by the tiniest of clues – even insects. One of the earliest documented instances is to be found in a Chinese book written in 1235 by Sung Tz'u, a legal and medical expert who lived during the Song Dynasty. *The Washing Away of Wrongs* was a handbook for coroners and one of the first works ever to cover forensic criminal detection methods. It features the case of a man whose body was found by a roadside with ten savage injuries. Initially he was thought to have been attacked by highway robbers, but an official at the inquest into his death noted that the victim's personal effects were still with him.

Examination of the wounds helped the official determine that they were probably made by a sickle, a farmer's tool. The man's wife was asked if he'd had any enemies. She could not think of any, but she did recall a man who had recently borrowed money from her spouse. The official then ordered all of the victim's neighbours to bring their sickles before him. In due course, seventy of the implements were collected and laid outside on the ground for inspection. All appeared to be clean. However, the weather that day was hot and suddenly flies began to swarm around one sickle in particular. When the owner of the sickle in question was challenged, he denied being the murderer. But the official told him, 'The sickles of the others in the crowd had no flies. There are traces of blood on the sickle, so the flies gather.' The accused, who happened to be the man who had borrowed money from the victim, immediately broke down and confessed to murdering his neighbour over the debt. The official had cracked the case by using his knowledge of the habits of flies to conclude that they had been attracted to the sickle in order to feast on the invisible residue of human remains still clinging to it.

The use of insect biology to help solve crimes is called forensic entomology. Today forensic scientists are often able to pinpoint the time of death from a corpse by analysing creatures that are feeding on the rotting body. However, it wasn't until the 1930s that this practice would successfully help secure a conviction in a high-profile case that became known as the Jigsaw Murders.

On the morning of 29 September 1935, a female holidaymaker taking a stroll across a bridge over a river near the town of Moffatt in the Scottish Borders noticed, to her horror, that there was a human arm protruding from a package on the bank below. Police eventually found seventy decomposing

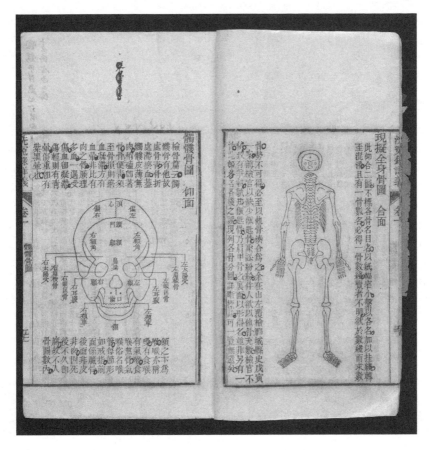

Washing Away of Wrongs book. (Courtesy of Wellcome Library, London)

body parts, including two heads, which they surmised had been carried up on to the banks when the river had last flooded on 19 September. However, anything that could help identification, like teeth or fingertips, had been purposely removed.

Some of the remains had been wrapped in a particular newspaper edition, dated 15 September, which was only available 100 miles away in the Lancaster area. Suspicion fell on a respected 36-year-old doctor living in the city, Buck Ruxton. His wife, Isabella, and their maid, Mary Rogerson, had been reported missing by their families. At first Ruxton had claimed that his wife – whom he'd accused of having affairs – had left him with her lover and that Mary had gone away to have an abortion. But adding to the unease about Ruxton's potential involvement in their disappearance was the fact that he had been stopped by police in his car on 17 September, following a collision with a cyclist in the Lake District. Ruxton appeared to have been on his way back from Scotland.

Now police needed to prove that the two dismembered bodies they had recovered were indeed the missing women. Some of the maggots feeding on the cadavers were sent to an entomologist at the University of Edinburgh. They were identified as maggots from a blowfly and about 12 to 14 days old, meaning that the bodies could not have been deposited in the stream since then. This chimed with the date of the newspaper and the last date that the two women had been seen at the Ruxton home. Another new technique was also used, where a photograph of the living Isabella was superimposed on to an image of one of the skulls which had been placed in the same orientation. It matched perfectly. Police also found bloodstains in the Ruxton home. It appears the doctor had strangled Isabella in a rage and then cut Mary's throat because she had witnessed the murder. Ruxton was hanged on 12 May 1936.

75... number of the grenade mine used in the Rayleigh Bath Chair Murder

The scene of carnage confronting police officers arriving at Hockley Road in the quiet town of Rayleigh in Essex on the afternoon of 23 July 1943 was just the kind of devastation that the designers of the Number 75 Hawkins anti-tank grenade had envisioned. There was a bloodied leg hanging from the branches of a nearby tree, another severed limb lying in a garden 50ft away, a torso on the tarmac and a tangle of twisted metal in the middle of the street. All this was due to the detonation of a single Number 75, a small but effective weapon. It had been developed following the evacuation of Dunkirk in 1940 and was intended to help Britain's meagre defence forces counter the threat of German armoured divisions following an invasion of the country, which was then considered imminent. But three years on, and with the threat of German landings now receding, the target of this particular device had not been a German Panzer tank advancing through the shires, but a humble wheelchair.

Its occupant was Archibald Brown, a 47-year-old former soldier and businessman who had already lost the use of both his legs through a motorbike accident in 1920. What remained of his body was now scattered across the suburban street thanks to the explosion of the grenade mine, one so loud it was initially assumed to have been the result of bombing by enemy aircraft. While there was nothing much left of Brown, somehow his nurse, Elsie Irene Mitchell, who had been pushing his metal 'bath chair', had survived with minor wounds.

Examining Brown's remains and the debris, the authorities quickly ruled out a bomb falling from the sky as the cause of the explosion, realising that Brown had been killed by something blowing up underneath him. The shrapnel indicated that the device responsible was British – the Number 75. Brown had been murdered, but by whom?

The brutality of the attack, purposely designed to obliterate the target, indicated that this was someone with a serious grudge against the victim, though the nurse's survival was something of a miracle. By chance, the velvet cushions of the chair and its frame had provided enough protection to shield her from the full impact of the blast. It was clear that the culprit didn't care if someone else was killed in their murderous attempt.

Mitchell was one of three nurses who helped care for the invalided Brown and regularly took him out for the afternoon in his chair. She was able to tell officers that at 1.45 p.m. on the day of the explosion she had gone to get the chair from the Anderson shelter in the garden of Brown's Rayleigh home, where it was usually kept. Strangely, she had found the shelter locked from the inside. Returning with Brown's wife, Dorothy, they encountered Brown's elder son, Eric, emerging from the shelter looking agitated. A little later Mitchell had wheeled Brown, clad in pyjamas and dressing gown, off for his outing. During the constitutional, he had asked her to stop so he could have a cigarette. Seconds later came the shattering blast.

Police turned their attention to Eric. His odd mannerisms had seen him fired from a job as a bank clerk in 1942. He had then joined the forces, serving in the 8th battalion, Suffolk Regiment. On the day of his father's death Eric had been on leave. But it emerged that he had recently been trained to use the very anti-tank weapon used to kill his father. Indeed, there were scores of the Number 75s primed and ready to be used at the camp stores.

Taken in for questioning, the 19-year-old had soon confessed to killing his father, claiming that Brown, embittered by his paralysis and pain, had become an overbearing bully to both him and Dorothy. Despairing, he had decided to end their suffering and, he said, his father's too. To do so he had stolen the Number 75, then adapted the mine so that it would go off, not under the pressure of tank tracks, but under the lighter weight of his father's body. When the device was strapped to the underside of the bath chair, a slight shift of weight on lighting up had been enough to trigger it.

At Eric Brown's trial, in Chelmsford, his mother confirmed that her husband had been a tyrant who would throw hot tea at her. It didn't stop her son being found guilty on 4 November. However, he was declared insane and ordered to be detained in an asylum, where he would languish for the next thirty-two years.

84... units of insulin found in murdered Elizabeth Barlow

Injecting insulin can saves lives. It's a hormone produced in the pancreas to help regulate blood sugar levels. But people with Type 1 diabetes don't produce enough insulin, and prior to the 1920s the condition could be a death sentence. Then scientists made the breakthrough discovery that would allow diabetes sufferers to be injected with insulin, enabling them to lead relatively normal lives. Yet within a few years, people were using the same method to commit suicide. Injected into a person without diabetes, the extra insulin can cause hypoglycaemia, or low blood sugar, potentially sending the body into fatal shock. It was inevitable that one day it would be used by a murderer and in 1957 came the first known case.

Before deciding to try and kill his wife, hospital nurse Kenneth Barlow had already boasted to a work colleague that he'd found the perfect murder weapon. He knew that insulin quickly dissolved in the bloodstream, making it virtually undetectable by anyone investigating a sudden death. Just before midnight on 3 May 1957, a doctor was called to the home of Barlow, 38, and his wife of eleven months, Elizabeth, in Bradford, West Yorkshire. The GP quickly determined that Elizabeth, lying in the bath, was dead. According to Barlow, his 32-year-old wife had vomited earlier that evening and, feeling sweaty, had decided to go and clean up. He had been shocked to discover her, at 11.20 p.m., submerged underneath the water in the tub. Barlow claimed he'd pulled out the plug and tried to perform artificial respiration but to no avail – she was already dead.

The doctor called the police who, in turn, called in a forensic pathologist, Dr David Price. A few factors were immediately suspicious. In spite of his version of events, Barlow's pyjamas were completely dry, as was the floor of the bathroom. Elizabeth's pupils were strangely dilated, as if she had been drugged, and tell-tale syringes were found in the kitchen. They also found Elizabeth's pyjamas covered in sweat.

Initial findings at the post-mortem, conducted by Price, were consistent with drowning. But he was convinced that Elizabeth (who was two months pregnant) had entered the water unconscious, and he sent samples of tissue away to be tested for a raft of common poisons. All came back negative. Re-examining the body with a magnifying glass, Price now found four tiny red marks – two in each buttock. They appeared to be puncture holes made by injections shortly before Elizabeth's death. The dilated pupils and sweaty pyjamas indicated hypoglycaemia and the investigation team now began to consider the possibility that Elizabeth had been injected with insulin. They were rewarded when further specialist tests recovered 84 units* of insulin from around the injection sites, easily enough to send Elizabeth's blood sugar levels plunging dangerously. Experiments with mice also showed that they would go into life-threatening diabetic comas when injected with some of the recovered tissue from the area.

Challenged about the injections, Barlow admitted giving his wife another drug, ergometrine, to induce an abortion. The scientific tests proved that, even if this was true, he had switched to giving her insulin, which hadn't been quite as untraceable as he'd imagined. As well as Barlow's statements to co-workers about identifying 'the perfect murder weapon', the forensic evidence would help see him sentenced to twenty-six years in jail. Barlow's motive for the murder was never clear, but his first wife had also died the previous year, aged just 33, apparently from natural causes. The coincidence was striking.

Since the Barlow case, insulin has cropped up in murder cases on more than fifty other occasions. One also involved a nurse, Beverley Allitt, who would end up convicted of murdering four children in 1991, as well as attempting to kill or cause harm to many more in the Lincolnshire hospital where she worked. Following an investigation of the unusually high death rate on the children's ward, it was found that the deaths and other incidents all had one thing in common – Allitt had been on duty. A number of drugs had been used, but insulin was found to have been given in large doses to at least two of her victims. Allitt was sentenced to at least thirty years behind bars and diagnosed with Munchausen syndrome by proxy, a condition which leads sufferers to crave attention.

In another celebrated case, Claus von Bülow was wrongly accused of trying to kill his rich wife, Sunny, using insulin. He was eventually cleared in 1985 after the hypoglycaemic comas Sunny had suffered – one of which had left her in a vegetative state – were found to be the result of her own health conditions.

* Insulin is officially measured in 'units'.

92... business cards in the strange case of the Tokyo Bank Poisoner

Those responsible for multiple murders often leave behind 'calling cards' at the scene of their crimes: perhaps particular items, writing or drawings. One serial killer in India left a beer can beside each victim. Another, in North America, drew a smiley face near each location where their victims' bodies were dumped. Sometimes, however, these calling cards can be more literal. In October 2002 the region around Washington DC in the United States was terrorised by a series of apparently random shootings which left ten people dead and three injured. Initially the crimes were thought to be the work of one individual, nicknamed the 'Beltway Sniper'. The shooter used a rifle and quickly fled, leaving the police with only sketchy details of the vehicles he might be driving. However, tarot cards, with cryptic messages, were left at several of the murder locations. On one, the Death Card, the words 'Call me God' had been written. In the end, ballistic and fingerprint evidence led to the apprehension and conviction of John Allen Muhammad, 42, along with an accomplice, Lee Boyd Malvo, 17, for the murders. The motive for their killing spree remains unclear.

In a case of mass murder from the 1940s, it was business cards that would form the basis of the investigation. On 26 January 1948, a man wearing an official-looking uniform arrived at a branch of the Imperial Bank in a suburb of Tokyo, Japan, just as it was closing. He told staff he was a public health official and had been sent by the occupying American forces to inoculate them against an outbreak of dysentery. The unsuspecting bank manager gathered together the sixteen people inside and all drank drops of the liquid 'medication' from teacups. Minutes later they were writhing on the floor in agony – poisoned. With ten of his victims already dead, two dying and four unconscious, the bogus medic then proceeded to rob the bank, fleeing with 180,000 yen.

A nationwide manhunt was launched, but police soon discovered that it was not the first such incident. There had been two other 'rehearsals' in banks, where a fake official had spun the same story and successfully given employees some 'medication' to take. In those incidents no one had fallen ill, but on both occasions the man had presented a business card. On the first occasion, the card turned out to bear a fictitious name. But the second time, he had used a card printed with the name of a real doctor, Shigeru Matsui, whom police were soon questioning.

Top murder detective Tamegoro Igii was brought in on the case, and Matsui himself was quickly ruled out as a suspect. But it was traditional and commonplace in Japan for business cards or *meishi* to be exchanged and for those received from others to be kept. Matsui had exchanged ninety-two cards of the type in question and recorded the times and locations of his meetings on the back of the ones he'd received in return. Using this information, Igii and his team were able to track down all the recipients, including 57-year-old Sadamichi Hirasawa, an artist from Otaru on the island of Hokkaido. When questioned by Igii, he claimed to have lost the card from Matsui. He was known to have been in Tokyo at the time of the crime, but he could not supply an adequate alibi as to his movements on the day.

There were more seemingly damning facts. Hirasawa had a similar amount of money in his possession to the amount that had been taken from the bank and had recently been in debt. Two of the survivors of the bank poisoning positively identified Hirasawa as the poisoner.

Hirasawa was arrested that August. At first, he protested his innocence, yet under interrogation he confessed to having used potassium cyanide to commit the killings. By the time his case came to trial, in 1950, Hirasawa had retracted this confession, but he was found guilty and sentenced to death.

From that moment on, doubts about Hirasawa's guilt would persist. There were allegations that his confession had been obtained through coercion, with later analysis of Hirasawa's confession showing that his account of how the crime unfolded was inconsistent with the known facts. Conflicting evidence from autopsies also suggested that the poison used on the victims may not have been cyanide but acetone cyanohydrin, a military agent linked to the activities of Unit 731, Japan's wartime biological and chemical research organisation. Hirasawa was unlikely to have had access to such a substance.

The Japanese government repeatedly deferred the death sentence on Hirasawa, who died in jail aged 95, in 1987, with supporters still proclaiming his innocence.

94.7... average IQ of a serial killer

Nathan Leopold had a reported IQ of 210, higher than that of the acclaimed scientist Albert Einstein. Richard Loeb's score was 160. Both were geniuses and high-flying graduates from wealthy backgrounds, and glittering futures appeared to lie ahead of them. Instead, the scheming duo would use their intellect for evil.

By 1924, Leopold, who had uttered his first words at just 4 months old, was aged 19 and could speak five languages. He was planning to attend Harvard Law School. Loeb had completed his degree aged just 17. The pair had become firm friends – and lovers – after studying at the University of Chicago together.

All too aware of their own academic brilliance, Leopold and Loeb were inspired by the works of German philosopher Friedrich Nietzsche to believe that they were *Übermenschen*, or 'supermen', who were not bound by the normal rules of society. They had also become fascinated by the idea of carrying out the 'perfect crime' and began to plot the kidnap of a young boy in order to collect a ransom. They intended to murder him, even if the money was paid, to prevent any chance of their being caught.

On the afternoon of 21 May, they went trawling around Chicago's suburbs for a suitable candidate. They soon came across a wealthy neighbour's son whom they knew, 14-year-old Bobby Franks, and lured him into their rented car. Soon afterwards Franks was callously beaten to death inside the vehicle with a chisel, his body then deposited at a culvert in a pre-arranged isolated location. Covering Franks' body in acid, in the hope of hampering identification, Leopold and Loeb then cleaned the car, burnt their bloodied clothes and returned home, delivering a ransom note demanding $10,000 to the boy's father, Jacob Franks. Their idea was to direct him to catch a certain train and then to throw the money out of a window at a particular location. They would simply collect the booty and make their escape.

But Leopold and Loeb's plan began to unravel almost immediately. Franks senior had called the police, and Bobby's body was quickly found and identified. The killers had also made several crucial mistakes. Chief among their blunders was accidentally leaving a pair of glasses by the body. Police were able to track the distinctively hinged pair of spectacles back to Leopold through the man who had sold them to him. Within ten days of the murder both men had confessed and they were later sentenced to life imprisonment.

Leopold and Loeb had been caught and successfully convicted despite their undoubted intelligence. In their case, there was only one victim. But serial killers, who, by the nature of their crimes, appear to outwit the authorities for long periods are often considered more cunning, perhaps even brighter, than the average murderer. A serial killer has been defined as someone who murders at least three people over at least one month, with a cooling-off period between each of the crimes. The FBI definition is 'unlawful killing of two or more victims by the same offender(s), in separate events'.

But are these multiple murderers really more intelligent? Analysis of data on over 4,000 serial killers amassed by Dr Mike Aamodt, a professor of psychology at Radford University, reveals that many of the best-known serial killers have possessed great intellect. American Jeffrey Dahmer, known as the Milwaukee Cannibal, who killed seventeen men and boys in the 1980s, had an IQ of 145, well above the average. He evaded capture for thirteen years. Another infamous serial killer with elevated intelligence was Ted Bundy. A bright and handsome university graduate, with a budding law career and an IQ of 124, he is known to have murdered at least thirty young women in the mid-1970s. John Wayne Gacy, known as the 'Killer Clown' and sentenced to death for sexually assaulting and killing at least thirty-three teenage boys between 1972 and 1978, had an above average IQ of 118.

However, Aamodt's figures suggest that when all serial killers (where the IQ is known) are taken together, the average is just 94.7, broadly in line with the average in the general population, considered to be 90–110. Among the most intelligent serial killers, according to the data, are those who use bombs to despatch their targets. Although better classed as a domestic terrorist than a serial killer, Unabomber Ted Kaczynski killed three people and had an IQ of 167. It took the authorities seventeen years to capture him (see page 181).

99... explosive devices in the Columbine School massacre

Criminologists distinguish between serial killers, who tend to have a 'cooling off' period between their crimes, and other types of multiple murderer. Mass murderers are usually defined as those who kill four or more people in one cataclysmic event, while spree killers tend to go on a rampage at more than one location. Where both of these latter types of crime are carried out by individuals, what is often startling is the sheer amount of firepower and weaponry they use.

The United States, which has a high level of firearm ownership, has a larger proportion of mass shootings than anywhere else in the world. One of the first to shake the country took place on 1 August 1966. Ex-marine Charles Whitman, 25, first killed his wife and mother, then took the lift to the twenty-seventh floor of the clock tower at the University of Texas, where he had been a student. With him he carried a swan off-shotgun, two rifles, an M1 Carbine, three handguns and knives, plus 700 rounds of ammunition. Making his way to the observation deck, Whitman then began firing at random targets 231ft below. By the time he himself was shot dead, ninety-six minutes later, fourteen more people were dead.

In the months running up to the 2012 killing of twelve people at a cinema complex in Aurora, Colorado, 24-year-old James Holmes was able to buy 6,000 rounds of ammunition for a rifle, shotgun and pistol over the internet. Dressed in combat gear, he fired tear gas and seventy-six rounds into an audience watching a Batman movie. Holmes was apprehended and police subsequently diffused explosive devices in his booby-trapped apartment, discovering thirty homemade grenades. He was later sentenced to spend the rest of his life behind bars.

Massacres at educational institutions provide some of the most upsetting examples of mass murder. Seung-Hui Cho, a 23-year-old student at Virginia Tech University in Blacksburg, chalked up the worst death toll for this sort of crime when he killed thirty-two people on 16 April 2007, using two semi-automatic pistols. He fired 174 rounds, finally taking his own life too. Equally distressing were the twenty-six lives lost, including twenty children, at the Sandy Hook Elementary School in December 2012. During the shooting there Adam Lanza, who would also commit suicide, fired 154 rounds from a rifle in five minutes. An array of firearms and 1,700 rounds of ammo were found at the home that the 20-year-old had shared with his mother, whom he'd also shot dead.

Though the Columbine School massacre of 20 April 1999 in Colorado involved fewer deaths, deranged students Eric Harris, 18, and Dylan Klebold, 17, had certainly planned to kill more people. In advance, they had also constructed an incredible ninety-nine improvised explosive devices, only a few of which detonated as they enacted their murderous plan. Two 20lb propane tank bombs, which they had planted in the cafeteria, failed to go off, at which point they decided to march onto the campus and use their arsenal of guns to shoot twelve people dead, before killing themselves. Had the cafeteria bombs gone off, hundreds might have perished.

The slaughter at Columbine echoed a much less well-known massacre from 1927 when Andrew Kehoe used dynamite to blow up a school in Bath, Michigan, killing forty-four people including thirty-eight children. Only a portion of the 1,000lbs of explosive that the disgruntled school board member had planted in the basement had gone off, meaning a higher death toll was only narrowly avoided. Kehoe, 55, also took his own life, blowing himself up in a truck.

The phenomenon of shooting sprees is far from merely an American problem. One of the worst incidents anywhere involved the 2011 Norwegian far-right extremist Anders Breivik, 32, who killed eight people in an Oslo bombing and shot dead sixty-nine others on the island of Utøya.

In the UK, the Hungerford massacre of 1987 saw 27-year-old Michael Ryan (licensed to carry seven guns) shoot dead sixteen people around the Berkshire town in a six-hour time-frame, using two rifles and a Beretta pistol. In 2010 Derrick Bird, 52, killed twelve people with a shotgun and rifle as he rampaged through Cumbria. Perhaps most shocking of all was the murder of sixteen children and a teacher at Dunblane Primary School in Scotland on 13 March 1996. Thomas Hamilton, 43, carried four legally owned pistols and revolvers plus 743 cartridges of ammunition, firing a total of 105 shots in little more than three minutes.

A fundamental difference in the responses to these mass shootings in the UK as compared to the USA was the introduction of tough restrictions on firearm ownership, particularly a ban on handguns after Dunblane. Britain has one of the lowest homicide rates involving guns in the world.

100... miles in a Hitler murder mystery

Adolf Hitler is remembered as the man who sparked a world war and masterminded the mass murder of 6 million Jews. Thanks to this catalogue of slaughter, it's not surprising that the death of one woman in his life, eight years before the outbreak of the Second World War and two years before he became chancellor of Germany, has been relegated to a footnote of history. Eva Braun is, of course, the woman most readily associated with the dictator, becoming his companion and briefly his wife at the end of the conflict. Yet earlier in his life Hitler had another important female relationship and one that was just as intense. In fact, it's said that Angela 'Geli' Raubal, Hitler's half-niece, was the only woman whom he ever really loved.

From 1929 the vivacious and attractive Geli shared his apartment at No. 16 Prinzregentenplatz in the city of Munich. Despite the fact that Hitler was nineteen years older than Geli, the pair seem to have had a romantic relationship. At the very least there was, as the historian Ian Kershaw puts it, a 'sexual dependence'.

On the morning of 19 September 1931, Geli was dramatically found dead at the apartment, with Hitler's gun, a Walther 6.35mm pistol, at her side. She was 23. The death was quickly ruled to be suicide, but from the outset there were rumours that 'Uncle Alf', as Geli called Hitler, might have had a hand in what happened.

Hitler, by then leader of the Nazi party, is known to have taken a domineering attitude towards Geli, intervening to stop her seeing other men, including his chauffeur. There are suggestions that he forced Geli to indulge some of his wilder sexual fetishes – even that she was pregnant when she died. For her part, Geli may have harboured some jealousy when Hitler began seeing the 17-year-old Eva Braun. Whatever the truth behind their strange liaison, it seems that in the run-up to Geli's death the pair argued about her professed desire to move to Vienna.

There are conflicting accounts of who discovered Geli's body and whether the door to the room where she was found was locked from the inside. Nazi party bigwigs, including Rudolf Hess, were certainly on the scene before the police were alerted.

When a doctor cursorily examined the corpse, he found that rigor mortis had set in, concluding that Geli had died the previous evening. There was a wound above her heart and a single fatal bullet had pierced her lung, lodging just above her hip.

Despite the official verdict of suicide, there was no note. Instead, near the prostrate body, was an unfinished letter to a friend, one that was surprisingly upbeat for someone evidently about to take a gun to their own breast. It ended mid-sentence. There was no inquest and Geli's body was quickly taken out of the country to be buried in Vienna.

Hitler claimed not to have been at the apartment when Geli died. Indeed, on the face of it he seems to have been 100 miles away in Nuremberg, on his way to a rally in Hamburg. But was he? Could he have murdered Geli in a jealous rage or as a potential inconvenience as he prepared for a political breakthrough? Following the death, Hitler denied allegations that he'd violently argued with Geli on the day she died. Meanwhile, the risible party line given for the supposed suicide was that Geli was worried about her hopes of becoming a singer.

Hitler reportedly stayed at a hotel in Nuremberg on the night of the 18th. His best alibi was a speeding ticket picked up the next day as his Mercedes supposedly sped back to Munich after he was told about the death. Of course, his hotel stay and the ticket could have been faked after the event, and given that no one heard the shot that killed Geli, even if the time of death was slightly awry, he could still have travelled to Nuremberg that night. More likely was that Geli was exterminated by someone else on the orders of party officials or Hitler himself.

There were like-minded people in power who could have helped with any cover-up. The presiding Minister of Justice in Bavaria was a Nazi sympathiser, while the first detective involved in the case, Heinrich Müller, would go on to head the Gestapo.

Catholic priest Johann Pant, who officiated at Geli's burial on consecrated ground, later said, 'They pretended she committed suicide … from the fact I gave her a Christian burial you can draw your own conclusions.'

Questions have also been asked about the trajectory of the bullet through Geli's body. She would have had to hold the gun pointing downward, above her heart, which seems unnecessarily awkward. She certainly seems to have had little clear motive to take her own life, and while Hitler is said to have plunged into a depression following her death, it's interesting to note that he did not find time to go to the funeral.

101...
room number in the murder of John Welch

> You asked me once, what was in Room 101. I told you that you knew the
> answer already. Everyone knows it. The thing that is in Room 101 is the worst
> thing in the world.

In George Orwell's book *Nineteen Eighty-Four*, Room 101 is a basement
torture chamber where citizens who do not conform to the regime must face
their worst nightmares. Back in 1980 there was a chilling real-life echo of this
fictional horror when, on the evening of 26 November, a porter came across a
grizzly scene at room 101 of the Swallow Hotel in Newcastle. In the en-suite
bathroom lay the battered body of a man. He'd been hit over the head several
times with a blunt instrument and turned out to be John Welch, 45, from
Lincoln, who had been in the city on business. The father-of-two had been
due to have dinner with representatives of a local casino. When Welch didn't
show up at the restaurant as arranged, they phoned his hotel to check on him.

Detectives assigned to the case determined that Welch had gone to answer a
knock on the door and that his killer had promptly beaten him over the head.
He'd died from his injuries. Oddly, despite the hotel being almost full that
night, no one else heard or saw anything suspicious. Welch had checked in just
a few hours earlier and no visitors had been officially admitted to see him; nor
had he received any phone calls. Adding to the mystery was the fact that his
vehicle, a Ford Cortina, had been taken from the hotel car park, before being
abandoned in nearby Jesmond. Yet nothing had been stolen from his room.

In what had the hallmarks of a professional hit, police thought a business
associate could be responsible, but struggled to find a motive for the murder
despite conducting 6,500 interviews and taking 3,200 statements. In 1990,
two men were arrested in connection with the crime, but charges were later
dropped. Welch's killer remains at large.

Hotels have often featured in famous cases of homicide. There was,
for example, the shooting of Prince Ali Kamel Fahmy Bey in suite 41 at
London's grand Savoy Hotel in 1923, with his wife sensationally acquitted
of his murder. In 1929 Rosaline Fox appeared to have died in a fire at the
Metropole Hotel in Margate, Kent, but forensic evidence showed she'd first
been strangled. Her son, Sidney, went to the gallows for the crime. And, in

1968, there was the assassination of civil rights leader Martin Luther King on the balcony of room no. 306 at the Lorraine Hotel in Memphis.

But there was one hotel that made even Norman Bates' motel in the film *Psycho* seem like a vaguely appealing place to stay. Nineteenth-century serial killer Henry H. Holmes would actually build his own hotel in which to carry out wholesale murder. He originally trained as a doctor before working as a pharmacist, then bought a piece of land in Chicago on which he constructed a three-storey building that would later be dubbed 'murder castle'.

The World's Fair Hotel was begun in 1887 and took five years to complete. Holmes hoped that he could cash in by accommodating visitors to the city's World Fair of 1893. However, this was no ordinary hotel. It contained a series of windowless and soundproof rooms, with hidden partitions and secret passageways. Gas pipes were connected to these rooms so that Holmes could asphyxiate unwitting residents. He also installed special chutes so that bodies could be delivered to a basement. Unsuspecting guests, lovers, children and employees would arrive here, and then Holmes could go about disposing of their bodies via an oven or acid bath. He would also dissect and dismember his victims, sometimes stripping off the flesh and selling on the skeletons to medical schools.

As well as a killer, Holmes was also a master conman who pulled off a series of insurance scams. What was going on in his hotel only came to light when he was convicted of murdering fellow fraudster Benjamin Pitezel in 1895. Holmes also murdered three of Pitezel's children. The police would go on to find human remains around Holmes' hotel, and he eventually confessed to a total of twenty-seven murders, though some believe the real tally could be much higher. Holmes would claim, 'I was born with the Devil in me.' He was hanged in Philadelphia on 7 May 1896.

105... kilos in the Gouffé affair

In April 1935, a 14ft tiger shark was captured off the coast of Sydney, Australia, and put on display to the public at an aquarium. A few days later it suddenly regurgitated a human forearm. There were no more body parts inside the shark, but forensic examination of the limb revealed that it had been severed with a knife, not by shark teeth. The arm sported a distinctive tattoo of two boxers. This body art helped police identify the dead man as small-time crook Jim Smith. It turned out that Smith had been murdered and his body put in a tin trunk and dumped in the ocean, but that the arm had come free, ending up inside the shark.

Unfortunately, in that instance, the prosecution team could not make the case against their prime suspect stick. But, half a century earlier, the case of another mystery body in a trunk in France saw science and detective work combine brilliantly to bring a pair of killers to justice.

After a road worker found a decomposing naked body in a sack by a river near Lyon on 13 August 1889, an autopsy was carried out by Dr Paul Bernard. He recorded that the corpse was male, probably about 35, and had been the victim of strangulation. A murder enquiry was launched but police struggled to establish the identity of the victim. Four days later a broken wooden trunk turned up not far from the first discovery. Since it smelled as bad as the sack, it was deduced that it had previously contained the body. There was a faded railway label stuck to the trunk, revealing that it had been sent to Lyon from Paris by rail on 27 July. The year was indistinct, but the local police believed the numbers to read 1888.

When Assistant Superintendent Marie-François Goron of the Sûreté, in Paris, heard about the case, he began to speculate that this date might actually be 1889. For, on 27 July that year, a wealthy, sex-obsessed Parisian bailiff, Toussaint-Augustin Gouffé, had gone missing. Goron arranged for Gouffé's brother-in-law to go to Lyon and view the festering corpse. He decided that the cadaver could not be Gouffé because it appeared to have black, rather than chestnut-coloured hair. The body was speedily buried.

Goron wasn't satisfied. He took the details from the trunk labels to the station in Paris and asked if there were any records of a trunk being sent to Lyon on 27 July 1888. There were none. When he checked the same date in 1889, there it was: Train No. 3; 11.45 a.m.; No. 1231; Destination: Lyons-Perrache; One trunk, 105 kilograms. The weight was just about right for a trunk holding a body.

Travelling to Lyon to interview Bernard, Goron examined some strands of the 'black' hair that had been retained from the corpse and had the idea to wash them. To Bernard's chagrin, dirt and blood fell away to reveal a chestnut colour.

The body was exhumed and, that November, examined by pioneering forensic pathologist Alexandre Lacassagne. He discovered that the right knee of the victim was deformed, indicating that he had walked with a limp, just as Gouffé had. Looking at the wear on the dead man's teeth, he estimated the actual age as 50. Gouffé was 49. Lacassagne also used a microscope to compare hair from the corpse with some from a hairbrush owned by Gouffé. It matched in colour and diameter – 0.13mm.

In the meantime Goron had discovered, from an informant, that two days before he'd disappeared Gouffé had been seen in a bar with conman Michael Eyraud and his mistress Gabrielle Bompard. They had also vanished.

Goron decided to commission an exact replica of the trunk, which was then put on public display. Soon, a man living in London, who had seen a photo of it in a newspaper, got in touch to say that a French couple had formerly stayed with him and bought an identical one. Goron managed to trace a receipt bearing Michael Eyraud's name.

The case was now a sensation and images of the two suspects were published around the world. In January 1890 Eyraud suddenly wrote to Goron from the United States declaring himself innocent, pointing the finger at Bompard. Then Bompard dramatically turned herself in at a Paris police station, accusing Eyraud. She was detained, while Eyraud was eventually picked up in Havana, Cuba.

Eyraud confessed that he and Bompard had plotted to kill the bailiff for cash. Bompard had distracted Gouffé by appearing to seduce him, then Eyraud had pounced, strangling him with his hands. In fact the hapless duo got away with next to nothing, dumping the body far away and hoping their crime would remain undiscovered. Eyraud went to the guillotine in February 1891. Bompard was sentenced to twenty years in prison.

126... cabin number in the 'Porthole Murder'

In Agatha Christie's book *Death on the Nile*, published in 1937, Hercule Poirot investigates the puzzling murder of a wealthy young heiress, Linnet Ridgeway, found shot dead in her cabin aboard the paddle steamer SS *Karnak*. After identifying a string of potential suspects, the Belgian sleuth eventually deduces how she was killed and who did it. Ten years after the book's publication there was a chilling echo in a real-life case, where a glamorous young woman would die in a ship's cabin in suspicious circumstances. The details of the affair would have fascinated Poirot, for the body of the woman, actress Gay Gibson, had disappeared altogether.

The 21-year-old beauty, real name Eileen Isabella Ronnie Gibson, had been trying to make her name as an actress, performing in low-paid roles in South Africa. On 10 October 1947, she booked a passage alone, home to England, aboard the liner *Durban Castle*. But eight days later, with the ship 150 miles off the coast of east Africa, she was reported missing. Captain Patey hurriedly turned the ship around to make a search. Had Gay fallen overboard? She had last been seen at 1 a.m., leaning against a rail on deck, wearing a black evening gown and complaining of the heat. The unmarried performer was certainly troubled, having told friends in South Africa that she was three months pregnant. And it later emerged that a nightclub owner had paid for her £350 first-class berth. Sadly no trace of Gay could be found in the shark-infested seas.

Captain Patey ordered an investigation. One of the crew reported that he had gone to Gay's cabin, no. 126, at 3 a.m. after its service bell had been rung frantically. He had been surprised to find James Camb, a 31-year-old ship's steward, opening the door slightly, insisting, 'It's alright.' The crew member assumed Camb was answering the passenger's call and so thought nothing more of it until the emergence of Gay's disappearance the next morning.

Camb, dubbed 'Don Jimmy' by the crew because of his reputation as a womaniser, was challenged about the night's events and denied having been in the cabin, but he appeared to have some curious scratches on his arm. Once the ship docked in Southampton, police interviewed the slippery steward, who now changed his story. He admitted that he had been in the cabin after all and that he'd enjoyed consensual sex with Gay, but said that that she'd suddenly died during intercourse. Camb told officers that he'd panicked and shoved Gay's lifeless body through the cabin porthole. However, later statements he made seemed to indicate that Gay had struggled and been alive when he bundled the body out of the ship. He even recalled how her body had made a 'helluva splash' when it hit the water.

At Camb's trial, in March 1948, an entire replica of cabin 126 was constructed inside the Winchester courtroom and the original porthole even brought in as an exhibit. Crucial to the prosecution's case was the cabin's original linen, which proved to have both Gay's blood and urine on it. A pathologist gave evidence that this was probably emitted during strangulation. Despite the absence of a body, Camb was convicted and given a life term in jail.

Murder on the high seas was, of course, nothing new. The notorious Captain Kidd, executed in 1701, had been tried not just for piracy but for the murder, during a voyage, of one of his crew. He'd bludgeoned William Moore to death with an iron-bound bucket. Another case saw skipper William Stewart murder seven men aboard his ship, the *Mary Russell*, in 1828 using a crowbar and axe. Incredibly, there was even another case of a missing woman and a porthole that led to police investigating murder in 1933. That December, Yugoslavian Ivan Poderjay had married American lawyer Agnes Tufverson in America. A few weeks later Agnes mysteriously disappeared, but not before withdrawing $25,000 from her bank. The same month Poderjay travelled alone back to Europe aboard the RMS *Olympic*. Witnesses reported that he had barely left stateroom C86 during the voyage. Some of Agnes' belongings then turned up at Poderjay's flat in Vienna, along with another wife! Detectives found that the porthole in Poderjay's cabin aboard the Olympic was, at 17in, easily wide enough for a body to pass through. They surmised that Poderjay had killed Agnes for her money, then smuggled her aboard the ship in his luggage before pushing out her corpse. However, no firm evidence could be found and Poderjay was convicted only of bigamy.

131... years to find Julia Martha Thomas' skull

Disposing of a body is invariably a troublesome affair for any murderer. In February 1983, a plumber was called to investigate a strange smell emanating from a drain at No. 23 Cranley Gardens in London's Muswell Hill. The workman soon discovered the source of the odour – small human bones and fat. Police discovered that Dennis Nilsen, the occupant of the property's attic flat, had tried to flush them away. A search of the apartment turned up more body parts from some of Nilsen's fifteen victims, stuffed in bin bags, including a boiled head.

Nilsen picked up many of his young male victims in pubs. When, in 1879, Kate Webster faced a similar dilemma of what to do with the body of the woman she had murdered, pubs would also play a part, but this time in her bid to get rid of the corpse, while making a tidy profit on the side.

In 2010 building works at the defunct Hole in the Wall pub in Richmond-upon-Thames turned up a lone human skull in foundations that had been in place for decades. It was on top of a layer of Victorian tiles, part of the hostelry's old stables. Forensic tests showed that it was from a woman in her 50s and at least 130 years old. Low collagen levels suggested that the fractured skull had also been boiled. Police immediately made the connection between the findings and a murder that had shocked Victorian London.

Julia Martha Thomas, a former schoolteacher and widow, had lived in a cottage just 100yds away. In January 1879 she had taken on a maid, an Irish woman called Kate Webster, unaware that her new employee was a habitual drunk and convicted thief. On 2 March their increasingly strained relationship would reach a crescendo in a dispute about the amount of time Webster was spending in the pub.

A couple of days later, Webster went to see friends in Hammersmith. After an evening spent drinking in local bars, she asked a Robert Porter to help her move a heavy box, which she subsequently threw into the River Thames at Richmond Bridge. The next morning a coalman found the same box washed up further down the river near Barnes Bridge. Opening it, he was startled to see the severed torso and legs of a woman. It appeared that the flesh had been boiled. Soon afterwards a single human foot turned up at an allotment in Twickenham. The identity of the remains could not be established and an inquest recorded an open verdict.

Meanwhile, neighbours of Mrs Thomas were becoming troubled by her apparent disappearance and the fact that her furniture was being removed from the cottage, having been sold to the landlord of another pub for £68. Webster had even taken to wearing her employer's clothes and using her name. She had also begun offering jars of 'best dripping' for sale at local pubs. When confronted by Elizabeth Ives, who actually owned the Thomas cottage and the one next door, Webster fled, making her way back to Ireland.

When police searched the cottage, they found suspicious bloodstains, pieces of charred bone and a fatty substance. Webster was soon traced to her uncle's farm in Ireland and arrested. She was put on trial for her employer's murder in July 1879 and found guilty.

Sentenced to death, Webster lied that she was pregnant to try and avoid the gallows, but finally, before her execution at Wandsworth Prison on 29 July, she confessed her guilt to a priest and explained what had actually happened.

Webster said that on Sunday 2 March, Thomas had returned from church and taken her to task about her timekeeping. She admitted flying into a rage and throwing Thomas down the stairs, before choking her. Using a razor, meat saw and carving knife, she had then cut up the body and boiled it, burning some of the bones too.

It was alleged that after cleaning up the cottage, she proceeded to try and get rid of some of the remains by trying to sell fat from the body as 'best dripping'.

Oddly, in her confession Webster implicated a man called Strong in the murder, but he was never found. Just how the skull came to be at the pub is unknown, but it's believed that Webster may have been carrying Thomas' head around for days in a canvas bag before hiding it at the back of the pub. In 2011 a coroner agreed that the skull found in the Hole in the Wall was that of Thomas and recorded a verdict of unlawful killing.

150... rounds used to kill the outlaws Bonnie and Clyde

The story of Bonnie and Clyde, the 'lovers' whose crime spree gripped Depression-era America, is largely remembered as the romantic adventures of a wily duo who robbed banks and evaded blundering police, whilst the nation revelled in their largely victimless antics. In fact, Bonnie Elizabeth Parker and Clyde Chestnut Barrow, along with their gang, are reckoned to have murdered thirteen people, killing both lawmen and civilians who got in their way.

Parker and Barrow both hailed from poor families in Texas. Parker dreamed of becoming a movie star but by the age of 16 was already married to a man about to be sentenced to a five-year stretch for robbery. Leaving him, at the age of 19 she met Barrow in 1930, at a mutual friend's house. Barrow, 20, was already a petty thief, and within months he was also behind bars. When he emerged from prison in 1932, Barrow had become a hardened criminal, described as possessing the character of 'a rattlesnake'.

But 4ft 11in Parker was besotted and quickly joined Barrow's gang. Their initial crimes mainly involved robberies from petrol stations and grocery stores, but within a year Barrow and his associates had already killed five people along the way, including police officers and a grocery store worker who tried to stop them from stealing his car.

Bonnie and Clyde. (Courtesy of the FBI)

Criss-crossing Texas, Oklahoma, Missouri, New Mexico and Louisiana, the gang began robbing banks, always staying one step ahead of the police. Before long their exploits were grabbing headlines as they continued to elude the authorities amid failed raids on their hideouts. The image of Parker and Barrow as a glamorous criminal couple stemmed partly from photographs recovered from one of these raids. The playful pictures, released to the media, showed a gun-toting Parker chewing on cigars whilst larking with her man. It bolstered the myth of Parker as a gritty gangster's moll. In fact, she was rarely more than a getaway driver and probably never fired a gun in anger. Indeed, her influence meant that many robbery victims and witnesses were kidnapped and eventually released unharmed rather than being killed.

Yet Parker was undoubtedly an accomplice to a string of murders. And as the killings went on, the public mood towards Bonnie and Clyde began to sour, especially after Barrow and accomplice Henry Methvin, with Parker in tow, cold-bloodedly gunned down two Texan highway patrolmen in spring 1934, also killing a 60-year-old constable a few days later in Oklahoma.

With rewards now being offered for Bonnie and Clyde's 'dead bodies' hard-bitten Texas ranger Frank Hamer was brought out of retirement to hunt them down. By May he'd discovered that the pair were holed up in a hideout near the Methvin family home in Bienville Parish, Louisiana.

Hamer set up an ambush along a quiet, tree-lined country road, State Highway 154, near the town of Sailes. His information told him that Parker and Barrow were likely to travel along the road in a stolen Ford V-8 sedan. Hamer had a posse of five hand-picked officers with him, all heavily armed with shotguns, automatic rifles and pistols, and packing armour-piercing bullets for good measure. Despite later protestations that they had acted in self-defence, it was clear Hamer's men meant to put an end to Bonnie and Clyde's rampage once and for all.

In the early morning of 23 May, after more than twenty-four hours of waiting, the posse intercepted Henry Methvin's father in his truck and set it up in the road to look broken down, as bait, hoping Barrow would slow down to help if he passed.

At 9.15 a.m. the tan-coloured V-8 finally came into view. One of the lawmen, who knew Parker and Barrow by sight, gave the nod that it was them. Sure enough, Barrow slowed past Methvin's truck.

Deputy Sheriff Prentiss Oakley was the first to open fire; Barrow was hit immediately in the head. His foot slipped from the brake and the car lurched forwards. By now all the officers were firing, emptying their weapons into the vehicle. They didn't stop even after the car had careered into a ditch. It was peppered with a deafening '150 rounds' according to one cop and in a timespan of just sixteen seconds. Edging carefully towards the vehicle, the officers found the dead bodies of Barrow and Parker slumped in their seats. They hadn't had time to fire a single shot in reply.

The official coroner's report later showed that there were a total of seventeen gunshot wounds in Barrow's body. Parker, who had survived just long enough for her piercing screams to have been heard by the officers, had twenty-six wounds.

It was, perhaps, the pair's bloody demise that cemented Bonnie and Clyde's reputation as the devoted couple, defying the law to the last and going down in a blaze of glory. Some 20,000 people would turn out to Parker's funeral.

Over the next decades, the couple's blood-spattered V-8, complete with 167 separate bullet holes (some caused by single bullets entering and exiting the car) ended up touring a string of carnivals and being housed in several museums before finding a home in the foyer of a Nevada casino.

158... microscopic specks of blood in the Billie-Jo Jenkins murder

There are 5 litres of blood in the average human body. So it's not surprising that when someone is brutally murdered it can get pretty much everywhere. Blood of the victim is likely to be left not only at the scene but on the killer too. However, blood found on a suspect or their clothing was of limited use to those investigating murders until the turn of the twentieth century, when a German scientist called Paul Uhlenhuth discovered that different species have distinctive proteins in their blood. It enabled him to devise a test to distinguish whether a blood sample came from an animal or a human.

In 1901 this technique helped crack a murder case on the Baltic island of Rügen. Police had arrested a suspect over the killing of two children whose bodies had been found dismembered in some woods. They found recently washed clothing in carpenter Ludwig Tessnow's wardrobe that appeared to show traces of blood. He claimed that they were actually stains from wood dye. Uhlenhuth was called in and analysed over 100 individual stains. He found that some were from wood dye, some from sheep and that others were human. Tessnow was convicted and executed.

Around the same time, another scientist, Karl Landsteiner, identified that humans have different blood types such as A, B, AB and O. Further research allowed even greater differentiation, providing police with the ability to rule suspects in or out of an investigation, while the more recent development of DNA testing of samples has made blood hugely important in linking killers to their crimes.

Blood spatter analysis can also provide vital evidence. The direction in which blood hits a surface reveals different patterned stains and this can offer up invaluable clues to whether a death was accidental or a murder, where a victim and a suspect were during an attack and even the sort of murder weapon that was used. It can also prove whether someone was at the scene of a murder or simply arrived afterwards.

However, the issue of blood spatter can be controversial, and never more so than in the case of Dr Sam Sheppard. In the early hours of 4 July 1954, his wife, Marilyn, was bludgeoned to death in their home on Lake Erie, Ohio. Sheppard claimed to have been asleep in the lounge when he heard his wife screaming upstairs. He'd run to her aid, and found an intruder grappling with her, but he was then knocked out. Coming round, he saw the prostrate body of his wife. Sheppard managed to run out and tussle with the fleeing attacker, but he was again knocked out. Recovering consciousness, he raised the alarm.

Marilyn had been beaten thirty-five times, and there was plenty of blood spatter around the bedroom. The house had been ransacked, but only Sam Sheppard's watch, keys and a ring had been taken (presumably from his unconscious body). These were later found in a bag in nearby shrubbery.

Police suspected that Sheppard had actually killed his wife, staging the robbery. The couple's dog had not barked at any intruder, and if Sheppard had really wrestled with the attacker, or checked his wife for signs of life as he'd stated, why was he not covered in smears of blood?

Yet if Sheppard had been the attacker, he would surely have been covered in blood spatter from his victim. Police experts did find evidence of blood spatter on the recovered watch, indicating it had been near Marilyn when she was attacked. Sheppard was initially convicted of second-degree murder, but he was sensationally acquitted at a retrial in 1966, when another expert testified that the blood on Sheppard's watch was not spatter but transfer smears obtained when he had checked his wife for a pulse.

Blood spatter was also at the heart of the mystery surrounding the murder of Billie-Jo Jenkins, 13, in February 1997. She had been beaten around the head with an 18in tent peg found at the scene. Her foster father, teacher Sion Jenkins, claimed that he'd returned home from the shops in Hastings, East Sussex, to find Billie-Jo lying dying outside. Analysis of his clothes found 158 tiny spots of blood spatter. At his 1998 trial, conflicting evidence was presented by the prosecution and defence teams about whether this could have been the result of Jenkins being her murderer or of Billie-Jo's last breath peppering him with blood as he rushed to her side. Jenkins was convicted, but two retrials followed and he was acquitted in 2006. New evidence indicated that a blockage had been stopping air escaping from Billie-Jo's lungs. When

Jenkins examined her body the air had been released, covering him with fine spatter. Intriguingly, there had been reports of a prowler in the area at the time, but the real killer remains at large.

200... assassins aiming to murder Queen Elizabeth I

In the early evening of 27 June 1850, Queen Victoria was getting into her carriage when former soldier Robert Pate ran up and tried to bludgeon her over the head with a brass-tipped stick. The deranged Pate was bundled away, but he had drawn blood and caused severe bruising. Only a sturdy bonnet had saved the 31-year-old monarch from greater injury. Undeterred, she went on with a visit to the opera, shooing away staff worried about her wounds, insisting, 'Everyone shall see how little I mind it.'

Her stoicism echoed that of her predecessor Queen Elizabeth I. In July 1579, while Elizabeth was travelling by royal barge down the Thames, shots rang out. A bullet whizzed past within feet of the queen and badly injured an oarsman. Without losing composure, she handed him a handkerchief to help stop the flow of blood and observed casually, 'That bullet was meant for me.'

The reigns of the two queens may have been separated by three centuries, but they both showed great bravery in the face of multiple threats of murder. In fact, given the number of very real assassination attempts against the pair, it's somewhat surprising that both died of natural causes in their beds, notching up a combined total of more than 100 years on the throne.

In 1583 Elizabeth wrote to the French ambassador that there were, 'two hundred men of all ages who, at the instigation of the Jesuits, conspire to kill me'. Repeated threats against her person meant that in later life Elizabeth even kept a sword by her bedside. And while it emerged that the incident on the barge had in fact been the result of an accident, no one could have blamed Elizabeth for being paranoid. By the time she had written that letter, one serious plan to kill her had already been exposed. In 1570 Pope Pius V had declared Elizabeth a heretic, absolving English Catholics of any allegiance to their queen and, in 1571, a plot centring around Italian banker Roberto Ridolfi aimed at killing Elizabeth and putting the imprisoned

Elizabeth I. (Courtesy of Wellcome Library, London)

Mary Queen of Scots on the throne. It was foiled when damning letters came to light, but it would be followed by two more plots to assassinate Elizabeth and overthrow her government, one in 1583, led by Francis Throckmorton, and another in 1586, led by Anthony Babington. Intelligence uncovered both before they could be enacted, and when Mary's involvement in the latter became apparent, it led to her execution.

Elizabeth was also the target of murder plots by lone madmen including Catholic John Somerville, from Warwickshire, who set out for London in October 1583 aiming to shoot her with his pistol and put her head on a pole. Somerville made the mistake of telling anyone who would listen what he intended to do and was arrested before he could get close to the sovereign.

Mentally unstable individuals made up the bulk of those who attempted to kill Queen Victoria during the nineteenth century. Pate was actually the fifth of seven would-be assassins to attack Victoria, and after evidence about his weak state of mind, he got seven years transportation for his crime. Unemployed barman Edward Oxford, 18, had been the first man to try and murder Victoria, firing at the pregnant queen's open carriage as it went by, near Buckingham Palace in June 1840. He missed and was later found not guilty by reason of insanity.

Despite two more insane assailants brandishing guns at the queen in 1842, she continued to make risky public appearances, just as her predecessor Elizabeth had done. There was another badly botched attempt to shoot Victoria by an unemployed Irishman in 1849. Then, in 1872, 'feeble-minded' Arthur O'Connor climbed a fence at Buckingham Palace and was only prevented from gunning down the queen when quick-thinking servant John Brown seized him. Frustrated poet Roderick McLean, who incidentally had a strange obsession with the number four, fired at the queen's carriage at Windsor in 1882, once again failing to hit the diminutive monarch, and was caught when a group of schoolboys set about him with umbrellas. McLean would also be declared insane by a court.

Elizabeth and Victoria seem to have had more than their fair share of near misses, but Queen Elizabeth II also had a close call. In 1981 six shots were fired at the Queen as she rode her horse along the Mall. They turned out to be blanks and Elizabeth was able to calmly control her startled steed, but had gunman Marcus Sarjeant used real bullets and had better aim, he could easily have achieved his fantasy of becoming the most famous – or at least the most infamous – teenager in the world.

237... cases that prove arsenic was the Victorians' favourite poison

It has been dubbed the 'king of poisons', a toxic killer with a trail of death leading back through history to the time of ancient Rome. Arsenic was the murder weapon of choice for the infamous Agrippina, who used it in a string of murders, including that of her husband, as she schemed to have her son Nero made emperor. Down the centuries the poison would continue to be much favoured by members of elites aiming to do away with rivals. The notorious fifteenth-century nobleman Cesare Borgia, for example, used it liberally to murder those who got in his way.

Gradually, more ordinary folk saw the advantage of arsenic as a homicidal agent. In seventeenth-century Italy a woman called Giulia Toffana was implicated in the deaths of 600 people, having supplied it to women wanting to kill their husbands. In Britain in 1712 Elizabeth Mason killed her employer by putting arsenic in her coffee, while in 1752 Mary Blandy was hanged for killing her father using the poison. Above all, it was the Victorian age that would become synonymous with arsenic poisoning.

Arsenic trioxide, produced by smelting certain ores, was odourless, tasteless and dissolvable in water, allowing the lethal white powder to be easily slipped into food or drink. The symptoms it induced, including abdominal pain, diarrhoea and vomiting, followed by a lingering death, could easily be attributable to a natural illness, such as cholera.

Arsenic was becoming cheaper and more easily available too, as it was often used to kill vermin. Half an ounce, a quantity which could easily kill a score of people, could be bought for a penny. There's no doubt that its use for murder was widespread. In her study of over 540 criminal cases involving poisoning that occurred between 1750 and 1914, the historian Katherine Watson identified that arsenic featured in 237. The next most common poison, opium, was a long way behind.

Ironically, the nineteenth century also saw the introduction of legislation ordering sellers to keep records of who bought arsenic and new forensic tests that could identify the presence of arsenic in a corpse. Yet the popularity of using arsenic for murder failed to wane fast, with courts somewhat chary of finding defendants guilty by relying on a science that was in its infancy. With such a prevalence of arsenic in homes (it was even present in a host of over-the-counter health remedies), defence lawyers were often able to sow doubt in the minds of juries as to how the poison had come to be in the system of the deceased. Annual cases of accidental arsenic poisoning ran into the hundreds.

In 1857 a verdict of 'not proven' was given at the trial of Madeleine Smith, from Glasgow, despite substantial evidence suggesting that she had murdered former lover Emile L'Angelier, who had been blackmailing her over some letters. A huge amount of arsenic was found in his stomach and Madeline, 21, was known to have purchased large amounts of the poison just prior to L'Angelier's death. The prosecution alleged that the accused had sprinkled it into his cocoa. Yet it was successfully argued that she had bought the arsenic innocently, as a cosmetic, and that 33-year-old L'Angelier could have been using arsenic medicinally and accidentally killed himself.

American Florence Maybrick would not to be so lucky. By 1889 both she, then aged 26, and her English husband, James, a 50-year-old cotton broker, had been unfaithful to each other. When he died, on 11 May, at their Liverpool home after a short illness, James' brother, who knew of Florence's affair, brought in police. In the days before her husband died, Florence had

Bottle of arsenic. (Courtesy of Wellcome Library, London)

been seen by a nurse putting something – which later turned out to be arsenic – into some meat juice that was destined to be given to James as a tonic. He hadn't taken it, but enough suspicion was aroused for an autopsy to be conducted, which identified a small amount of arsenic in James' body. Florence was charged with murder.

It was alleged that her affair gave Florence a motive to kill James, that she had tampered with the meat juice he was due to consume and had bought a quantity of flypapers with the purpose of soaking them to remove the arsenic, which she had then administered to James in small doses.

Her defence pointed out that James was known to have regularly taken small doses of arsenic for his health, possibly as an aphrodisiac. In an echo of the Smith case, Florence stated that she had been extracting the arsenic from the flypapers to use cosmetically. She also swore that it had been James who had asked her to add a mystery white powder to the meat juice. Thanks in part to biased summing up by the judge, Florence was found guilty, though her sentence was later commuted to life in prison. In the end she served fifteen years.

The twentieth century would see more convictions involving arsenic poisoning, but cases began to decline as detection methods improved and access to the poison became restricted.

250... calls to a TV show that led to the capture of John List

On the evening of Sunday, 21 May 1989, the sixty-sixth episode of the hit show *America's Most Wanted* was broadcast in the United States. The series featured appeals about unsolved crimes, and this particular programme would include an 8-minute segment devoted to a missing man, still wanted for the callous murder of five members of his own family back in 1971. The problem for the police, who had been investigating the crime in vain, was that the only photograph they had of their suspect, John List, was now more than twenty-five years old.

The show's producers brought in a forensic sculptor, Frank Bender, whose work led to the capture of many fugitives over the years. With the help of a criminal profiler and photos of List's parents, Bender constructed a clay model of what he thought the much older List might look like. After the item went out on the show, complete with the lifelike bust of List's head, the telephones in the studio began ringing. And one call out of the 250 that came in that night would prove crucial in helping detectives track down their man.

John List, a failed accountant who was deeply in debt, had planned the murders down to the last detail and executed his scheme in a most cold and calculated manner. On 9 November 1971, the 46-year-old had calmly shot his wife in the back of the head at their eighteen-room home in Westfield, New Jersey. After killing 45-year-old Helen, he then turned his gun on his mother, Alma, 84, leaving her dead too. Then, when his three children, Patricia, 16, John Jr, 15, and Frederick, 13, returned home from school, he shot them as well.

Thanks to the family's reclusive lifestyle, it was nearly a month before the bodies were found. List's car was tracked to the local airport, but he hadn't taken a flight anywhere. However, it was clear he had been the culprit, for the supposedly devoutly religious List had left behind a letter for his Lutheran pastor. In it List explained that he was concerned that his debts would lead to the breakdown of his family. His twisted logic was that he had killed them all to save their souls and now needed to start a new life so that he could make amends. List made it difficult for the police to trace him, cutting himself out of every photograph in the house.

One of the calls that had come into the programme was from a woman in Denver, Colorado. She thought the figure resembled a neighbour of hers who had since moved to Richmond, Virginia. The churchgoing man in question called himself Bob Clark, worked as an accountant and had been married to an army clerk called Dolores Miller for four years.

The FBI followed up a number of calls to the show, but when they confronted the bewildered Dolores at her home with the 'aged' image of her husband, she agreed it looked just like him. Finding Clark at his office, agents were amazed to find that he was, indeed, the spitting image of Bender's bust, down to the receding hairline, tortoise-shell glasses and scar behind one ear. At first Clark denied he was List, but his old army fingerprints soon proved otherwise. He had somehow fashioned a whole new identity for himself, but in 1990 he was convicted of five counts of first-degree murder. List died in jail in 2008.

In its first twenty-five years of being on air, BBC's *Crimewatch*, a similar programme to *America's Most Wanted*, was reckoned to have helped catch fifty-seven murderers. One of its most memorable success stories was in the case of a shocking double murder on a country lane in Chillenden, Kent, on 9 July 1996. Lin Russell, 45, and her daughters Megan, 6, and Josie, 9, had been battered over the head with a blunt weapon. Lin and Megan died from their injuries but Josie survived. Police had little forensic evidence to go on but were able to put together an e-fit of the attacker.

When *Crimewatch* featured a reconstruction of the killings, detectives were inundated with 600 calls. One came from a psychiatrist, who reported that a former patient, Michael Stone, not only matched the e-fit but had fantasised about killing women and children. Despite protestations of innocence, Stone would eventually end up convicted of the murders.

313... crucial frame in a film of JFK's assassination

The home movie taken by dressmaker Abraham Zapruder, of President John F. Kennedy's motorcade making its way through Dallas on 22 November 1963, became the most famous 26.6 seconds of footage on celluloid. Shot in colour, but without sound, the Zapruder film captured the 46-year-old president's assassination as his open-top limousine travelled through the city's Dealey Plaza. It has since been used to suggest that Lee Harvey Oswald did not act alone in murdering the president and that his death was the result of a conspiracy.

Grainy but graphic, the 8mm film contains 486 frames in total. It shows the president's motorcade passing Zapruder's position and how Kennedy is dramatically shot in front of well-wishers at 12.30 p.m., as well as the reaction of both his wife, Jackie, and the president's security detail as they scramble to his aid. It is the most complete recording of Kennedy's final moments, and as well being made public to a shocked world, it became a vital exhibit at the Warren Commission, the official investigation into the assassination. This would conclude that 24-year-old Oswald had shot the president from the sixth floor of the nearby Texas School Book Depository building, using a high-powered Italian Carcano M91/38 bolt-action rifle. Oswald had been captured the same afternoon after shooting a Dallas police officer elsewhere in the city. After the firearm was found in the building, it was linked to Oswald.

There was one frame of the Zapruder film that was, for many years, excluded from publication – no. 313. Zapruder himself felt it was too upsetting. The frame shows the president's head being hit by a bullet and 'exploding'. This was considered to be the fatal shot. The preceding frames show Kennedy's Lincoln Continental emerging from behind a sign and the president clutching his throat – the result of the first bullet to hit him. In the frames that follow 313, we see the results of the president's head wound as skull and brain matter fly outward.

The Warren Commission concluded that Oswald had fired three shots and that Kennedy was hit by two, one missing, with Governor Connally, sitting in front of him, hit by one of the same rounds that also hit the president.

Some experts have argued that the Zapruder footage, from frame 313, shows the president's head being thrown backwards by the impact – clear evidence that he has been shot from the right and front. Other forensic and ballistic analysts have countered that it proves nothing of the sort – that a person's head doesn't always snap back in that way when shot from the front, and that what we see could be due to an automatic reaction of the body's nerves and muscles to a blast from behind. Other evidence has indicated that from frame 312 to 313 the president's head may have actually jerked forward, this being the actual moment that the bullet entered the president's body.

If there was a shot from the front, it couldn't have been fired by Oswald, as his supposed position in the book depository was behind Kennedy. It implies another gunman. Those who believe that a shot was fired from the front point to the fact that it would have been hard for Oswald to have fired so many shots in the available time-frame and highlight that some witnesses claimed to have heard a shot fired from behind a picket fence on a grassy knoll overlooking the scene.

In the late 1970s, the United States House of Representatives Select Committee on Assassinations determined, on the basis of a recording made by a motorcycle cop's walkie-talkie, that a fourth shot had been fired. It concluded that, while Oswald was involved, there had been a second gunman and 'a probable conspiracy', but it did not offer an opinion on who might be behind it. Much doubt would later be cast on what the recording really did prove, but the idea of a conspiracy was fostered by Oliver Stone's movie *JFK*, which made a lot of how the president's head went 'back and to the left'.

What is certain is that the Zapruder film reveals in horrifying detail how the president died. However, it does not appear to provide conclusive evidence to prove or disprove the existence of a second gunman. Nor has

Assassin Lee Harvey Oswald. (Courtesy of the FBI)

any firm evidence emerged to suggest that the president's death was due to a plot involving the Soviet Union, mafia, CIA or anyone else.

Kennedy's assassination was not the only murder caught on film. At 11.21 a.m. on 24 November, TV cameras captured the moment when Oswald was gunned down at a police station. This time there was no debate about the identity of the killer. Nightclub owner Jack Ruby could clearly be seen shooting Oswald at close quarters. While the official verdict was that Ruby had also acted alone, his actions only added weight to the idea that unseen, sinister forces were at work.

340...

characters in the Zodiac killer's unsolved cipher

Serial killers love nothing more than attention and glory, while maintaining their superiority and control over those trying to catch them. While still at large, they often contact the authorities directly, or through news outlets, with messages to taunt pursuers and provide tantalising clues as to their own identity. During 1888 scores of letters ended up being sent by people claiming to be responsible for the killings of prostitutes in the East End of London. Many were obvious hoaxes, but a few were taken seriously by police. The so-called 'Dear Boss' letter, sent to a news agency on 27 September, following the murders of Mary Ann Nichols and Annie Chapman was signed 'Jack the Ripper', establishing the name by which the world's most notorious criminal would henceforth be known. The author promised to carry on killing, saying that he would 'clip' the next lady's ears off. Three days later Elizabeth Stride and Catherine Eddowes were murdered on the same night by the Ripper. Eddowes' right ear was cut. In October, another letter headed 'From Hell' was mailed to the chairman of the Whitechapel Vigilance Committee along with half a human kidney, the other half of which the Ripper claimed to have eaten. Eddowes' left kidney had been removed by the killer.

While it was never confirmed that the real Ripper had sent these missives, in the late 1960s another serial killer appeared to be on the loose and even keener on communication. In December 1968 and July 1969, two young couples in parked cars were shot near Vallejo, California, resulting in three deaths. A few weeks later, newspapers in the state each received a handwritten anonymous letter purporting to be from the killer. Each contained a third portion of a 408-character cryptogram and was signed with a crossed circle. Unlocking the cipher would reveal his identity, said the writer. After this was published, it was a local history teacher and his wife who managed to crack the code first. The first line read: 'I like killing people because it is so much fun.' However, the text also revealed that the author had decided not to reveal his name after all – it would slow down his ability to collect 'slaves for the afterlife'.

By this time another letter had arrived, in which the killer referred to himself as the 'Zodiac' and revealed details only the murderer could know. He soon killed again. On 27 September, a man wearing a hood with a crossed circle stabbed another young couple, picnicking at Lake Berryessa, leaving one dead. He drew his trademark symbol on their car too, beside the dates of the previous murders. Then, on 11 October, taxi driver Paul Stine, 29, was shot dead in San Francisco. The Zodiac subsequently sent a torn piece of Stine's shirt to a newspaper.

Witnesses helped work up a composite sketch of the killer, but detectives were no closer to identifying the Zodiac when, on 8 November, the *San Francisco Chronicle* received another cryptogram. This one had 340 characters, made up of sixty-three different symbols. However, it did not follow the substitution patterns used in the earlier cryptogram and introduced more symbols. It was either highly complex or made no sense. Even if the symbols somehow represented twenty-six letters of the alphabet, the possible combinations ran into many trillions.

In the course of their enquiries, detectives investigated 2,500 potential suspects but the focus fell upon Arthur Leigh Allen: on the day of the third attack he had told his family that he was going to the location in question. A friend also said he referred to himself as the Zodiac before the killer's moniker was made public. Allen also wore a Zodiac wristwatch – the brand used a similar symbol. Survivor Michael Mageau would later identify Allen as the stocky white male who had attacked him.

However, Allen's handwriting did not seem to match those in the letters and police couldn't bring a case against him. Furthermore, when DNA from saliva on one of the stamps used in the Zodiac letters was tested in 2002, it was found not to be Allen's.

The Zodiac, or someone pretending to be him, went on sending letters – some with encrypted sections – until 1984. In total he claimed to have killed thirty-seven people. Many unsolved murders were linked to the Zodiac, but there was never definitive proof that he'd killed more than five people.

Many believe the key to the Zodiac's identity is contained within the 340 cipher, but until someone can crack it, it will be hard to argue with his jeer that 'The police shall never catch me because I have been too clever for them.'

400... infants murdered by Amelia Dyer – Britain's worst ever killer?

Victorian Britain was an age of industrialisation and a booming population, with legions of children whose parents were not in a position to care for them. Infanticide was rife. Between 1863 and 1887, an incredible 63 per cent of all homicides involved infants. Given the social stigma surrounding illegitimacy, single mothers in particular were often left in an unenviable position, without the freedom or finances to bring up their own offspring.

It was in this climate, with no formal adoption or foster care arrangements in place, that the practice of 'baby farming' grew up. It involved paying either a regular fee or a lump sum to someone else, usually another woman or a couple, to take in a child. But it was open to large-scale abuse, with many of the youngsters simply neglected. In the case of lump sums – with the prospect of no more money to come – some children were simply allowed to starve; others were murdered for a profit.

As the century progressed, several sickening such cases began to emerge. The first person to be convicted was Margaret Waters, from Brixton, south London. Using an alias, she advertised in local papers, offering to adopt children for as little as £4. A police investigation discovered eleven drugged and emaciated babies at her home, many of whom subsequently died. In 1870 Waters, 35, was convicted of the murder of just one of them, John Walter Cowen, and hanged, though she was thought to have been responsible for the deaths of nineteen youngsters.

Cases of baby farming would continue to come before the courts into the twentieth century, until legislation came into force to better protect children, but there was one case that surpassed all the others in the scale of its inhumanity.

On 30 March 1896, a bargee on the River Thames happened to fish a package out of the water. He was horrified to discover that inside was the body of a 15-month-old child, later identified as Helena Fry, the illegitimate child of a servant girl from Bristol. There was a length of white tape tied tightly around her neck – she had been strangled. Using a faint address found on the parcel's wrapping paper, police were eventually able to trace a woman using the alias 'Mrs Thomas' to an address in Reading. Her real name was

Amelia Dyer and she was in her late 50s. Upon raiding the property, the police found that the house reeked with the smell of human decomposition. There were no actual bodies, but they did uncover evidence that in just a few months twenty children had been placed in Dyer's care.

In fact she had been using a string of noms de plume and had a long history of taking in babies for cash, and then either allowing them to die or murdering them. In the 1870s Dyer had even served a period of hard labour for neglect, after a doctor became concerned about the number of death certificates he had to sign for children who had supposedly been in her care. Yet Dyer's incarceration only served to bring a temporary halt to her murderous designs. Once released, she took up her old trade again and simply began secretly disposing of the bodies and changing addresses frequently to avoid detection.

The day before the discovery of Helena Fry, Dyer had been in Cheltenham, Gloucestershire, posing as 'Mrs Harding', to receive 4-month-old Doris Marmon from her mother, Evelina. The 25-year-old barmaid had replied to a newspaper advert that read: 'Married couple with no family would adopt healthy child, nice country home. Terms, £10.' Knowing that she was unable to care for Doris herself, Evelina agreed to hand over her baby to 'Mrs Harding' for the fee, assured that Doris was going to a good home. Instead Dyer took the baby to London, where she used her trademark white tape to strangle the child. Then Dyer placed Doris, together with another murdered infant, Harry Simmons, into a carpet bag weighed down with bricks and threw it into the Thames.

After the Reading raid, police ordered the Thames be dredged. Six more infant bodies were found, including that of Doris. Dyer soon confessed to being a multiple murderer, stating that police would know her victims 'by the tape around their necks'. At her Old Bailey trial in May 1896, Dyer was convicted of Doris Marmon's murder, with Evelina appearing in court to identify her. She was later hanged in Newgate Prison. However, given that Dyer had been plying her trade for twenty to thirty years, it's estimated that there were many more unknown victims, perhaps as many as 400, a total which would make Dyer a rival for the unenviable title of the worst killer in British history.

414 ...
bricks recovered from the wall of the St Valentine's Day Massacre

In 1997 an unusual bidding war took place at Christie's, the famous auction house in London. It was for a rather unremarkable gilt pocket watch dating from the Edwardian era. However, this timepiece had a rather macabre provenance. For it had once belonged to Dr Hawley Harvey Crippen, hanged in 1910 for the murder of his wife, Cora. The watch was sold to a retired banker for £10,000, ten times its pre-sale estimate.

The trade in 'murderabilia', artefacts related to well-known homicides and infamous killers, has long been controversial. Although top auction houses have occasionally sold historic items, the internet site eBay went as far as banning the trade in true crime collectibles in 2001. However, the market remains buoyant online, even though some of the items up for grabs are truly bizarre – including everything from Christmas cards mailed by serial killer Ted Bundy to locks of hair from the head of murderous cult leader Charles Manson.

The desire to grab such grizzly souvenirs goes back a long way. In 1827 William Corder shot his lover, Maria Marten, and buried her body in a barn at Polstead, Suffolk. The Red Barn murder, as it became known, was a Victorian sensation, with every detail of the case eagerly lapped up by the public. Corder was hanged for the crime at Bury St Edmunds in 1828 in front of 7,000 people, and the story of Maria's slaying inspired songs and plays. There was also a fascination with any items even vaguely related to the story. Pieces of the rope that was used to hang Corder were sold for a guinea a time, while the barn itself was stripped of its wooden planks, which were cut up and marketed as commemorative toothpicks.

One of the oddest collections of murderabilia ever recovered was from the St Valentine's Day massacre, which took place on the morning of 14 February 1929 in Chicago. After reports of a shooting, police arrived at a garage on the city's north side to find seven men dead or dying inside the lock-up, their bodies riddled with bullet holes. They turned out to be members or associates of 'Bugs' Moran's gang. He was a fierce rival of another of the city's top gangsters, Al Capone, nicknamed Scarface. This was the era of prohibition, and Capone was engaged in a fierce turf war with Moran to take control of Chicago's organised crime racket.

Al Capone. (Courtesy of the FBI)

Detectives discovered that, on the 14th, Moran's men had been expecting a delivery of bootlegged whiskey to the address at 2122 North Clark Street. But they had surrendered when confronted by four other men who had walked in brandishing guns. Two of them were wearing police uniforms. But Moran's gang had been tricked. These were not officers of the law but assassins, who promptly lined their targets up against the garage wall and gunned them down in cold blood. At least seventy rounds of ammunition were fired from their Thompson machine guns, with the few slugs that didn't find flesh ricocheting off the red brick walls. Just one of Moran's men, Frank Gusenberg, survived long enough for police to question him. Peppered with fourteen bullets, he was asked who'd shot him and replied, 'No one, nobody shot me.' Though Capone was suspected of having ordered the hit, neither he nor anyone else was ever brought to book for the murders. Capone was jailed for tax evasion in 1931.

Nevertheless the St Valentine's Day massacre went down in mob history, and in 1967, when 2122 was demolished, the crime was still famous enough for 414 of the blasted bricks from the north wall of the garage to be put aside, each carefully lettered and numbered. This 7 by 11ft section was then bought by canny Canadian businessman George Patey. He turned it into a mobile display, touring fairs and exhibitions, before placing the bricks in a Vancouver nightclub he owned, where they formed the backdrop to the venue's urinals. Today the majority have been turned into a reconstruction of the wall in an exhibit at The Mob Museum in Las Vegas.

The brick wall from the St Valentine's Day Massacre. (Courtesy of The Mob Museum, Chicago)

While the trade in more esoteric souvenirs linked to the likes of serial killers seems to have been deemed distasteful, auction houses have shown fewer qualms when it comes to selling items owned by Al Capone, still history's most notorious gangster and undoubtedly responsible for multiple murders. In 2011 Christie's listed a revolver that had belonged to Capone and was made just a few months after the St Valentine's Day hits in 1929. The nickel-plated Colt .38 six shooter was snapped up for a cool £67,250.

421... soil samples that led to the brewery heir killer

On 11 September 1960, a hiker stumbled upon a pair of discarded trousers in the foothills of the Rocky Mountains, and looking in the pocket, he came across a penknife bearing the initials ACIII. He alerted police, who soon turned up skeletal remains nearby. They had finally found the body of Adolph Coors III, seven months after the brewery heir had gone missing. Pathologists ascertained that Coors had been shot twice in the back. What had been a kidnapping investigation now turned into a murder case. FBI agents working on Coors' disappearance had not yet found his killer, but they did have a firm suspect in mind as well as his burnt-out car, which would provide them with vital evidence to help prove the man's guilt.

Listing the abilities of the great literary detective Sherlock Holmes, his assistant, Dr Watson, noted that he 'tells at a glance different soils from each other' and that, after walks, he 'has shown me splashes upon his trousers and told me by their colour and consistence in what part of London he had received them'. It would be more than a decade after these words appeared in print that fiction would become reality as forensic analysis of different dirt and soil samples would yield a conviction for murder.

In 1904 German seamstress Eva Disch was found in a bean field, strangled with her own scarf. Next to her body was a filthy handkerchief. The forensic scientist George Popp was called in to analyse it. Along with the mucus, he found that it contained particles of coal and the mineral hornblende. A suspect, Karl Laubach, was identified – he worked at a coal-burning gasworks and a quarry, where there was lots of hornblende. Both substances were found

WANTED BY THE FBI

INTERSTATE FLIGHT – MURDER
JOSEPH CORBETT, JR.

FBI No. 605,861 A

Photograph taken 1959   Photographs taken 1951

Aliases: James Barron, Joe Corbett, Walter Osborn, William Osborn, Charles Osborne, W. William Osborne, Walter Osborne and others

DESCRIPTION

Age: 31, born October 25, 1928, Seattle, Washington (not supported by birth records)

Height: 6'1" to 6'2"	**Complexion:** fair
Weight: 160 to 170 pounds	**Race:** white
Build: medium	**Nationality:** American
Hair: light brown	**Occupations:** alkyd cooker (paint manufacturing), clerk-typist,
Eyes: hazel	laboratory technician, laborer, warehouseman.

Scars and Marks: mole under chin, crescent-shaped scar right thumb, scar right side of abdomen.

Remarks: allegedly left-handed and nearsighted; reported to be proficient typist and neat dresser.

Fingerprint Classification: 19 O 29 W 100 20
I 27 W 100

CRIMINAL RECORD

Corbett has been convicted of second degree murder.

CAUTION

CORBETT SHOULD BE CONSIDERED ARMED AND EXTREMELY DANGEROUS. HE REPORTEDLY IS A GUN ENTHUSIAST AND EXPERIENCED IN USE OF FIREARMS.

A Federal warrant was issued at Los Angeles, California, on March 21, 1960, charging Corbett with unlawful interstate flight to avoid confinement after conviction for murder (Title 18, U. S. Code, Section 1073).

IF YOU HAVE INFORMATION CONCERNING THIS PERSON, PLEASE NOTIFY ME OR CONTACT YOUR LOCAL FBI OFFICE. TELEPHONE NUMBER IS LISTED BELOW.

DIRECTOR
FEDERAL BUREAU OF INVESTIGATION
UNITED STATES DEPARTMENT OF JUSTICE
WASHINGTON 25, D. C.
TELEPHONE, NATIONAL 8-7117

Wanted Flyer No. 241
March 22, 1960

Joseph Corbett Jr. (Courtesy of the FBI)

under his fingernails. When Popp examined Laubach's trousers, he discovered more pertinent evidence. They were encrusted with two layers of soil. The layer nearest the cloth was consistent with that of the murder scene. On top of that was a different layer of soil, which matched that from a path leading back to Laubach's home. Confronted with this evidence, the suspect confessed and was convicted of the murder.

From these early days, forensic geology would prove increasingly useful in criminal cases and was fundamental in making the case against the man who had murdered Adolph Coors. The 44-year-old father of four had been abducted near his ranch in Morrison, Colorado, on 9 February 1960, while driving to work at the family brewery. Coors' car was found abandoned with its motor running on a bridge over Turkey Creek. Spots of blood and the victim's glasses and hat were found at the scene. A ransom note soon turned up, but the kidnapper never got in touch again to collect the money. The FBI had little to go on, but a witness had seen a yellow Mercury car hanging around the area before the abduction and recalled part of the number plate. It was traced to 31-year-old Joseph Corbett Jr, already a convicted murderer, who had bought the car using an alias, but whose whereabouts were unknown.

By March the FBI had found the yellow Mercury, now a charred wreck, in an Atlantic City dump – more than 1,500 miles away. Enough of the vehicle remained for the engine serial number to be identified and for it to be confirmed as Corbett's. Investigators also found several layers of mud and soil underneath the fenders of the car and began analysing them.

After Corbett's description was circulated, he was captured in Vancouver, Canada, in October. But the FBI still had to link him to Coors' death.

Corbett's typewriter was matched to the ransom note, but much of the attention at his trial the following year was focused on the four layers of dirt and particles taken from the yellow Mercury, which had been picked up on unpaved roads. These were compared to 421 other soil samples. Unsurprisingly, the first layer contained dirt from the road into the dump, but the other three layers showed a geological make-up that was consistent with the samples from the Rocky Mountains and around Denver. The experts were able to go further, linking the next layer down to a mineral composition that matched the location where Coors' body was found. The third layer matched the type of earth to be found around the Turkey Creek bridge on the Coors ranch. On 29 March 1961, Corbett was found guilty and sent to prison for life. Although Corbett maintained his innocence, it appeared that Coors had died during, or in a struggle shortly after, the kidnapping.

477 ... milligrams of antimony found in the body of Maud Marsh

Countless candidates have been put forward for the true identity of Jack the Ripper, the still unknown serial killer who terrorised London's East End in 1888 leaving at least five women dead. But among the more serious suspects is George Chapman, a name taken by Polish man Severin Klosowski, who moved to Whitechapel about the same time as the Ripper murders began in that area of the capital. Indeed, Frederick Abberline, who headed the police investigation into the Ripper attacks, later became convinced that Chapman was the man responsible for the series of violent murders of prostitutes, which had proved impossible to solve. One of his reasons was that Chapman had medical training. The way in which the Ripper's victims were mutilated suggested to some that he had the skills of a surgeon. What is certain is that Chapman was a serial killer and knew a lot about murdering women.

Spending time in the United States in the early 1890s and then returning to England to work as both a barber and the landlord of several pubs, he had a turbulent love life, attacking a former wife with a knife and leaving his later mistress Annie Chapman when she fell pregnant, taking only her surname with him. By 1895 Chapman had met a woman in her 30s called Mary Spink. They lived together in both Hastings and then London, where they ran a pub. But, tiring of Mary, Chapman began poisoning her using antimony, a poison with similar effects to arsenic. Odourless and virtually tasteless, the soft metal was readily available at chemist's shops, in the form of a white powder known as tartar emetic, as it was used in small doses medicinally. Chapman is known to have purchased 1oz of it in April 1897 for twopence.

Later that year, Mary began to get vomiting attacks, diarrhoea and terrible stomach pains. She died on Christmas Day afternoon. At the time, her passing was put down to tuberculosis. Soon Chapman had taken up with 32-year-old Bessie Taylor, who helped him run a different pub, but by December 1900 she began suffering with similar symptoms to Mary. By Valentine's Day 1901 she was also dead, but again her death was officially recorded as being the result of natural causes. When a third partner, Maud Marsh, began suffering from vomiting and diarrhoea from July 1902, she ended up in hospital, where a doctor diagnosed peritonitis. She recovered, but on returning to the hostelry where she lived with Chapman, Maud fell ill again and died on 22 October 1902.

This time, however, her family and a doctor who'd treated Maud were suspicious. A post-mortem was performed and it identified the presence of antimony in large quantities in Maud's stomach, bowel and even brain. In all there were 477mg of antimony in the cadaver. In the light of this, Mary Spink's and Bessie Taylor's bodies were both exhumed, and doctors were amazed at the state of their preservation, a known side-effect of antimony. Both corpses contained high levels of antimony. Bessie's remains, for example, contained 693mg. A single dose of 120mg could be enough to kill. Chapman had spent weeks adding small amounts to the food and drink of his victims, slowly putting pressure on their organs and causing them to get weaker through lack of proper nutrition as their bodies reacted to the poison.

Chapman, 37, was put on trial, found guilty of murder and executed on 7 April 1903. His motives for the killings remain shadowy, and while the small inheritance he received as a result of one of the murders may have been an inducement, his main spur appears to have been a peculiar hatred of women. Yet, given his modus operandi, it seems unlikely that he was the Ripper, who had butchered his targets violently and with a blade.

While there is no doubt that Chapman was a poisoner, an earlier case involving antimony threw up a mystery that perpetuates to this day. When the lawyer Charles Bravo died in 1876 at his home in south London, from a fatal dose of tartar emetic, an inquest found that he had been murdered. Suspicion fell upon his wife, Florence, but nothing could be proven and ultimately no charges were brought. Theories about what really happened in the case have abounded ever since. Had the unfaithful Florence decided to do away with the bullying Bravo? Was it Bravo who had actually been secretly poisoning Florence and taken too much of the antimony himself by mistake? Or had the 31-year-old merely committed suicide? The truth may never be known.

500...

circulars written by poisoner Dr Thomas Neill Cream

Had sexual sadist Dr Thomas Neill Cream not craved both attention and money, along with the twisted gratification he took from his victims' agonising deaths, he might never have been brought to justice for any of the vicious slayings for which he had been responsible across two continents. Instead, through boasts, blackmail and a series of bizarre public pronouncements, Cream would precipitate his own end.

Born in Scotland, Cream received medical training in Canada and England between 1876 and 1878. During this time, his wife, Flora, died in mysterious circumstances, and in 1879 another pregnant lover, Kate Gardener, was found dead behind Cream's surgery in London, Ontario. She had died from chloroform poisoning. Though Cream was believed to be involved in her death, no charges were brought.

Cream moved to Chicago, where he scaled up his illegal abortion business. In 1880 prostitute Mary Anne Faulkner died while in his care, but once more Cream evaded prosecution. When Ellen Stack died from taking pills laced with the poison strychnine, which Cream had prescribed, he tried to blame the pharmacist for the overdose. Cream avoided jail, but when he tried to use the same ploy in the death of railway worker Daniel Stott, he wasn't so lucky.

Stott had been taking a remedy devised by Cream for his epilepsy. But Cream connived with Stott's wife, with whom he was having an affair, to add fatal quantities of strychnine to the mixture once it had been made up by the pharmacist. Stott died in June 1881, and his death was put down to natural causes. Yet Cream would not let Stott lie. Desperate to preserve his medical reputation, he sent a telegram to the coroner blaming the relevant pharmacist, saying, 'I want you to have a post-mortem examination made … have stomach examined, suspect foul play.' Sure enough, the strychnine was found in Stott's body, but it was Cream, not the druggist, who was charged. Found guilty of murder, he was sentenced to life.

Probably through corruption, Cream managed to get an early release, and by the autumn of 1891 he was in Britain, where he took to poisoning young women in London. His first victim was Ellen Donworth, 19, a Lambeth prostitute, who died in agony after Cream added strychnine to her drink.

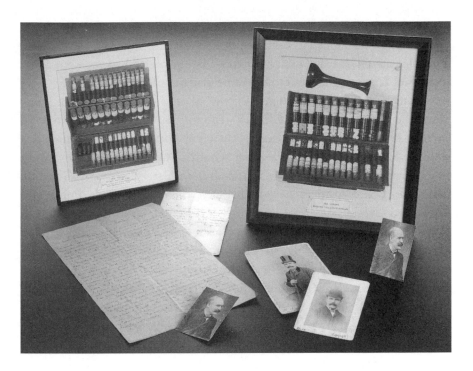

Photographs of Dr Neill Cream and his cases of poison. (Courtesy of Wellcome Library, London)

Despite her deathbed description of Cream's distinctive squint, top hat and 'bushy whiskers', he was not identified. But Cream did write a wild and risky note to police as 'A. O'Brien, Detective', offering information that could help solve the case in return for £300,000. He also used a pseudonym to try and blackmail politician Frederick Smith, randomly accusing him of Donworth's murder. On a visit back to Canada, he even had 500 circulars printed up, to be sent to the guests at London's Metropole Hotel. These, signed 'W. H. Murray', were intercepted by a clerk but were deemed to be an eccentric hoax and so went unreported to the police. Yet the tone of the handbill was emblematic of the bombast that would eventually lead to Cream's downfall: 'I hereby notify you that the person who poisoned Ellen Donworth on the 13th of October last year is today working at the Metropole. Your lives are in danger as long as you stay in this hotel.'

By April 1892 Cream was back in London; that very month, he killed two prostitutes, Alice Marsh, 21, and Emma Shrivell, 18, by putting strychnine in their bottles of Guinness. He sent more blackmail letters to a top physician and a peer, using aliases, but this time mentioned the 'murder' of Matilda Clover. The 27-year-old had died back in October, but her death had been put down to alcohol. Exhumed, she was found to be a victim of strychnine too.

Cream would finally be caught by showing off about how much he knew about the crimes – including Clover's – to a visiting American detective and then an officer from Scotland Yard. Police put him under surveillance and tracked down Lou Harvey, a woman whom Cream mentioned as having been murdered. He thought he'd killed her with strychnine pills, but Lou had actually thrown them away and later testified against him. Police also unearthed Cream's criminal past in the United States and found him in possession of a case containing scores of deadly strychnine pills. Convicted of murder, he was hanged at Newgate Prison in November 1892. His penchant for killing prostitutes led some to think he could have been Jack the Ripper. Yet Cream was actually in jail in 1888, when most of the Ripper's killings occurred, and his alleged cry of 'I am Jack the …' as he plunged to his doom on the gallows is likely to have been a final, and characteristically arrogant, plea for notoriety.

568 ... components in an Identi-Kit system used to catch the Antique Shop Killer

During their investigation into the 'Glamour Girl Slayer', Harvey Glatman, the Los Angeles police made use of a new facial composite system, giving them a striking image of their suspect. TV repairman Glatman's modus operandi was to pose as a photographer for crime magazines and modelling agencies. In this way he managed to persuade women to allow themselves to be tied up for bondage-style pictures. Once they were bound, he raped or sexually assaulted them. Glatman then strangled his victims, dumping their bodies in the desert. Three women died in this way between 1957 and 1958. Glatman was finally caught when another potential victim, Lorraine Vigil, fought back and was lucky enough that a passing policeman spotted what was happening and intervened. When detectives compared the composite of their suspect to Glatman, they were amazed at the likeness. Glatman went to the gas chamber for his crimes in 1959.

Until this time, police had to rely on witness descriptions of killers, helped by likenesses drawn up by skilled artists. But with the introduction of the Identi-Kit system, two-dimensional facial composites of suspects could be produced more easily, often by detectives themselves. The original box kits contained 568 printed sheets of sketches, each showing different facial characteristics, such as chins, eyebrows, hairstyles and noses, from which a likeness would emerge with the help of the witness. Although it was patented in the United States by Smith & Wesson, Identi-Kit's first big success came in helping to solve a British murder case in 1961.

On 3 March, antique dealer Louis Meier discovered the body of his assistant, Elsie Batten, lying dead in his shop in Cecil Court, just off London's Charing Cross Road. The 65-year-old had been stabbed three times – once in the neck, once in the back and once in the chest, where an ivory-handled dagger was still buried to a depth of 8in. Interviewed by police, Meier described how a young man of Indian heritage had visited the shop on the previous day, enquiring about buying a dress sword and some daggers, but had left without making a purchase. The sword was now missing. Questioning other local antique dealers, the police ascertained that a man matching the same description had tried to sell the sword in the hours following the murder.

As luck would have it, just two days earlier police officers in the capital had attended a course on using the new Identi-Kit system, which had just been introduced from America. Detective Sergeant Raymond Dagg was one of them and decided to put it into action. He worked with Meier and one of the other antiques traders, Paul Roberts, to build up likenesses of the man they had encountered using the Identi-Kit sheets. His superiors were so impressed with the similarity between the two composites that they were circulated to police forces across the country and to the media.

Just five days after the murder, on 8 March, Constable Arthur Cole was on duty in Old Compton Street, not far from where the murder had been committed. He noticed a man of Asian descent and immediately recognised that he matched the Identi-Kit images of the Elsie Batten murder suspect that he'd seen. Cole arrested the 21-year-old, who turned out to be Edwin Bush.

Questioned at the police station, Bush initially denied killing Elsie, saying he was with his mother. But she couldn't back up his alibi and, after Roberts picked Bush out of a line-up, he broke down and confessed, saying, 'I am sorry I done it. I don't know what came over me.' He went on to explain that when he had gone back into the shop to buy the sword, he had become impatient when Elsie had haggled over the price. She had also, according to Bush, made a racist remark. Bush was found guilty at the Old Bailey on 12 May 1961 and hanged at Pentonville Prison on 6 July.

Many more convictions using the Identi-Kit system followed, and over the years more sophisticated techniques of producing facial composites were developed. From the 1970s, use of the Photofit system, containing 560 real photographs of facial features, to produce likenesses became widespread. And in more recent times a host of different software programmes, such as E-Fit, have emerged that can produce detailed computerised images of suspects.

629... flight number of the plane Jack Gilbert Graham blew up for cash

On 11 September 2001, two airliners, hijacked by members of the terrorist group al-Qaeda, ploughed into the Twin Towers of the World Trade Center in New York. Two more flights were brought down that day and the attacks resulted in the loss of nearly 3,000 lives. It was the most horrifying case of murder in the skies in history, yet these were far from the first people to perish in an aircraft following a terrorist incident. We have become sadly accustomed to planes being targeted by killers for political reasons since the invention of powered flight. However, murder has sometimes been committed on aeroplanes for rather more mundane and personal motives.

In the summer of 1949, Canadian Albert Guay, 31, was in financial difficulties and desperate to be free of his wife, Rita. Living in Catholic Quebec, it was almost impossible to obtain a divorce, yet he wanted to win back a beautiful teenage waitress, Marie-Ange Robitaille, with whom he had been having an affair. She had left Guay, apparently because of his marriage. So Guay came up with an extreme solution to his problems, one that would get rid of Rita and make him some money into the bargain. The jewellery trader persuaded Rita to take a plane across the country to pick up some suitcases of merchandise for him. On 9 September 1949, Rita boarded Canadian Pacific Air Lines Flight 108 at Quebec City airport. But, 41 minutes into the flight, the Douglas DC-3 exploded, killing all twenty-three people on board.

Before the plane had left, Guay had bought a $10,000 insurance policy on Rita's life. With his wife now dead, and looking forward to collecting the money, he invited Marie-Ange over, telling her that they were free to be together. She told him that it made no difference – she no longer wanted to pursue the relationship.

Worse news was to come for Guay. Rita's plane had been delayed for five minutes before take-off. Guay had convinced his employee, Généreux Ruest, to make him a crude bomb using dynamite, batteries and an alarm clock, and Ruest's sister Marguerite Pitre had arranged for the package that it was concealed in to be placed in the mail aboard Rita's doomed aircraft. Guay had set the bomb to go off when he calculated that it would be over the wide St Lawrence River, giving police little chance of finding remains of the device. Yet the plane's late departure meant the debris had, instead, come down on land. Once detectives knew a bomb had caused the crash, it took them little time to link the crime to Guay, especially after Pitre confessed to her part in the plot. Guay was hanged on 12 January 1951, exclaiming, 'At least I die famous.' Ruest and Pitre were also executed.

Whether or not Jack Gilbert Graham knew of his predecessor's fate, he would become even more notorious for attempting to pull off murder in the air for profit just six years later. Graham, 23, was on bad terms with his mother, restaurant owner Daisie King, 53, and the pair frequently argued, not least because she had, for a time, put Graham in an orphanage as a child.

On 1 November 1955, Daisie was taking United Airlines Flight 629 to Portland, Oregon, from Denver en route to see her daughter. Despite their stormy relationship, Daisie was waved off at Stapleton Airport by Graham. A few minutes after the Douglas D-6 took off, it plunged to earth in a fireball. All forty-four people on the plane were killed. Graham later called the airline's office to ask if his mother had been killed in the crash. Told that it was likely, he replied flatly, 'Well, that's the way it goes!'

FBI forensic experts determined that the plane had been brought down by a bomb made of dynamite and traced it back to Daisie King's suitcase. When they started looking into her background, they discovered that Graham had a string of convictions for crimes such as forging cheques. An explosion at Daisie's restaurant earlier the same year had suspiciously ended with an insurance payout to Graham. He was set to inherit a large portion of Daisie's

Killer Jack Gilbert Graham. (Courtesy of the FBI)

estate and had also bought a $37,000 insurance policy on her life from a vending machine at the airport (though the policy wasn't signed and was, in fact, worthless). When police found bomb-making equipment at Graham's home, he confessed to putting the explosives in his mother's luggage. Graham was only charged with his mother's murder, as there was, at the time, no specific law against blowing up an aircraft. He ended up going to the gas chamber on 11 January 1957, but not before stating, 'The number of people to be killed made no difference to me; it could have been a thousand. When their time comes, there is nothing they can do about it.'

666... times Satanic killers stabbed their victims

'The Devil made me do it.' This chilling phrase, or versions of it, has been uttered many times from the lips of some of history's most callous killers. There are numerous cases where murderers have attempted to explain away their hideous crimes by putting the real blame at the door of Satan. Some even claim to be Beelzebub himself.

On 8 August 1969, pregnant actress Sharon Tate and four other house guests at 10050 Cielo Drive, Los Angeles, were brutally murdered by members of the so-called Manson family. When screenwriter Wojciech Frykowski had asked one of the crazed gang, Tex Watson, what he was doing there, moments before Frykowski was shot and stabbed to death, Watson replied, 'I'm the Devil and I'm here to do the Devil's business.' Crazed cult leader Charles Manson, found guilty of conspiracy to commit the murders in 1971, would also go on to tell the press, cryptically, 'I am the Devil.' Manson would be sentenced to serve nine life sentences for the crimes he and his followers committed, while Watson was convicted of a total of seven murders. Driven by his own demons, lone killer Mark Chapman, who gunned down musician John Lennon on 8 December 1980 outside his New York home, later revealed that he had appealed to the Devil to give him the strength to commit the act.

Symbolism is often important to those who dabble in the occult, and some of the most infamous symbols can crop up in the crimes of murderers said to be inspired by supernatural forces. Richard Ramirez, known as the 'Night Stalker', killed random residents of California during the 1980s. In the course of his killings he would demand victims swear their love for Satan and often left a pentagram (a five-pointed star often associated with Satanic worship) behind as his signature. Using lipstick, Ramirez drew one of these on the thigh of Mabel Bell during a gruesome attack in her home. The 84-year-old would later die of the injuries she had sustained at his hands. Police eventually tracked down the sadistic serial killer from a single fingerprint left on the rear-view mirror of a car. In his cell awaiting trial, Ramirez drew both pentagrams and the number 666 in blood on the floor. Referred to in the Bible as the 'number of the beast', these digits were also proudly displayed on the palm of his hand by Ramirez during his trial. It ended with his conviction for thirteen murders in 1989.

The Night Stalker wasn't the only serial killer to be obsessed with the number 666. Wayne Nance, a truck driver from Montana, had been a Satan worshipper since his teens and once branded his own flesh with the number 666 using a white-hot coat hanger. Responsible for at least five murders, Nance was shot in the head, aged 30, in 1986, by a man he had been trying to kill. Nance's trail of human destruction was only uncovered after his death.

Vampire-loving couple Daniel and Manuela Ruda murdered their friend Frank Hackert, 33, by hitting him over the head with a hammer and stabbing him multiple times at their flat in Witten, Germany, on 9 July 2001. They then carved a pentagram into his skin. Having met through a lonely hearts column two years earlier, the Rudas had sealed their Satanic union by getting married on the sixth day of the sixth month, deciding to kill Hackert on 6 July 2001. Put together, the dates fitted the figure 666 and presumably gave them some kind of twisted satisfaction. After the killing they drank Hackert's blood and prayed to Satan. Fortunately, they were caught before they could carry on killing, after a tip-off to police from Manuela's mother. She had become concerned after receiving a letter from her daughter in which she'd said, 'I am not of this world.' The Rudas were locked up in secure psychiatric units in 2002.

Incredibly, their devotion to the 'number of the beast' did not go as far as the gang of Satan worshippers responsible for the murder of teenagers Anya Gorokhova, Olga Pukhova, Varya Kuzmina and Andrei Sorokin in Russia's Yaroslavl region in 2008. They had been forced to drink alcohol, then each stabbed 666 times. One of the culprits reportedly stated that 'Satan will help me avoid responsibility.' In the end, however, Lucifer's powers were found lacking and the killers received hefty sentences.

700 ...

cases of missing women examined in the Brighton Trunk Murders

Before the age of airliners, travel trunks were routinely used to transport belongings by ship or rail. Due to their relatively large size, they were sometimes used by murderers to convey bodies too. In 1889, France had been gripped by the Gouffé affair (see page 99), in which a piece of luggage bought in London was used to bundle the victim out of Paris. Then, in 1927, London itself was the scene of a shocking discovery – the chopped-up corpse of 36-year-old prostitute Minnie Bonati. The body parts had been found wrapped in separate parcels inside a trunk deposited at Charing Cross Station. Minnie was identified via a pair of knickers found inside. Her killer, John Robinson, was eventually tracked down via an address where a taxi driver recalled he had picked up a man with a large trunk, heading for the terminus. Robinson would admit cutting up Minnie and was hanged, aged 36, at Pentonville Prison on 12 August.

Charing Cross Station was little more than an hour's train ride from the station at Brighton on the south coast of England, and Minnie's demise was still fresh in the memory when, in June 1934, a strange smell began emanating from a trunk there too. Police were called and inside, under layers of paper and cotton wool, they found a woman's torso. An alert was put out and the following day a pair of legs was found in another trunk left at King's Cross Station in London. They belonged to the same pregnant woman, aged about 25.

Without the victim's head or arms, or even a precise cause of death, police launched a huge investigation, reviewing the cases of 700 missing women as well as following up suspected abortionists and making public appeals for information. This led to a tip-off about the disappearance of a 41-year-old prostitute, Violette Kaye, known to be associated with a small-time crook, Tony Mancini. Witnesses said that the pair had often quarrelled. Mancini, 26, was questioned but not arrested, and he went on the run.

Meanwhile, police investigating the trunk murder had already been making searches of homes near the station. A painter alerted them to a strange smell coming from No. 52 Kemp Street, where Mancini had been living. Inside they found another trunk, which Mancini had been using as a coffee table.

Opening it, they made the gruesome discovery of Violette's body. She had been bludgeoned over the head.

After a short manhunt, Mancini was apprehended and brought to trial in December 1934 at Lewes Assizes. His defence was that one day in May he had come home to find Violette dead. Mancini maintained that he had panicked and bundled Violette's body into the trunk. Despite an overwhelming amount of evidence, including a hammer said to have inflicted the fatal blow, bloodied clothing and a woman whom Mancini had met in London who claimed that he'd asked her to give him an alibi, Mancini was found not guilty. His brilliant defence counsel, Norman Birkett, had managed to argue that one of Violette's clients could have killed her and that her injuries might have been sustained by falling down some steps. He said that Mancini had no apparent motive.

Some forty years later Mancini confessed to a newspaper that he had indeed killed Violette during a row. Oddly, however, there has never been any evidence to connect him to the body in the first trunk, which had led to the discovery of the second murder. Apart from the type of container used, the crimes were almost certainly unrelated. But the puzzling coincidences didn't end there, for the 1934 trunk murders had not been Brighton's first.

In July 1831 bigamist John Holloway had been desperate to do away with his estranged wife, Celia Bashford. The painter had managed to get both her and his mistress, Ann Kennett, pregnant and was facing financial ruin. On the pretence of making up with Celia, he invited her to an address on Donkey Row, then, asking for a kiss, pulled a rope around her neck. Once his victim had been strangled, Holloway set about dismembering Celia's body, putting the head and limbs in an outside privy and the torso in a trunk. Holloway then trundled the trunk out to a wooded area. He buried the body in a shallow grave, broke up the trunk and scattered it. Rain soon uncovered the torso and the remains of the trunk, which was identified as having belonged to Celia. It didn't take long for the rest of her body to be found. Holloway was hanged for murder that December.

800... dollar insurance payout in the case of 'The Man Who Wouldn't Die'

In 1737 an apothecary based in Southwark, London, took out an insurance policy on the life of his wife and then poisoned her so he could collect the payout. It was the first known case where a killer sought to gain financially as a result of cashing in on this kind of cover; it would not be the last. Ever since life insurance policies began being offered in the eighteenth century, the practice has gone hand in hand with murder.

When Ann Palmer died in 1854, at the age of 27, it did not cause much of a stir. A cholera epidemic was rampant and the disease was blamed. Meanwhile, her husband, William, a doctor from Rugeley, Staffordshire, quietly pocketed the £13,000 payout from her life insurance policy. It was only when he was later found to have murdered his friend John Cook that Ann's body was exhumed and traces of the poison antimony were found in her system. Palmer, responsible for a string of other deaths to fund his gambling habit, was hanged in 1856, having tried to cash in a policy on his dead brother Walter too.

The case was just one of many where a greedy relative has contrived to make themselves a beneficiary of a large sum in the event of the death of a supposed loved one, then murdered them before having to pay out too many premiums. Yet perhaps the most beguiling case of all insurance-related homicides was one where the killers sought to murder a complete stranger.

By the time former fireman Mike Malloy began drinking at Tony Marino's Depression-era speakeasy in New York, he was aged 50–60, homeless and an alcoholic. One day, in 1932, Marino and some of his associates were considering how to raise some easy cash when they glanced over at Malloy and hit upon what they considered a cunning plan. Marino, along with undertaker Francis Pasqua, grocer Daniel Kriesberg and bartender Joe Murphy, figured no one would miss him. Malloy had no family and was already drinking himself into an early grave.

With the help of a corrupt insurance agent, they managed to take out three separate policies on Malloy's life, with themselves as the beneficiaries in the event of his death. In all, they were in line for more than $3,500. All the plotters had to do now, they thought, was ply Malloy with enough free whisky to kill him. They hadn't accounted for Malloy's constitution. However much he drank, it didn't look like finishing him off any time soon. The gang took things up a gear, adding antifreeze to Malloy's drinks. They were astonished when he simply slept it off.

Over the coming weeks, the conspirators served Malloy an increasingly bizarre array of free food and drink in a frantic attempt to kill him while making his death look due natural causes for insurance purposes: bad oysters, sardine sandwiches laced with pins and, finally, rat poison. To their astonishment Malloy seemed to be impervious to it all.

The free booze, and paying those insurance premiums, was beginning to hurt Marino and his pals, who now resorted to desperate measures. One

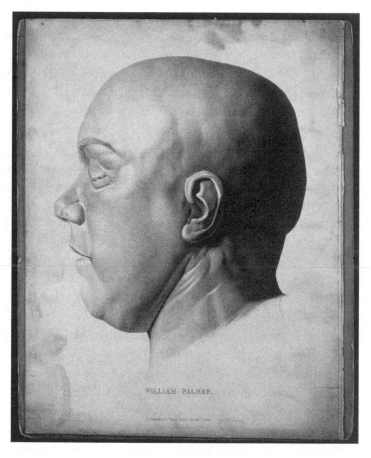

William Palmer. (Courtesy of Wellcome Library, London)

January night, when Malloy was comatose with drink, they bundled him into a local park, then ripped off his shirt and poured 5 gallons of water on to his chest. They left him out in temperatures of -26 degrees Celsius, expecting him to freeze to death. Instead Malloy turned up at the bar the next day, complaining of a 'bit of a chill'.

The next scheme, to make Malloy appear to have been the victim of a 'hit and run', fared no better. For a slice of the loot, taxi driver Hershey Green was persuaded to hit Malloy in the street with his car. Seizing an opportune moment, he ran over his target at 45mph, reversing over the body for good measure, before fleeing the scene. Again 'Iron' Mike survived, recovering from relatively minor injuries in hospital.

'The Murder Trust', as they would later be dubbed by the press, had already spent $1,875 trying to bring about Malloy's untimely end and now lost patience. On 22 February 1933, they got him drunk, then dragged him to a rented room where a gas pipe was shoved into his mouth. Even he couldn't survive that. Thanks to an unscrupulous medic, Malloy's death was officially ascribed to pneumonia and he was quickly buried. One of the insurance policies, worth $800, paid out. But the other company involved was suspicious and police had got wind of rumours circulating on the street about Malloy's legendary resilience.

Malloy's body was exhumed and the real reason for his death – asphyxiation by carbon monoxide – discovered. Four members of 'The Murder Trust' would end up convicted of murder and go to the electric chair, with Green getting a lesser sentence after spilling the beans.

931... number of victims of the world's worst serial killer?

The history of murder in the last century has featured some seriously prolific serial killers, individuals whose staggering number of victims make Jack the Ripper look like a rank amateur. Some of those with the highest body counts include the depraved doctor Harold Shipman (see page 61) as well as American Gary Ridgway, the so-called Green River Killer, convicted of the murders of forty-eight women in the 1980s and 1990s. The real death toll is believed to be around ninety – by Ridgway's own admission, he lost count. Lesser known, but responsible for even more killings, is Luis Garvaito, the chilling Colombian nicknamed 'The Beast', who was convicted of murdering 138 young boys in the 1990s but has been linked to a total of 300 or more. Countryman Pedro Lopez, dubbed the 'Monster of the Andes', also killed at least 300, in his case young girls, in the 1970s.

According to criminologists, there may be at least two unknown serial killers at large in a country like the UK at any one time, but other research reveals that the number of serial killers appears to be declining, with figures from Radford University in the United States suggesting that, at least in America, cases reached a peak in the 1980s. Better forensics and the ability of police forces to analyse data and make links between crimes certainly mean that it's now easier to identify such criminals early, before they manage to notch up multiple victims. Yet serial killers have always been with us and to pinpoint those with the highest number of victims it's worth peering past the high-profile cases of recent decades, further back into history.

There are tales of killers with hundreds of victims dating back to at least the sixteenth century, though the contemporaneous accounts of their exploits often tend to be laced with supernatural overtones, making it hard to know if the numbers were exaggerated or, indeed, if the supposed culprits were really responsible for the horrors of which they were accused. Roving robber Peter Niers, for example, was said to have killed 544 people before being executed in 1581, helped in his murderous deeds by the Devil himself.

His terrifying tally was evidently topped by Elizabeth Báthory, who became known as the Blood Countess after her crimes were associated with vampirism. There is no doubt that the Hungarian aristocrat existed. She was married to a warrior called Nadasdy who spent much of his time away from home, fighting the Ottomans, while she looked after their estates. Starting as early as the 1580s, a string of teenage servant girls began to die at Báthory residences amid whispers of depraved goings-on behind closed doors. When she opened an etiquette academy and girls higher up the social scale started disappearing, an investigation was launched. It uncovered a catalogue of sexual sadism and murder that eventually led to several trials of accomplices and Báthory's own imprisonment, with one maid testifying that there had been 650 separate victims. Báthory died in 1614, aged 54, apparently still incarcerated in a small room of her own castle.

It wasn't until the eighteenth century that the legend of how Báthory had bathed in her victims' blood became established. But, if the large amount of testimony from witnesses assembled during her lifetime was to be believed, her crimes had certainly been vile enough not to need this elaboration.

By the time the myth about Báthory began to grow, a mysterious sect in India was murdering thousands of victims every year. They were called the Thugees, from which we derive the English word 'thug', and roamed the country robbing and strangling strangers. Their modus operandi was to befriend travellers and gain their confidence before striking. Lower estimates have the Thugs murdering 1,000 people a year, but some estimate a million victims between 1740 and 1840.

When, in the early nineteenth century, India's new British rulers began trying to supress the cult using informants, the bloody extent of Thugee crimes became evident and among their ranks there emerged some particularly skilled killers. In 1837, Captain James Paton recorded the confessions of some captured Thugs. One, called Ramzam, was linked to the deaths of 604 people; another, Futty Khan, to 508. Heading the list, however, was Buhram Jemedar. He had become expert in despatching victims using a scarf featuring a medallion. He claimed to have killed, or been present at the murder of, 931 people during a forty-year reign of terror. Tried in Lucknow, he would be hanged in 1840. Whether criminologists would classify Buhram as a classic serial killer is a moot point, but as a one-man killing machine he must certainly rival many of his modern criminal counterparts.

936... picograms of lead in the rib of Pope Clement II

There is an old adage among policemen and forensic experts that, if a credible suspect has not been identified in the first forty-eight hours after a murder is committed, then the chances of solving the crime plummet by half. Certainly new evidence becomes more difficult to collect after this time and a perpetrator harder to apprehend. In spite of this, some murder cases have been solved years after the event.

On 5 November 1961, three cavers were exploring an old lead mine at Brandy Cove, on the Gower peninsula in south Wales, when they made a shocking discovery. Inside was a rotting sack, a human skull and other bones. Nearby were two rings and a hair clip with some strands still attached.

Home Office pathologists reassembled the skeleton, identifying that it belonged to someone about 5ft 4in. The pelvis indicated a female. By examining sutures on the skull, the experts reckoned that the woman had been in her mid-20s at the time of death. A lack of tissue meant they couldn't be sure how she'd died, but from marks on the bones, it was evident that the body had been sawn into three sections. She was the victim of a crime.

Locals believed they knew who the victim was. Former chorus girl Maime Stuart had gone missing in 1920, aged 26. Her age and height matched the pathologists' findings, and when an old photograph was superimposed on the retrieved skull, it matched exactly. An elderly woman, who had known Maime, confirmed that the rings were hers.

In 1918 Maime had married marine surveyor George Shotton, thirteen years her senior, and they moved to a cottage on the Gower. Suddenly, in 1919, both disappeared. Police soon found Shotton, who was back living with another wife, whom he'd married in 1905. He claimed not to know where Maime was, saying they'd fought over her infidelity and broken up. Despite nationwide appeals, police could find no trace of Maime. Although they were convinced Shotton had killed her, he was convicted of bigamy alone.

In December 1961 an inquest heard testimony from an 83-year-old postman who recalled having seen Shotton acting shiftily as he removed a heavy sack from his cottage just before Maime's disappearance was reported. The court concluded that the body in the mineshaft was indeed Maime and that she'd been murdered by Shotton. When police tried to track down the killer, they discovered that he'd died in 1958, aged 78, alone and in poverty.

The emergence of DNA evidence (see page 167) would enhance the ability to connect killers to their murders from samples they had left behind years before. One of the coldest cases cracked this way was the murder of Colette Aram. The 16-year-old trainee hairdresser had been abducted on 30 October 1983, at Keyworth, Nottinghamshire, en route to her boyfriend's house. Her body was found the next day in a field. She had been raped and strangled.

Blood and semen were found in an abandoned stolen car and blood was also found on a recovered paper towel that a suspect had used to wash his hands in a local pub. However, at the time, no one was caught for the crime.

In the light of advances in the use of DNA, the case was later reviewed and, in 2007, experts managed to identify Colette's DNA in blood samples extracted from the paper towel as well as the full DNA profile of the man who was undoubtedly her killer. Sadly this didn't match any already on the police database.

In 2008, Jean-Paul Hutchinson was arrested over a motoring offence and a DNA swab was routinely taken. When another trawl of the database was made, his profile was found to be a near match to Colette's killer. Jean-Paul hadn't been born at the time of the murder, but the guilty man had to be a relative. When the DNA of his father, Paul Hutchinson, was tested, it matched the murderer's profile exactly. The 51-year-old pleaded guilty at Nottingham Crown Court in December 2009 and was jailed for a minimum of twenty-five years.

Other techniques have allowed the investigation of even older mysteries. From the time of his death in 1047, it was suspected that Pope Clement II had been poisoned, probably by agents of ousted pontiff Benedict IX. When, in 1959, German scientists were given permission to open Clement's sarcophagus and test a rib bone from the remains, they discovered that it contained 936 picograms of lead. A picogram is one-trillionth of a gram. It might not sound like a lot, but the scientists calculated that in terms of parts per million this was far in excess of the amount you'd expect to see. The findings suggested that Clement was poisoned with lead sugar, probably added over time to his wine.

999... the mystery emergency call in a country murder

When the 999 telephone number service was introduced in Britain, on 30 June 1937, one advert advised people how to use it by saying, 'Call 999 if, for instance, the man in the flat next to yours is murdering his wife.' In its first week of operation, 1,000 people called 999 to report various emergencies, and by 2012 the service was fielding 600,000 calls a week. Similar systems were adopted across the world. In 1968, the United States got its own number – 911.

Emergency numbers have often been used to report a murder, perhaps most famously when a terrified David Smith dialled 999 on 7 October 1965 to alert police after he'd watched 17-year-old Edward Evans battered to death with an axe. His call, at 6.07 a.m. from a coin-operated telephone box, set in chain the investigation that ultimately led to the conviction of the Moors murderers, Ian Brady and Myra Hindley.

Chillingly, some 999 operators have had to endure listening to murders being committed at the other end of the line, after people have phoned for help while being attacked. In January 2009, Lakhvinder Cheema rang 999, effectively to report his own murder. He said he felt extremely unwell after eating a chicken curry and thought that he might have been poisoned by his ex-girlfriend. Indeed he had. The 39-year-old died later the same evening. In 2010 Lakhvir Singh was convicted of his murder after being found to have put deadly aconite in her former partner's food.

Killers have also used 999 to report their own crimes. When, in 2014, 19-year-old Lewis Daynes slit the throat of teenager Breck Bednar, he called 999 asking for police and forensic teams to be sent to his flat, calmly admitting that he had grabbed a knife and stabbed his victim 'in the back of the neck'.

Dale Cregan, a man already wanted for a double murder, called 999 with the intention of luring two police officers to their deaths. On 18 September 2012 he used a false name to report that someone had thrown a concrete slab through the window of his home in Mottram, Manchester. It was a trap. When constables Nicola Hughes, 23, and Fiona Bone, 32, arrived at the property, Cregan opened the front door and immediately began firing his Glock pistol at them, unleashing thirty-two shots in thirty-one seconds as well as throwing a grenade at the pair. Both were killed. Cregan later handed himself in at a police station.

The strangest murder involving a 999 call relates to the case of Lieutenant-Colonel Robert Workman, 83, whose body was found by his carer at 7 a.m. on 8 January 2004 lying across the doorstep of his idyllic country cottage, Cock House, in the village of Furneux Pelham, Hertfordshire. The victim, a widower who lived alone, had been shot dead at point-blank range with a 12-bore shotgun.

At 8.15 p.m. the previous evening, neighbours had heard a loud bang but had dismissed the sound as a car back-firing. Later, at 4.49 a.m., a man had called 999 from a telephone box in the nearby village of Braughing. He requested that an ambulance should be sent to 'Hollycock Cottage' in Furneux Pelham. It referred to a name of the cottage – actually Hollyhock Cottage – that had not been used for many years. An ambulance was dispatched but as the wrong name for the house had been given to them, the crew could not find the address and dismissed the call as a hoax.

Once it was clear that a murder had occurred, police focused on the identity of the mystery 999 caller, but with no apparent motive to go on, the investigation stalled. It wasn't until several years later that pest controller Christopher Docherty-Puncheon, who was behind bars in Bedford Prison, confessed to killing the colonel. He was inside for another murder, that of his friend Fred Moss, 21.

At his trial for the Workman killing in 2012, the court heard that Docherty-Puncheon had told a fellow inmate that he'd had a homosexual relationship with the ex-serviceman and had shot him after an argument. He had also claimed to be a hitman. In court the 33-year-old accused denied all this, but the prosecution alleged that he had ended up killing Moss because he knew too much about the colonel's murder.

A witness said that he'd seen a Range Rover in the vicinity of the murder, with a number plate that spelt SOHO, on the night of the killing. Docherty-Puncheon drove one with the plate N50H0. A lorry driver had seen a 4x4 parked by the phone box at the time of the 999 call. However, while Docherty-Puncheon was convicted of the colonel's murder, the identity of the mystery 999 caller was never definitely established.

1,000... cuts in a Chinese execution used for killers

For much of history, and across every continent, the death penalty has been the default sentence for those found guilty of murdering their fellow humans. Despite its gradual abolition by many nations, at least 100 countries have retained capital punishment into the twenty-first century.

When it comes to executing killers, a huge variety of methods have been used. Hanging has been one of the most common ways to despatch murderers down the centuries, and it is thought to have originated as a punishment for criminals in Persia, 2,500 years ago. It was brought to Britain in the fifth century by the Saxons, but it only became a regular punishment from the time of Henry I. London's Tyburn would become one of the most popular places to hang criminals, with 50,000 perishing on its gallows over 600 years. In the nineteenth century, 1,353 people in England and Wales were hanged for murder. The punishment was only abolished following the hanging of Gwynne Evans and Peter Allen in August 1964, after they murdered a van driver during a robbery.

In the United States, the first person to be officially hanged for murder was John Billington, in 1630. The 40-year-old had sailed for New England aboard the famous *Mayflower* but later had killed rival John Newcomen. Hanging remains a potential punishment in two states and Billy Bailey, 49, was hanged in 1996 for murdering two people.

Other common punishments for murder have included electrocution, lethal injection, the gas chamber, guillotine, crucifixion, beheading and stoning, as well as being shot; firing squads are used in cases of military murder by a number of nations.

There have also been some less familiar forms of execution for murder, such as being burnt at the stake. From medieval times, women in England could suffer this penalty for killing their husbands, with Catherine Hayes the last woman to be burned alive for such a crime in 1726. Being boiled alive in water or tar is another gruesome punishment that has occasionally been used to end the lives of murderers. Richard Roose had the ignominy of suffering this fate in 1531, on the personal orders of Henry VIII, after being found guilty in a case of poisoning. Up until 1772 those accused of murder, who refused to plea, could be crushed with stones. England has even seen murderers flung off cliffs or torn apart by wild horses, like the clergyman who killed the Earl of Huntingdon's infant son in the twelfth century.

In Scotland and elsewhere, killers were once 'broken on the wheel'. The convicted person would be strapped to a wheel and beaten until they died. From the nineteenth century, the garrotte was used in Spain to strangle criminals, including murderers. It involved the condemned person being tied to an adapted seat or chair and then asphyxiated. It was used in cases of murder until 1974.

The macabre list doesn't end there. In ancient Rome, murderers could be 'thrown to the lions', while those who killed their fathers would be placed in a leather bag filled with snakes or other animals, then drowned at sea. Versions of this punishment were later used in medieval Germany and the Far East. In south-east Asia, until the nineteenth century it was a common sentence for murderers to be crushed, in public, using elephants.

Of particular infamy was the Chinese method of executing criminals, which became known in English as 'death by a thousand cuts'. Known in China as *lingchi*, meaning literally 'humiliating and slow', it has also been

Model of cuts. (Courtesy of Wellcome Library, London)

called 'death by slicing'. The way in which *lingchi* was carried out varied across time and place, but it generally involved being tied to a pole, before a series of cuts were made to the body, followed, perhaps, by dismemberment and a final, fatal cut to the heart or decapitation. This type of execution had been in use for at least 1,000 years until its formal abolition in 1905 and was usually reserved for cases of multiple murder or patricide. One of the last of those condemned to die in such a manner was Wang Weiqin, put to death publicly in Beijing in 1904. He and his criminal gang had murdered twelve members of the same family. In practice, 'death by a thousand cuts' was a misnomer, as death usually occurred well before such a number of incisions could be inflicted.

1,300... guns tested in the 'Jockey Cap Murder'

Some guns are famous because of the high-profile crimes in which they are involved. Take, for instance, the Browning pistol used by Gavrilo Princip to assassinate Archduke Franz Ferdinand on 28 June 1914, in Sarajevo. The firearm, which helped spark the crisis which led to the First World War, is now a museum piece. Other individual weapons are notable because they represent important landmarks in the history of forensic ballistics. This was true of the Webley .455 MkVI revolver used to shoot Police Constable George Gutteridge in 1927. The crime itself, though brutal, was not especially remarkable, but the way in which the perpetrators were brought to justice showed how crucial scientific analysis of guns was becoming in securing convictions.

Forensic evidence from firearms was used for the first time to solve a crime in 1784, after carpenter Edward Culshaw was shot through the head with a muzzle-loading flintlock pistol while travelling near Liverpool. A post-mortem was conducted, and from the wound a surgeon retrieved both a ball and some wadding, used to pack the powder into the gun. This scrap of paper was found to have come from a song sheet. When 18-year-old John Toms became a suspect, he was searched. In his pocket was a song sheet with a piece ripped out – the missing segment was shown to match exactly that found on the victim. Toms was hanged.

With the development of guns over the next two centuries came new techniques in the emerging study of forensic ballistics. Rifling inside modern guns involves grooves inside the barrel which give the bullet spin and accuracy. The 'lands' and grooves in a barrel leave marks known as striations on the bullet. These can be individual to each gun – even when the result of mass production – because the wear on tools used to manufacture them will make each firearm very slightly different. When bullets are recovered, examination of these marks can help provide police with information about what kind of gun they're looking for in a murder case. The invention of the comparison microscope, in the 1920s, permitted comparison of bullets side by side, allowing these tiny marks to be compared to see if they had been fired from exactly the same gun.

Marks left on shell casings, by firing pins or when they are ejected, can also serve up vital ballistics information, and it was this kind of clue that became critical in the Gutteridge case. The 36-year-old was found murdered in an Essex country lane on 26 September 1927. He had been shot four times, including through both his eyes. As Gutteridge was still clutching a pencil, with his notebook next to his body, investigators surmised that he had probably tried to stop a suspicious car to question the drivers. A Morris car was known to have been stolen locally. Gutteridge must have been shot by the thieves, who had then made their escape.

Sure enough, the Morris was quickly found in London. Inside there were traces of blood and a single spent cartridge under the passenger seat. Scotland Yard detectives had already called in the gunsmith and renowned ballistics expert Robert Churchill to analyse the bullets found at the murder scene. From the rifling marks on them Churchill concluded that they came from a .455 Webley revolver. There was also a mark on the base of the cartridge, resembling the shape of a jockey's cap. Churchill believed this must have been made by an unusual flaw in the breech block of the gun.

At the start of 1928, known petty crook Frederick Browne, 46, was picked up over the theft of another car, and at his garage officers found a fully loaded Webley, serial number 299431, in yet another vehicle he used. It contained the same sort of ammunition that had been used to kill Gutteridge. Using a comparison microscope, Churchill was able to tell that the Webley was the very same one that had fired the spent cartridge in the Morris. When he test-fired 1,300 other Webley revolvers, none made the unique jockey cap mark on the cartridge. Powder traces from the ammunition also matched those found on the dead man.

Shortly after Browne's arrest, an accomplice, William Kennedy, 36, was also apprehended. He admitted being present at Gutteridge's murder but said that it was Browne who had shot him. For his part, Browne strongly protested his innocence, saying that he had only acquired the gun from Kennedy after the date of the murder. However, with the ballistics evidence at the heart of the prosecution's case, both ended up being found guilty of murdering Gutteridge. They went to the gallows on 31 May 1928.

1,505... suspect number of John Duffy

Over a period of sixteen years, a series of explosions rocked New York City, the result of crude bombs left mostly in public places, such as phone booths, stations and libraries. While no one was killed, many people were injured. The bombings appeared to be the work of one person, who had sent a series of letters and notes to the police. These indicated a grievance held towards the Consolidated Edison energy company. However, with police increasingly frustrated at their inability to catch the perpetrator, they turned to psychiatrist Dr James Brussel for help. By studying police files on the bomber and the letters he'd written, Brussel came up with a profile for the individual he thought responsible: probably a former employee of Con Ed, middle aged and a paranoid loner, probably of Slavic descent, neat and tidy, and possibly living with an older female relative. Brussel felt he was likely to be a man who favoured wearing double-breasted suits.

When a clerk at Con Ed read the profile, which had been published in the newspapers, she turned up the file of ex-worker George Metesky, who had been injured in an accident at work in 1931. Phrases in his correspondence matched those in the bomber's letters. It led to Metesky's arrest and the discovery of his bomb-making equipment. Metesky was found to be 54, of Polish extraction and living with his older sisters. He was taken to the station wearing a double-breasted suit. Brussel's profile had proved startlingly accurate.

It was one of the first occasions where offender profiling helped bring a criminal to justice. Psychological profiling is based on studying the criminal's modus operandi and the patterns of behaviour exhibited by past criminals to help formulate a picture of the likely culprit. It can sometimes provide clues to investigating teams about where they should be looking.

In the early 1980s a series of violent rapes were carried out near railway stations in and around London, then murders too. The body of 19-year-old Alison Day was found in the River Lea in December 1985. She had been raped and strangled. Two more victims, Maartje Tamboezer, 15, and Anne Lock, 29, followed. Helped by blood group evidence, police linked the crimes but struggled to narrow down their list of 2,000 suspects.

Psychologist David Canter was called in to help and studied all the crime scenes and victim statements. By mapping the offences, he was able to tell police that the culprit was likely to live in the Kilburn area. Among other pointers he also suggested that they should be looking for a 25- to 30-year-old man with a semi-skilled job and an interest in martial arts, and who liked to keep souvenirs of his victims.

John Duffy was number 1,505 on the police suspect list, but he matched many of the characteristics that Canter had pinpointed. Duffy was a 28-year-old former British Rail carpenter and martial arts fan from Kilburn who had previously been arrested over raping his ex-wife. When police searched his home, they found string and fibres linking him to the murdered women. Duffy had also kept thirty-three door keys from his victims.

In all, thirteen of the seventeen traits Canter had listed proved to be correct. At his trial in 1988, Duffy was found guilty of two murders and four rapes. He later admitted to a psychologist what Canter and the police already suspected – that he had not always acted alone. An accomplice, David Mulcahy, was convicted in 2001 for his involvement.

Although it didn't help catch the killer, one of the first profiles of a murderer had been drawn up a century earlier, as police in London searched for the elusive Jack the Ripper. In November 1888, surgeon Thomas Bond wrote a report for the police, reviewing the cases and detailing the likely character of the killer. Bond had just conducted the post-mortem on one of the victims, Mary Jane Kelly, whose heart appeared to have been taken in the attack.

There was speculation that, given the level of mutilation of the women whom the Ripper had killed, he was a man with medical knowledge. Bond dismissed this, saying that he showed no more skill than a 'common butcher', but he concluded that five of the murders of London prostitutes were the work of the same man, someone of 'physical strength and great coolness and daring', who was 'subject to periodical attacks of homicidal and erotic mania'. Bond further suggested that he was middle aged and 'likely to be a quiet inoffensive looking man', who was living among 'respectable persons'. He added that the Ripper probably wore a cloak to disguise the blood that his brutal attacks must surely have left upon his person.

2,000 ... volts used to kill the first man to die in the electric chair

William Kemmler was an illiterate alcoholic, endeavouring to make a frugal living as a fruit pedlar. Having left his first wife, Ida, after discovering she was already married, he'd shacked up with Matilda, or 'Tillie', Ziegler, who had fled from her own unfaithful and unemployed spouse. By 1889 Kemmler, Matilda and her daughter, Ella, were living in Buffalo, New York, where they rented rooms in a run-down district of town.

On the night of 28 March a drunk Kemmler returned to the dingy apartment and had one of his habitual quarrels with Tillie. Their rows usually concerned his drinking, but Kemmler was also convinced that she was having an affair. The next morning he grabbed a hatchet and struck Tillie over the head as she was washing the breakfast dishes. He hit her twenty-six times, inflicting 'several mortal wounds'. Ella had watched the whole thing and rushed in to tell the landlady, living next door, 'Papa has killed Mama.' Kemmler, dripping with blood, immediately admitted his crime, saying, 'I have killed her and I'll take the rope for it.'

Normally this run-of-the-mill domestic murder would notch up little more than a footnote in history. But it was Kemmler's eventual fate that would see his name firmly logged in the annals of crime. He would not be hanged as he'd thought. For the law had recently changed in the state of New York to allow execution by electrocution. By virtue of the fact that he was simply next in the queue, Kemmler would become the first person to die in the electric chair.

Hanging had been used for centuries to despatch condemned criminals, but it was notoriously inefficient, and disquiet over the number of botched hangings was growing. Electrocution had first been suggested as a method of execution by Buffalo dentist Dr Alfred Southwick after he'd witnessed a drunkard die, seemingly painlessly, from touching the terminals of an electrical generator. Electrical power was the new wonder of the age, already lighting some streets and homes. During the 1880s, officials seized on the idea of electrocuting those convicted of capital crimes as a 'humane' alternative to hanging and ordered the development of an electric chair that could apply sufficient power to kill a human being instantaneously.

The project soon became caught up in the so-called 'war of the currents' – a dispute over the best way of transmitting power, with George Westinghouse's alternating current (AC) and Thomas Edison's direct current (DC) at odds commercially. Although inclined against capital punishment, Edison became convinced that if there was to be an electric chair, Westinghouse's AC should be used as it would allow him to portray it as the more dangerous form of current.

One of Edison's associates, Harold P. Brown, began electrocution experiments on dogs and a horse using AC and satisfied experts on a New York state committee that it could deliver enough power to kill a man instantly. On 1 January 1889, the Electrical Execution Law prescribed that three electric chairs should be established in New York State prisons.

But exactly how much power would be needed? Brown had estimated that around 1,000–1,200 volts would be sufficient. There was only one way to find out.

Kemmler had swiftly been convicted of first-degree murder on 10 May. Three days later the judge ordered his death by electrocution. Suddenly his case became a national talking point. Kemmler's defence counsel objected to his sentence on the basis that it had not been determined how much current would be needed to kill him. The legal wrangling dragged on for months, but ultimately Kemmler's appeal was turned down.

At 6.30 a.m. on 6 August 1890, the 30-year-old was led into a small chamber in Auburn Prison where the new electric chair was located. Electrodes were then attached to his head and spine. The switch was flipped and a current of 1,000 volts passed through his body for 17 seconds. Kemmler's body stiffened – he appeared to be dead. But on examination by a doctor, it was found that blood was still pumping out of a cut on his hand. With horror, the execution party realised that he was still alive. The current was turned on again and this time ramped up to 2,000 volts for several minutes. Kemmler gave a groan and finally expired. Smoke was rising from his head and the room was filled with the smell of burning flesh.

The execution had been a mess. Westinghouse himself later commented, 'They would have done better using an axe.' Despite continued misgivings, the electric chair would become the established method of execution throughout the United States. The typical current used into the twenty-first century was still 2,000 volts applied for fifteen seconds, with the aim of inducing unconsciousness and stopping the heart.

2,247... the laundry mark that solved the Luton Sack Murder

During the Second World War some 60,000 civilians in Britain were killed by enemy bombs. So in July 1942, when the body of a woman was found underneath a bomb-damaged Baptist chapel in Kennington, south London, the immediate assumption was that she had simply been another of the unfortunate victims killed in the area during an intense raid by the Luftwaffe back in March 1941.

But when suspicions about the origin of the mummified remains grew, police called in a pathologist who quickly determined that the body's injuries were not the sort likely to have been inflicted by bombs and falling masonry. It had been purposely dismembered and various crude attempts had been made to disguise the person's identity. Despite this, he was able to link the corpse's upper jaw to a local missing person, Rachel Dobkin, via her dental records.

It turned out that local fire-watcher Harry Dobkin had murdered his estranged wife, Rachel – possibly because she was trying to blackmail him – and then buried her in the ruins of the chapel, assuming nobody would investigate further. He was hanged for the crime on 7 January 1943.

It was not the only remarkable case involving a seemingly unidentifiable woman that detectives would have to handle during the conflict. Ten months after Dobkin went to the gallows, some workmen pulled a sack out of the River Lea near Luton, Bedfordshire. They were stunned to find that it contained the naked and badly beaten body of a woman in her thirties. She had been strangled just twenty-four hours earlier, and the culprit had gone to considerable efforts to try and destroy any clue as to who she was, including the removal of her false teeth. Police circulated a description of the woman locally, including photographs of a reconstruction of her face, yet to no avail.

However, Detective Chief Inspector William Chapman was not a man to give up easily. He had ordered a search to be made of local dumps for clothes and rags that might be linked to the victim. It paid off. Three months into the investigation, remains of a black coat were examined. Suspiciously, it had been viciously ripped apart. On one fragment was a tag bearing the number 2247.

It was traced to a branch of Sketchley's dry cleaners, where it had previously been left for dyeing by Caroline Manton, who lived on Regent Street in Luton. Chapman soon discovered that Caroline had, indeed, disappeared, but when he interviewed her husband, Horace Manton, the 40-year-old driver in the fire service claimed that his wife had decided to leave him and their four children, settling in Hampstead, north London.

Caroline did appear to have sent letters to her mother confirming this, but Chapman found it suspicious that she'd regularly misspelt the name of her new home town as 'Hamstead'. Chapman asked for a sample of Horace Manton's handwriting. It matched the letters. Caroline's dentist was also able to confirm from X-rays and plaster casts of her remains that the recovered body was indeed his patient, and a single thumbprint found on a pickle jar in the Manton home was also matched to the body.

Confronted with mounting evidence, Horace Manton soon confessed to the killing. He had hit his wife with a heavy wooden stool after an argument and then dumped her dead body in the river. He'd decided to get rid of Caroline's coat at the dump to make his story about her sudden decision to up sticks look more plausible. After all, she would hardly have left without it. In trying to cover his tracks, Manton had made a crucial error that would see him convicted of murder the following year.

A laundry mark was also pivotal when it came to identifying a murdered young woman who had been discovered on a Great Yarmouth beach on 23 September 1900, having been strangled with a bootlace. She'd been lodging in the town but no one knew her real name. The number 599 on some of her clothes was eventually linked to a laundry in London and the body identified as belonging to Mary Jane Bennett of Bexleyheath. Her husband, Herbert Bennett, was alleged to have taken a gold chain from his wife's body: the chain was found in his possession. Police maintained that it was Mary Jane's because she could be seen wearing it in a photograph she had posed for in Yarmouth before her death.

However, work records and witnesses seemed to put Herbert elsewhere at the time of her demise. Bennett was hanged for the murder at Norwich in March 1901, still claiming to be innocent, and doubts about his guilt grew further when a woman was found strangled on the same beach in 1912. The murder weapon? A bootlace.

2,300... South African rand – the fee in a 'murder by request'

If someone begs you to kill them, you'd be wise not to agree, however much you might sympathise with their plight. For history is not kind to those who allege that they have carried out 'murders by request'. The defence is always a shaky one, not least because the individual who is alleged to have asked for help in terminating their own life is no longer around to back up the killer's narrative.

On the morning of 25 March 1961, a South African landowner, Baron Dieter von Schauroth, was found dead on a road outside Cape Town. The 36-year-old had been shot in the back of the neck twice. His car was found abandoned some distance away. There were some uncut diamonds lying by his body. Investigating von Schauroth's background, police discovered that he'd been having financial difficulties and there were rumours that the baron was involved in shady gem deals. Detectives also determined that, just prior to his death, von Schauroth had taken out large life insurance policies, totalling 360,000 rand. A known associate of the dead man, Marthinus Roussow, was questioned by police but maintained that he hadn't seen von Schauroth on the night of the 24th. It turned out that he'd been lying about his movements, and the 23-year-old was soon arrested and charged with murder.

At the trial, held in September 1961, Roussow admitted that he had indeed killed von Schauroth, but caused a sensation by claiming extenuating circumstances – that the dead man had actually requested his own death. Roussow's story was that von Schauroth had business problems, had been unhappy in his marriage and wanted to end his life. However, if he committed suicide, his insurance policies would not be paid out to his family.

Roussow said that, prior to the killing, von Schauroth had given him 2,300 rand, saying that he might need him to shoot someone on his behalf. On the night of 24 March, after a drink, von Schauroth had driven the pair out to a lonely spot, got out of the car and produced a gun. Then, according to Roussow's version of events, he said, 'I want you to shoot me.' Roussow said that he initially refused, but was eventually convinced to go through with the deadly deed, with von Schauroth insisting that he would be in the clear because the police would simply think it had been a diamond transaction gone wrong.

There were some problems with Roussow's story. If von Schauroth had been so unhappy with his 19-year-old wife, why was he so desperate to see her get the insurance money? How did a few diamonds which had been in Schauroth's pocket come to be scattered around the body? At the trial a forensics expert cast doubt on Roussow's description of the shooting and it also emerged that he was broke. The prosecution alleged that he had simply got the 2,300 rand by choosing to murder von Schauroth. It took the jury under an hour to find Roussow guilty, and he was hanged at Pretoria Central Prison on 20 June 1962.

The case echoed the death of George Jones on 11 June 1919. The 60-year-old had treated homeless 17-year-old William Adams to a meal and drinks in a pub in Tooting, south London. But later that night Jones had been stabbed six times by Adams in a south London park. Jones lived three days, long enough to name his attacker and state that he had no idea why he'd been stabbed. At his trial, in Guilford, Adams maintained that Jones had informed him he was in trouble over an income tax bill. Jones had, Adams alleged, told him that he would be doing him a 'good turn' if he killed him. Jones then selected the spot in Sutton for his own demise, even taking off his hat and coat, before advising Adams on the best part of his neck at which to plunge in the shoemakers' awl, a weapon which he had provided.

At least, this was Adams' version of events. Intriguingly, Adams said that a third man, Charlie Smith, had been present and could confirm his story. Jones did in fact corroborate Smith's presence before he died. But the police never found Smith and, whether or not they believed Adams, the jury had little choice but to find him guilty of murder, though his sentence was commuted to life imprisonment, probably because of his age.

2,800 ...

pounds of fertiliser and fuel oil in the Oklahoma City Bombing

At 9.02 a.m. on 19 April 1995, a huge explosion rocked Oklahoma City in the United States, ripping apart the Alfred P. Murrah Federal Building. It left 168 people dead, including nineteen children. An act of international terrorism was initially suspected, but it was soon clear that the appalling crime was the result of a home–grown conspiracy. Thankfully the main instigator, Timothy McVeigh, would end up in custody the same day, but that he and his main accomplice were brought to justice for the heinous mass murder was the result of some serious detective work.

Some of the final numbers involved in the FBI's OKBOMB investigation would be truly staggering. In its quest to uncover what had happened, and the full extent of the conspiracy involved, the Bureau would collect 3.5 tons of evidence, carry out 28,000 interviews, search 1 billion records, follow up 3,450 leads as well as review 16.3 million hotel registration and vehicle rental records.

It was a hidden portion of an official Vehicle Identification Number (VIN), PVA26077, that would provide the agents' first vital clue. It was found on a piece of mangled wreckage thrown 500ft from the scene, which turned out to be from a truck that investigators believed had been used to contain the bomb. Each VIN number is unique to that vehicle and FBI agents were able to use it to trace the truck to a rental company branch in Junction City, Kansas. Employees there helped forensic artists to produce a sketch of the man who had rented it on 17 April under a false name. This image was recognised by a local motel owner as being Timothy McVeigh, who had stayed there on the nights before the bombing. In this case it turned out he had given his real name.

Ninety minutes after the explosion on the morning of the 19th, a state trooper had happened to stop McVeigh driving north from the city on I-35, in a yellow Mercury Marquis without a licence plate. In the car he found an unregistered gun. McVeigh was detained. No immediate connection was made to the bombing, but when the FBI made routine checks on the morning of the 21st, using the information garnered from the motel owner, they discovered McVeigh was already under arrest.

Just forty-eight hours after the bombing, the FBI had a suspect. Now they needed to prove he had planted the bomb. Forensic teams estimated that the device had consisted of 4,800lbs of ammonium nitrate (also commonly used as fertiliser by farmers) and fuel oil. FBI agents discovered that, along with accomplice Terry Nichols, McVeigh had bought a total of 4,000lbs of ammonium nitrate in a Kansas store in autumn 1994. One of McVeigh's fingerprints was on a receipt for 2,000lbs of the stuff. Furthermore, the clothes McVeigh was wearing when he was arrested were found to be covered with explosive residue compatible with that found at the scene. At their subsequent trials, many more items would be introduced as evidence to show how the pair had spent months carefully planning the bombing.

Criminal profilers had judged that the man responsible for it would likely be someone in their twenties with a military background and a grudge against the government. McVeigh was a 27-year-old Gulf War veteran. When arrested, he had been wearing a t-shirt that bore a picture of President Abraham Lincoln with the words 'Sic Semper Tyrannis', meaning 'Thus always to tyrants.' These were the words used by assassin John Wilkes Booth as he gunned down Lincoln in 1865. McVeigh had developed a deep hatred

Scene of the McVeigh bombing. (Courtesy of the FBI)

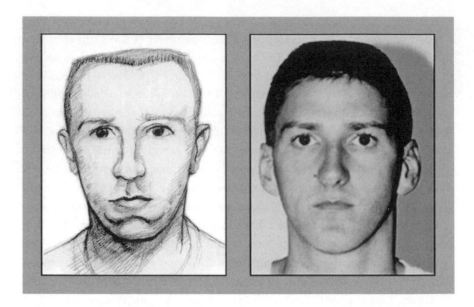

Timothy McVeigh. (Courtesy of the FBI)

of the US government and was partly motivated by revenge for the 1993 government siege of the Branch Davidian compound in Waco, Texas, that ended in the deaths of seventy-six people.

Along with Nichols, 40, McVeigh had decided to send a message by targeting government workers at the Federal Building. It emerged that on the morning of the bombing, McVeigh had parked the truck packed with barrels of explosives outside the Federal Building, then calmly lit the fuse and walked away before making his getaway in another car.

In June 1997 McVeigh was convicted on eleven counts of murder and conspiracy, and he was later sentenced to death. He showed little remorse and was executed by lethal injection in 2001. Nichols was also convicted and ended up being locked up for life, while another man who knew about the plot, Michael Fortier, was sentenced to twelve years in prison for not revealing what the others had planned.

5,500 ... samples taken in the first murder solved with DNA fingerprinting

'Every contact leaves a trace' was the mantra of pioneering forensic scientist Edmond Locard. In the early twentieth century, the Frenchman established what he called 'the principle of exchange', which holds that a criminal will always leave some trace evidence at a crime scene and take some away with them. This could involve fibres, fingerprints, blood or semen. Locard's notion would transform forensic science, with the development of techniques which would successfully link criminals to their victims.

The discovery of genetic fingerprinting would go on to give Locard's principle a new and exciting dimension, as DNA profiling allowed samples collected from crime scenes to be linked to individuals with pinpoint accuracy.

Humans share 99.9 per cent of our DNA, the chemical code that determines who we are. It was in 1984, while studying the material that makes us all different, that scientist Dr Alec Jeffreys discovered a way of identifying each person's genetic fingerprint. Further work established that DNA could be extracted from samples from a crime scene and that, from these, the DNA profile of an individual could be identified. The chances of it matching anyone else's were tiny.

Criminals can always avoid leaving fingerprints at a crime scene by wearing gloves. Tests of samples for, say, blood type might provide only a partial clue as to a suspect. But the ability to extract DNA from traces of bodily fluids, skin cells or hair and then produce a unique profile from them would revolutionise forensics. The techniques enabled investigators to see the signature of a killer in a way that had never been possible before. It was not long before Jeffreys' work on DNA helped crack a double murder case that had played out not far from his lab at the University of Leicester.

On the evening of 21 November 1983, 15-year-old Lynda Mann left her home in Narborough to visit a friend, but on her way back she disappeared. Her body was found the next day on a lonely footpath. She had been raped and strangled. Tests on semen samples left behind by the killer allowed police to identify that he was a blood group A secretor. While this narrowed down the potential suspects to one in ten of the male population, few leads were forthcoming and the investigation stalled.

Three years later, another 15-year old, Dawn Ashworth from the nearby village of Enderby, was also found raped and strangled after she had gone to see friends. Again her body had been dumped on a secluded footpath, just over a mile from the first murder. Not only were the crimes strikingly similar but, once more, semen samples retrieved threw up the same blood type.

This time police had a particular suspect in mind, 17-year-old Richard Buckland, a hospital porter with learning difficulties who had been spotted near the scene. During a police interview he admitted to killing Dawn. However, he strenuously denied murdering Lynda. Police were frustrated when tests on Buckland's blood showed that it did not appear to match the type for which they were looking.

Detectives contacted Jeffreys, wondering if his new genetic fingerprinting technique might help prove that Buckland was the killer of both girls after all. When he extracted the DNA from the semen sample found on Mann's body, he discovered that the profile did not match a blood sample taken from Buckland. Sensationally, Buckland's DNA profile didn't match the

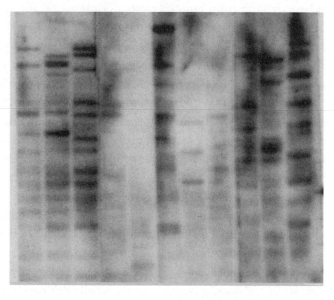

A DNA fingerprint. (Courtesy of Alec Jeffreys, Wellcome Library, London)

semen sample from Ashworth's body either. However, Jeffreys was able to tell police that the genetic fingerprint of the killer was the same in both murders.

With Buckland in the clear, police now began a renewed effort to find the killer, who was still at large. The investigating team decided on a bold course of action, taking blood or saliva samples from 5,500 local men. When Jeffreys and his team tested those with the right blood type, none matched the DNA profile of the killer.

Then came an unexpected breakthrough from a woman who had overheard a conversation in a pub. A baker called Ian Kelly had been boasting that he'd made £200 by agreeing to take a blood test on behalf of a colleague, Colin Pitchfork. She informed police, and when they questioned Kelly, he admitted it. Pitchfork, 26, was arrested. When his blood was taken, Jeffreys found that it matched the DNA profile of the killer. In 1988 Pitchfork was jailed for life.

This was the first case where DNA samples had helped solved a murder and it led to enhanced techniques meaning that DNA could be extracted from the tiniest speck of blood and from samples that were quite old. Thousands more convictions have followed.

DNA tests have also led to many innocent people being exonerated. In 1985 in the United States, Kirk Bloodsworth was convicted of murdering a 9-year-old girl. Several years later he became the first prisoner on death row to be exonerated by DNA tests on semen samples, which proved that he was not responsible.

7,000... quizzed in the search for 'Jack the Stripper'

While the story of Jack the Ripper is known around the world, and has spawned countless films, documentaries and books, there was another serial killer who likewise preyed on prostitutes, this time in the London of the 1960s. Just as in the case of the unsolved Whitechapel murders, the police failed to find the culprit. Yet the man dubbed 'Jack the Stripper' by the press may well have murdered more women than his nineteenth-century counterpart, and although his crimes are less well known, they throw up compelling mysteries of their own.

Jack the Ripper can only definitely be linked to five deaths in London's East End which occurred in 1888, but the Stripper is reckoned to have killed as many as eight in the capital's western suburbs. On 2 February 1964, the body of 30-year-old prostitute Hannah Tailford was retrieved from the River Thames near Hammersmith Bridge. She was naked apart from her stockings, which had been rolled down her legs. A piece of her knickers had been shoved down her throat. By analysing tide tables and currents, police determined that she'd been dumped into the river at Dukes Meadows Park in Chiswick. On 8 April the body of another prostitute, Irene Lockwood, 26, was found on the river bank in a similar vicinity. She'd been strangled.

More bodies began to turn up. Helen Barthelemy, 22, was found on 24 April in an alleyway in nearby Brentford. This was followed by the grim discovery of 30-year-old Mary Fleming's corpse on 14 July on a Brentford driveway, then that of Frances Brown, 21, who was found just off Kensington High Street on 25 November, and finally Bridget O'Hara, 28, found on the Heron Trading Estate in Ealing in January 1965.

All the victims had been sex workers, were typically short in stature and were found naked or partially clothed. Most had been strangled or asphyxiated. They'd been abducted between 11 p.m. and 1 a.m. and their bodies dumped between 5 and 6 a.m. Just as the Ripper took organs from some of his victims, the Stripper also kept grizzly souvenirs – removing teeth from several of the women.

The crimes bore an uncanny resemblance to the murders of prostitutes Elizabeth Figg in 1959 and Gwyneth Rees in 1963, both apparently strangled and found in a state of undress at or near Dukes Meadows.

Perhaps the most crucial clues were that some of the bodies were flecked with industrial paint and that some appeared to have been stored before being dumped. From the mummified remains of O'Hara, forensic experts worked out that she'd been kept in a small transformer building opposite a paint spraying workshop on the Heron Trading Estate.

However, police struggled to pin the killings on any individual despite interviewing 7,000 people. An Identi-Kit of a suspect was produced, based on the description given of a man whom Frances Brown had last been seen with, but it also failed to throw up any useful leads.

Police were also hampered by the fact that local man Kenneth Archibald falsely claimed to have killed Irene Lockwood. It was found he could not have committed the other murders and he later retracted his confession.

Detective Chief Superintendent John Du Rose was brought in to give the investigation new impetus. He announced that he believed that the culprit was driven by a penchant for erotic asphyxiation, and he rashly sent out female police officers undercover, dressed as prostitutes, to try and lure the culprit. Later he held press conferences pretending to have whittled down the list of suspects, first to twenty, then to three. Amazingly, this bold ploy seemed to work. There were no more murders that could be linked to the Stripper. Had he frightened off the killer?

In his memoirs, Du Rose said he believed that the murders ceased because the culprit had committed suicide. In March 1965 a man later identified as Mungo Ireland gassed himself at his home, leaving a note which read: 'I can't stick it any longer … PS. To save you and the police looking for me I'll be in the garage.' Ireland worked as a security guard at the Heron Trading Estate. Evidence has since emerged that Ireland was not in London at the time of O'Hara's murder, casting doubt on Du Rose's theory, and although he fitted the profile, there was no direct evidence that Ireland was the Stripper.

As in the case of the Ripper, there has since been speculation that the real Stripper was someone enjoying a high-profile position. Whoever he was, there's little reason to disagree with Du Rose's view that he deserved as 'prominent a place in the annals of crime as Jack the Ripper'.

9,656... prisoner number of the last woman to be hanged in Britain

On the morning of 13 July 1955, prisoner number 9,656 prepared to go to the scaffold inside London's Holloway Prison, dressed in a two-piece black suit, white blouse and black court shoes. The 28-year-old, 5ft 2in woman weighed 103lbs. The executioner had used this information to calculate the length of drop on the rope that would swiftly break her neck, delivering a quick death. He set it at 8ft 4in.

At 9 a.m. the condemned woman, her arms pinioned behind her back with a leather strap, was escorted the 15ft from her cell to the gallows, where another leather strap was put around her legs. A white cotton hood was put over her head, then the noose.

The safety pin was removed from the lever and the executioner pushed it forwards, plunging the prisoner through the trap door. The whole process took twelve seconds. Death, according to the official post-mortem, had been instantaneous.

For the hangman, Albert Pierrepoint, this had all been routine. He had already executed hundreds of people using the same method.

On this occasion his charge was the nightclub hostess Ruth Ellis. She had been convicted of murdering her lover, David Blakely, 25, outside a north London pub on the evening of Easter Sunday 1955, pumping four bullets from a .38 calibre Smith & Wesson revolver into his body.

No one thought Ellis, the eighteenth woman to be hanged in Britain during the twentieth century, was innocent. She'd been arrested at the scene and admitted the crime. But many felt there were mitigating circumstances. Evidence that Blakely had been violent, and once punched Ellis in the stomach causing her to miscarry, was not heard at her Old Bailey trial.

Her sentence of death led 50,000 to people petition the home secretary for a reprieve. When the execution proceeded regardless, it strengthened the movement that would see the death penalty abolished a few years later.

Despite having conducted 435 hangings in a career that marked him out as Britain's most expert executioner, Pierrepoint would also come to believe that capital punishment didn't work.

Yet Pierrepoint, born in 1905, claimed that hanging ran in his blood. His father and uncle were both hangmen, and at school the young Pierrepoint even wrote, 'When I leave school I should like to be the Official Executioner.' By his 30s, he had got his wish, and while working as a grocer and later as a publican, Pierrepoint would carry out executions on the side for a small fee (£15 by his retirement).

He had soon established a reputation for speed, efficiency and humanity in carrying out his duties. Pierrepoint was proud of mastering the process followed on the day of an execution and the careful calculations needed to deliver the 1,000 foot-pounds force of drop energy deemed ideal for a 'clean' death, avoiding strangulation or decapitation.

There was an official table of drops, based on a mathematical formula taking into account weight and height, but executioners would also take into account other factors, such as build, before determining the exact drop they felt appropriate to the individual.

Some of the most infamous murderers of the era would go to their death on Pierrepoint's watch. He executed acid bath murderer John George Haigh, Neville Heath and serial killer John Christie, the last of these 'in less time than it took the ash to fall off a cigar'. In fact Pierrepoint's record for a hanging was just seven seconds when he dispatched James Inglis, responsible for strangling a 50-year-old woman, in 1951.

During the Second World War, Pierrepoint hanged spies, and after the conflict he achieved fame when he was recruited to execute war criminals in Germany and Austria. He sent seventeen to their doom in one day.

Pierrepoint was even called upon to hang an acquaintance, James 'Tish' Corbitt, with whom he'd sung duets in his Lancashire pub. Corbitt had murdered his girlfriend, Eliza Wood, strangling her in a hotel room in Ashton-under-Lyne. Pierrepoint didn't baulk at the task, putting Corbitt at his at ease by using his nickname, 'Tish', before placing the noose around his neck at the execution in November 1950.

Just a year after he hanged Ruth Ellis, Pierrepoint resigned from his role as executioner in a row over his fees. In his later autobiography he shocked commentators by suggesting that he did not feel capital punishment was any sort of deterrent and that his work had not 'prevented a single murder'.

10,000... hours of CCTV footage in the case of the Suffolk Strangler

The twenty-first century has seen the growth of the so-called 'surveillance society'. Virtually every movement we make in towns and cities is monitored by cameras. Across the world we're being watched by 350 million of them. However, despite worries about privacy, closed-circuit television (CCTV) technology has been vital in recent decades for catching killers. One study of Scotland Yard murder cases, in 2009, showed that seven out of ten were solved with the help of CCTV cameras. Indeed, use of footage in criminal enquires has been widespread since the 1990s. CCTV helped the police to identify the killers of 2-year-old James Bulger, murdered in 1993 (see page 29). Camera footage also helped track down nail bomber David Copeland, who killed three people in April 1999. But CCTV has also been vital to police in catching and convicting serial killers.

In November 2006 police would receive reports of two missing women, both working as prostitutes, in the Ipswich area. Then, on 2 December 2006, one of them, Gemma Adams, 25, was discovered dead in a brook near the Suffolk town by a member of the public. Six days later the corpse of the other missing woman, Tania Nicol, 19, would be found not far away, also near water. On 10 December, 24-year-old Anneli Alderton was found, her body dumped in woodland. It was clear that the police now had a serial killer on their hands who was targeting sex workers and still on the loose. Women were warned to stay away from Ipswich's red-light district, but over the next five days two more bodies would be found, Paula Clennell, 24, and 29-year-old Annette Nicholls – both prostitutes. While the bodies were found naked, there were no signs of sexual assault, but both Nicholls and Alderton had, bizarrely, been laid out in the shape of a crucifix. All the dead women had died from asphyxiation or strangling.

As part of Operation Sumac, some 650 officers from all over the country were called in to catch the culprit. They would take 13,000 telephone calls, make 1,500 door-to-door enquiries, carry out 176 separate searches, take 6,650 statements and collect more than 10,000 hours of CCTV footage from 841 locations around Ipswich.

Before long they had made a breakthrough. DNA recovered from three of the bodies was identified as belonging to forklift truck driver Steve Wright, a man who had recently moved to Ipswich's red-light district. He had been added to the national crime database following a 2002 conviction for stealing £80 from a pub till. Wright, 48, was also a known user of prostitutes.

Trawling through the CCTV footage, officers were able to place Wright's dark-blue Mark III Ford Mondeo – with its distinctive air freshener and oddly positioned tax disc – cruising the red-light district on nights when the murders took place. The car was also seen on cameras leaving town in the early hours of the morning in the direction of the locations where the bodies would be found. Fibres from Wright's car and clothing would be linked to all five victims.

Wright was charged with murdering all five women that December. In February 2008 he was found guilty and ordered to spend the rest of his life in prison. This was just a few days before fellow serial killer Levi Bellfield, then 39, was convicted of the murder of two of his female victims. In 2003 Bellfield had bludgeoned 19-year-old Marsha McDonnell to death after she got off a bus in Hampton, south-west London, while Amelie Delagrange, 22, had died from head injuries after being found on Twickenham Green in 2004. During their investigation, police had studied 2,000 hours of CCTV footage and identified a distinctively marked white Ford Courier van in the same area and at the same time that Amelie was killed. An appeal to trace the van led to a call from wheel clamper Levi Bellfield's ex-girlfriend, who said he was violent. This in turn led to a man who had said he had sold his van of the same type to a wheel clamper – he even had Bellfield's telephone number.

It wasn't until 2011 that police would be able to construct a case against Bellfield for the earlier murder of 13-year-old Milly Dowler in 2002. Within 22 minutes of Milly being snatched off the street in Walton-on-Thames, Surrey, on her way home from school, the red Daewoo Nexia car that Bellfield was using at the time was caught on CCTV leaving the area.

11,419 ... number on a mugshot in the case of the Black Dahlia

There is something haunting about police mugshots of murderers. At the moment the photograph is taken, they are, of course, in custody and unable to pose a threat to the public. But, like caged tigers, those typically steely, expressionless gazes seem only to underline their menace, darkly hinting at the remorseless violence of which they are capable. Perhaps this is why the mugshots of Myra Hindley, Ian Brady, Charles Manson and Ted Bundy have become some of the best-known images of those particular killers.

In the case of the Black Dahlia it was a haunting mugshot of the victim that captivated the public and helped identify her. On 15 January 1947, the naked body of a young woman was found on a vacant lot by a woman out for a walk in the Leimert Park area of Los Angeles. From the outset the Los Angeles Police Department knew that they were dealing with no ordinary murder.

The corpse was lying face up, eyes open. It was in two pieces, severed at the waist. The parts had been positioned carefully, about a foot away from each other. The victim's intestines had been placed under her buttocks. The body had also been drained of blood and washed. There were cuts to her thighs and breasts and 3in slashes to the corner of her face, creating the effect of a 'smile'. Her hands had been placed by her head with the elbows bent; her legs splayed apart. The letters 'BD' may have been carved on her thigh, but there is no definitive proof of this.

An autopsy identified that the 5ft 5in female had been dead about 10 hours and that she'd died from blows to the head. Her wrists, ankles and neck showed evidence of rope burns, and police determined that she'd probably been tortured and killed elsewhere before being dumped.

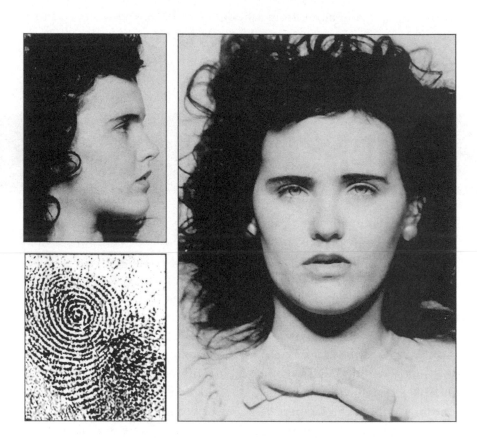

Elizabeth Short's mug shot and fingerprints. (Courtesy of the FBI)

SPECIAL
Daily Police Bulletin

Issued Daily Except Saturday Sunday & Holidays by Police Printing Bureau

For Circulation Among Police Officers Exclusively

OFFICIAL PUBLICATION OF POLICE DEPARTMENT, CITY OF LOS ANGELES, CALIFORNIA

CHIEF'S OFFICE, City Hall (Phone MIchigan 5211—Connecting all Stations and Depts.)   C. B. HORRALL, Chief of Police

Vol. 40   Tuesday, January 21, 1947   No. 14

WANTED INFORMATION ON ELIZABETH SHORT
Between Dates January 9 and 15, 1947

Description: Female, American, 22 years, 5 ft. 6 in., 118 lbs., black hair, green eyes, very attractive, bad lower teeth, finger nails chewed to quick. This subject found brutally murdered, body severed and mutilated January 15, 1947, at 39th and Norton.

Subject on whom information wanted last seen January 9, 1947 when she got out of car at Biltmore Hotel. At that time she was wearing black suit, no collar on coat, probably Cardigan style, white fluffy blouse, black suede high-heeled shoes, nylon stockings, white gloves full-length beige coat, carried black plastic handbag (2 handles) 12 x 8, in which she had black address book. Subject readily makes friends with both sexes and frequented cocktail bars and night spots. On leaving car she went into lobby of the Biltmore, and was last seen there.

Inquiry should be made at all hotels, motels, apartment houses, cocktail bars and lounges, night clubs to ascertain whereabouts of victim between dates mentioned. In conversations subject readily identified herself as Elizabeth or "Beth" Short.

Attention Officers H. H. Hansen and F. A. Brown, Homicide Detail.

KINDLY NOTIFY C. B. HORRALL, CHIEF OF POLICE, LOS ANGELES, CALIFORNIA

Police bulletin requesting information on Elizabeth Short. (Courtesy of the FBI)

There was nothing on the body to suggest the woman's identity, but police took her fingerprints and sent images of them to the FBI, with the help of an early type of fax machine. The Bureau ran them through its database of 104 million prints, quickly turning up the record of an arrest on charges of underage drinking in Santa Barbara, California, from 23 September 1943.

There was a mugshot, numbered 11419, to go with the prints, which revealed that the woman in question, Elizabeth Short, had been a striking beauty. The police soon discovered that the raven-haired 22-year-old had been an aspiring actress, but had been working as a waitress at the time of her death. When the mugshot image was released to the press, she was quickly dubbed the 'Black Dahlia', a play on a film noir of the time, *The Blue Dahlia*. The case fast became front-page news across the country.

Police ascertained that Elizabeth had last been seen on 9 January, wearing a black suit and heels near a cocktail lounge in Downtown LA, where she appeared to have been waiting for someone. A black luxury sedan had also been seen in the early hours of 15 January near the vacant lot where her body was found.

Elizabeth had moved around a lot and enjoyed dates with a string of men, making the potential number of suspects large. On 24 January someone purporting to be the killer sent a package to the *Los Angeles Examiner* with her birth certificate, social security card and an unused address book embossed with the name Mark Hansen, a nightclub owner with whom Elizabeth had boarded.

The following day, Elizabeth's handbag and a shoe were found at a dump, and in the weeks that followed more letters were sent from the 'Black Dahlia Avenger', but these dried up and did not reveal any useful clues as to who the killer might be.

Scores of men were interviewed as detectives worked their way through hundreds of potential suspects and also had to spend time ruling out sixty individuals who falsely confessed to the murder. Eventually the list of suspects was whittled down to twenty-two. As the skilful dissection of Elizabeth's body suggested some medical training, this list included several doctors. Hansen was also on the list, but no charges were ever brought against him or anyone else.

Intriguingly, five fingerprints were found on one of the 'Avenger' letters, but they did not match any in the FBI files, leaving one of the biggest mysteries in the history of crime and no mugshot of her killer for us to study.

25,000... francs charged by the 'Butcher of Paris'

France has had its fair share of cunning killers. One of the oddest was Alain Lamare, who was described as the 'perfect policeman' until he was unmasked as the infamous Killer of l'Oise. Operating in northern France in 1978–9, Lamare was in his 20s when he began running over women in cars and then took to picking up and shooting female hitchhikers. He even helped investigate his own case. Suspicions were aroused about Lamare from language in anonymous letters he sent, taunting officers leading the investigation. He was arrested but declared schizophrenic and unfit to face trial. Lamare was sent to a secure mental hospital.

Another French murderer, whose position in society belied his duplicity, was Marcel Petiot. Serial killers often prey on the vulnerable and Petiot was no exception, targeting terrified Jews who were trying to escape France following the nation's surrender to the Germans.

By the time the Nazis were occupying Paris in 1940, Petiot was a married father and working as a doctor in the city, despite a history of mental instability and shady financial dealings. He had moved to the capital from his native Burgundy, following the strange disappearance of some of those with whom he had been involved locally.

However, to Parisians Petiot seemed a model of respectability and a force for good, at least to those with reason to fear the Germans. Living at an upmarket mansion on the Rue Le Sueur in the 16th Arrondissement, Petiot let it be known that he could help people get out of the country using a secret Resistance network. There was no shortage of people willing to stump up the 25,000 franc fee he was asking in return for arranging their passage to neutral Argentina, via Lisbon in Portugal. Among those seeking his help were Jews attempting to avoid the horror of the concentration camps.

Petiot's so-called network didn't exist – it was all an elaborate ruse to satisfy his lust for money and murder. Using the nom de plume 'Dr Eugene', he would lure the would-be escapees to his house, urging them to bring their cash and valuables for the journey. Then, he would persuade them that they would need to be inoculated to enter Argentina. Instead, he promptly administered a lethal injection, watching his victims die in a room which he'd had specially soundproofed. Then Petiot pocketed their belongings.

Of course, few people missed his 'refugees', as they were supposed to have left the country. At first, Petiot disposed of the bodies in the River Seine or put body parts in bags and threw them into passing trucks, but when some of these were found he decided to start cutting them up and burning them at the house.

In March 1944 neighbours reported that foul smoke had been coming from the chimney of Petiot's house for days, but that the owner appeared to be away. Firemen and police let themselves in through a window to be met with a scene of utter depravity. In the basement they found a stove burning with coal and body parts. There were bits of decomposing bodies in sacks in the stairs and others buried in quicklime in outbuildings.

Initially, ten bodies could be definitely counted, but it was clear there were many more victims. Officers collected 33lbs of charred bones, 11lbs of human hair and many pieces of severed scalp from around the property. There were also forty-nine empty suitcases. The dead included men, women and children. Later it was found that among victims who could be identified were Jewish mother Margaret Kneller and her 7-year-old son René. Instead of getting out of France as they'd hoped, they had been injected with strychnine by Petiot.

When Petiot was finally arrested in a Métro station seven months later, he blustered that the bodies were those of Germans or collaborators killed by the Resistance. His excuses didn't wash. At his trial in 1946, Petiot was accused of twenty-seven murders. He now admitted being a killer but retorted, 'Not twenty-seven. I liquidated sixty-three persons but all were enemies of France.' Prosecutors pointed out that no one in the real Resistance seemed to have known him.

Petiot was convicted of twenty-six of the murders, but it's thought the real total could be much higher, making him one of the worst serial killers in France's history. During the course of his crimes he had filched 200 million francs. On 25 May 1946, Petiot, aged 39, went to the guillotine, telling the assembled crowd, 'Gentlemen, don't look. This won't be pretty.'

35,000 ...

word document that led to the Unabomber's capture

On 19 September 1995 the *New York Times* and the *Washington Post* did something very unusual. They simultaneously published a 35,000-word pamphlet called the *Industrial Society and Its Future*, having been asked to print it verbatim in a note by its author, 'FC'. If the thesis was not printed, the note threatened, a bombing campaign, one that had long caused mayhem and terror across the United States, would continue. By now the FBI knew that 'FC' was the Unabomber, a domestic terrorist, whom they'd been trying to catch for seventeen years. On advice from them, the newspapers went ahead with publication of what was dubbed the Unabomber's 'manifesto'.

The rambling 35,000-word essay railed against the detrimental effects industrialisation and technology were having on the human race. Its turgid style would, no doubt, have sent most of the newspapers' readers to sleep. But the FBI hoped that by giving into the Unabomber's demand, someone might recognise his writing and they'd finally get a lead.

The Unabomber had first come to the attention of the authorities in May 1978 when an unposted package was found in a car park at the University of Illinois. There was a return address on it for Buckley Crist, a professor at Northwestern University. The package was sent back to him but Crist became suspicious – he'd never sent it. He gave it to a policeman, Terry Marker, who did open it. The package blew up, leaving Marker with minor burns. A similar homemade device injured another man at the same university the following year. Then, in 1979, a bomb nearly downed a Boeing 727 passenger plane flying from Chicago to Washington DC. The device had filled the plane with smoke, causing it to make an emergency landing. The bomb only failed to detonate because of a minor fault.

Correctly identifying that there were similarities between the crudely constructed devices from the plane and those in the university incidents, the FBI initiated a nationwide manhunt, putting a huge team on the case, with the codename UNABOM (for UNniversity and Airline BOMbing). However, amid conflicting psychological profiling that suggested that the Unabomber could be anything from a disaffected academic to an airline mechanic, the investigation went nowhere fast.

Unabomber pipe debris. (Courtesy of the FBI)

Meanwhile, the Unabomber continued his campaign with ever more sophisticated bombs, seriously injuring an airline boss and three more university employees. Then, in 1985, a computer rental store owner, Hugh Scrutton, picked up an object outside his shop in Sacramento, California. It was a nail and splinter bomb that immediately went off, blowing open the 32-year-old's chest and tearing off his right hand. Scrutton died half an hour later. After another computer store owner was injured, there were no more bombs for six years. In 1993 the Unabomber made a dramatic return. Two university professors were maimed and the following year public relations executive Thomas Mosser died when he opened a package which exploded at his home. The following April, the president of a timber lobbying group was blown to pieces by a powerful bomb mailed to his office.

Yet the FBI were baffled. There was little forensic evidence to go on. The bombs, although lethal, were made out of easily available 'scrap' items. Moreover, although the bomber's victims were vaguely linked to technology, they seemed to be chosen randomly. The letters 'FC' (later found to stand for Freedom Club) were left on some devices but not others. The FBI believed that the perpetrator was a loner and originally from Chicago. But, the few witnesses they had could only come up with a vague description of a man in a hooded sweatshirt and sunglasses. By 1995 they were offering a $1 million reward for information that could lead to the Unabomber's capture.

Then, with the publication of the 'manifesto' came their big break. When David Kaczynski read the manifesto, he became convinced that his brother, whom he had not seen for ten years, might be the Unabomber.

Born in 1942, in Chicago, Ted Kaczynski had been a brilliant mathematician, who had taught at the University of California, Berkeley – where two of the Unabomber's devices had gone off. But in the 1970s Kaczynski had quit academia to live in a ramshackle 10ft by 12ft cabin in the woods of Montana, where he began developing his anti-technology philosophy and experimenting with bomb making.

David eventually handed the FBI documents that included a 1971 essay by Ted that bore similarities to the wording used in the manifesto. Linguistic experts who analysed them determined that the authors were almost certainly the same person.

On 3 April 1996, the FBI raided Kaczynski's cabin, where they found him bearded and bedraggled, surrounded by journals detailing his crimes – and a live bomb ready to be mailed out.

Kaczynski maintained he was not insane, but in 1998, after being diagnosed with paranoid schizophrenia, he pleaded guilty to thirteen bombing-related charges, including causing the three fatalities. He was given four life sentences plus an extra thirty years for good measure.

46,253... police record number of the first murderer caught by mass fingerprinting

It was at about 1.20 a.m. on 15 May 1948, while making her rounds at ward CH3 of Queen's Park Hospital in Blackburn, Lancashire, when nurse Gwendoline Humphreys noticed that 3-year-old June Anne Devaney was missing from her bed. The child, who had been recovering from pneumonia, had been there half an hour earlier, but now, with horror, Nurse Humphreys realised that June had vanished from the ward. It was unlikely that the youngster could have climbed out of the high-sided cot on her own. Tellingly, a string of muddy adult footprints was visible on the ward's polished floor. A porch door was open, as was a storeroom window. A bottle that had been on a trolley at the end of the ward an hour before was mysteriously lying on the floor beneath the cot.

Police rushed to the scene, and at 3.15 a.m., they made a grim discovery – June's bloodied corpse about 300ft away. Her head had been bashed in. A post-mortem suggested that June had died when she'd been gripped by the ankles and swung against a nearby wall. She had also been raped.

For detectives now hunting her murderer, one set of fingerprints on the bottle that could not be accounted for provided the chief clue. They had discovered that a taxi driver had dropped a man with a local accent by the hospital just before midnight. Chief Inspector John Capstick suggested that the fingerprints of the whole male population of Blackburn and the surrounding area aged over 16 should be taken in a bid to identify June's killer.

Over the coming weeks, police took nearly 50,000 sets of prints. One set, numbered 46,253, stood out. It belonged to Peter Griffiths, a 22-year-old ex-soldier and flour packer. Griffiths was arrested. He soon confessed to taking June from her bed and being responsible for her death. Griffiths admitted that at one point he had grabbed the bottle. He'd done so, he said, in case he was challenged. Griffiths was found guilty and hanged on 19 November at Liverpool Prison.

The case was the first in which mass fingerprinting had been used to catch a murderer, but fingerprint evidence had long been used to help convict killers. Back in 1892 Sir Francis Galton had calculated that the odds of two people bearing identical sets of fingerprints were 1 in 64 billion. In the same year, Juan Vucetich opened a fingerprint bureau in Argentina, and his techniques soon helped solve a murder case involving the killing of two children. Their mother, Francisca Rojas, had put the blame on a neighbour, Pedro Velázquez, but he appeared to have an alibi, and when a bloody thumbprint was found on a bedroom door, it turned out to match her own, not the man Rojas had accused.

Scotland Yard set up its own fingerprint bureau in 1901. Four years later, brothers Albert and Alfred Stratton were convicted of the brutal murders of 71-year-old shopkeeper Thomas Farrow and his wife, Ann, in Deptford, south-east London, carried out during a robbery. A thumbprint found on an empty cash box at the property was matched to a set taken from Alfred Stratton. It was key evidence in persuading the jury that he and his brother were guilty of the murders, and they were subsequently hanged on

23 May 1905. In 1911 burglar Thomas Jennings would become the first murderer to be convicted in the United States using fingerprint evidence, for shooting a man he was trying to rob, Clarence Hiller.

It is not merely the impressions of fingers that have snared killers. The ridges on the palms of hands can also be critical. On 29 April 1955, the body of Elizabeth Currell had been found near the seventeenth tee on a golf course near Potters Bar in Hertfordshire. The 46-year-old, who regularly walked her dog there, had been battered over the head with an iron tee marker found nearby. Upon it detectives found a single bloody palm print. The police embarked on an operation to take 9,000 palm prints from residents. That August a match was found (number 4,605) with Michael Queripel, a 17-year-old council worker. He was convicted of the seemingly motiveless murder that October at London's Old Bailey.

Toe and footprints have sometimes helped solved murder cases too. In 1936 the remains of missing socialite Grayce Asquith washed up in the harbour near Boston, Massachusetts. An Italian man she knew, Oscar Bartolini, had left a bare footprint in her bathroom and experts linked it to the handyman, who was later imprisoned for Asquith's murder.

50,000... people who watched the execution of the Mannings

Charles Dickens did not approve of public hangings, though it did not stop the famous novelist attending four such spectacles. He was present on 13 November 1849, when a murderous couple, Maria and Frederick Manning, were hanged outside Horsemonger Lane Gaol in Southwark, south London, and he wrote of his distaste: 'I believe that a sight so inconceivably awful as the wickedness and levity of the immense crowd collected at that execution this morning could be imagined by no man ...'

For hundreds of years in Britain, public executions were deemed an appropriate deterrent as well as a way of demonstrating the effectiveness of the justice system. These events, be they 'burnings' or even 'boilings', but more often hangings, also became a perfectly acceptable form of entertainment, with locations such as Tyburn, Smithfield and Newgate Prison in London drawing large crowds to watch the ghoulish proceedings. Executions of murderers were always a popular event, but they became a particularly big attraction in the nineteenth century when changes in the law reduced the number of other crimes that could attract the death penalty.

In 1840 François Courvoisier was hanged at Newgate for slashing the throat of his 73-year-old employer, Lord William Russell. Some 40,000 people swelled the streets to see the convicted man face the noose. They included author William Makepeace Thackeray, who admitted feeling 'shamed and degraded at the brutal curiosity that took me to that spot'. In 1856, 30,000 people attended the hanging of William Palmer for the poisoning of his friend John Cook. Many of them made the journey to Stafford by train, thanks to execution excursions arranged by travel companies.

On the day of a public hanging, crowds would be kept well supplied with food, drink and music, while special 'broadsides' – a type of commemorative flyer – would be printed up, detailing the crimes and confessions of the killers. In the case of the Mannings, some 2.5 million broadsides were sold, while 50,000 people – deemed the largest crowd ever to attend a public hanging in Britain – turned up to see the climax of a case that had captivated Victorian society.

On 9 August 1849, the Mannings had invited an acquaintance, customs official Patrick O'Connor, to dinner at their home in Bermondsey. Once he was there, Maria, a Swiss-born maid, shot O'Connor in the head, while failed publican Frederick finished him off by clubbing him over the head with a crowbar. The couple buried their guest under the property's flagstones. Then Maria went to his lodgings, talked her way in and stole O'Connor's railway share certificates and some money.

When O'Connor's disappearance was reported, suspicion fell upon the Mannings, who had already fled, separately, taking their rather paltry ill-gotten gains with them. Police searched their home and found the body of O'Connor. A description of the wanted couple was issued and the Mannings were soon caught, Maria trying to sell some of O'Connor's stock in Edinburgh and her husband hiding out in Jersey.

At their Old Bailey trial, the Mannings tried to blame each other for the murder, but they were both found guilty and went to the gallows side by side in front of a baying mob.

By the time Franz Müller was hanged outside Newgate in 1864 there was a growing revulsion at the behaviour of crowds at hangings. Müller had been condemned for murdering banker Thomas Briggs on a train, but his

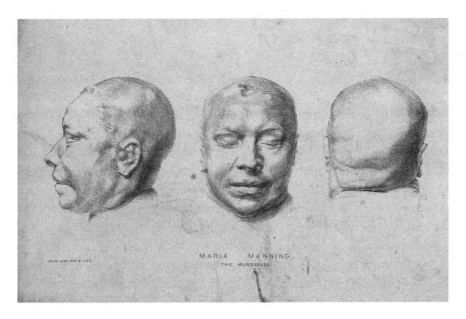

Lithograph of Maria Manning's death mask. (Courtesy of Wellcome Library, London)

execution had been conducted amid appalling scenes of debauchery and drunkenness. While there was little support for abolishing capital punishment entirely, worry that public executions were undermining the dignity of the justice system led to their abolition in 1868. Frances Kidder, 25, was the last woman to be publicly hanged, on 2 April, found guilty of murdering her 12-year-old stepdaughter. Fenian Michael Barrett was the last man hanged publicly, at Newgate, for a bombing in London that killed seven people.

In America, as in countries all over the globe, public executions had proved just as popular. A crowd of 12,000 turned out in Cooperstown, New York, to see schoolteacher Stephen Arnold hanged in 1805, after he had clubbed a child to death for mispronouncing a word. It was not until 1936 that Rainey Bethea, deemed responsible for the death of a 70-year-old woman, became the last person publicly hanged in the United States, and even by then 20,000 people made it an excuse for a day out.

Into the twenty-first century there are still some states, such as North Korea, carrying out public executions.

74,843... number of the luggage ticket in the Moors Murders

Methodically searching the bookshelves of a house at No. 16 Wardle Brook Avenue, Hattersley, in Cheshire on 20 October 1965, Detective Chief Inspector John Tyrrell came across a white prayer book. It had been given to Myra Hindley on her first communion in 1958 and was inscribed by her Auntie Kath and Uncle Bert. Examining the book more closely, Tyrrell noticed that inside the spine was a piece of paper which turned out to be left-luggage ticket 74843, for two suitcases which had been deposited at Manchester's Central Station.

Inside the recovered suitcases was damning evidence that would help convict one of the most notorious killer couples of all time. On 6 May 1966, at Chester Assizes, Ian Brady, 28, and his partner, Myra Hindley, 23, were convicted of multiple murders. They would eventually be linked to the brutal deaths of five children. But they had obstructed the police investigation at every turn and maintained their innocence until the end. It was only as a result of intensive detective work that they had been brought to justice.

By the time the police came to open the suitcases, they had already charged Brady with the murder of Edward Evans, 17, a lad he'd picked up at the station, luring him back to his house with the promise of drink. They'd been tipped off about the killing by Hindley's brother-in-law, David Smith, who had watched, horrified, as Brady had battered Edward to death with an axe at Wardle Avenue, then strangled him for good measure. On 7 October police found the body at Wardle Brook Avenue, 'trussed up in a plastic bag in the bedroom'.

At first Hindley was not arrested and in the meantime destroyed evidence, but she couldn't get back into their house, which was being searched. Notes were discovered, made by Brady, revealing the name of John Kilbride, a 12-year-old boy who had been missing since November 1963. Police also found lots of photos of Saddleworth Moor. Smith had told them how Brady had boasted about 'bodies on the moors' and also of the existence of the suitcases, saying that the pair had taken them from the house on the night before Evans' murder. A search of the city's left-luggage offices uncovered both on 15 October.

Inside, along with other items, was a thirteen-minute tape of a girl pleading for her life and screaming. The voices of Brady and Hindley could clearly be heard, taunting and threatening the child as well as asking her name, which she gave as Lesley Ann. Ten-year-old Lesley Ann Downey had been missing for nearly a year. A search of likely spots on Saddleworth Moor was made, and the following day Lesley's partially decomposed, but identifiable, body was found.

When the left-luggage ticket was found, it matched the two incriminating suitcases the police had in their possession. Notes made by Brady for P/B (prayer book) and TICK (ticket) now made sense – vital evidence that showed how the couple had planned the murders and attempted to cover them up.

They were both charged with Downey's murder on the 21st, the same day as John Kilbride's body was also found on the moors. At their trial Brady and Hindley both pleaded not guilty, with Hindley swearing that she had not taken part in the murders. The tape of Lesley Ann was crucial in proving her involvement. She was found guilty, along with Brady, of helping murder Evans and Downey, while Brady was found guilty of killing Kilbride too. They would both later confess to their parts in murdering two other children, Pauline Reade, 16, and Keith Bennett, 12.

The couple's murderous campaign had begun in 1963, two years after they had met when working at the same chemical firm. Brady talked of wanting to commit the 'perfect murder' and started looking for a likely victim. On 12 July, Hindley picked up Pauline Reade on her way to a dance, asking her to help look for a glove. Brady then joined them and they drove out to Saddleworth Moor, where Brady cut her throat. They then buried the body.

In November of the same year, Hindley and Brady offered John Kilbride a lift home in a hired car. They then took him to the moor where Brady strangled him with a shoelace. The following June, Hindley persuaded Keith Bennett to get into her car after asking him to help her with some boxes. Brady raped, tortured and strangled him before, once more, disposing of his body on the moor.

On Boxing Day 1964 they found Lesley Ann Downey at a fairground and convinced her to come home with them. They tortured her to death before burying her on the moor in a shallow grave.

Pauline Reade's body was found in 1987, but Keith Bennett's would remain undiscovered.

103,648...

number on the frame in the 'Green Bicycle' case

Throughout history there have been killers who have managed to evade justice, even when brought to trial, because the evidence against them wasn't strong enough, despite the fact that they were unquestionably responsible. Around others the air of suspicion still lingers heavily, despite their acquittal, though there is no concrete proof against them. Adelaide Bartlett was such a person.

French-born and pretty, Adelaide was believed to have poisoned her older husband, Edwin, in 1885, with the help of the Reverend George Dyson, with whom she was having an affair. A sixteenth of an ounce of liquid chloroform was found in Edwin's stomach, and Dyson was known to have purchased four small bottles on Adelaide's behalf. Everything seemed to suggest she was a murderess, but the prosecution had a problem. They could not explain how the chloroform had got into the dead grocer's body, for it had caused no burns to his mouth or throat, as would be expected. Delivering their verdict, the jury thought 'grave suspicion was attached to the prisoner' but were left with no option but to find her not guilty. After Adelaide's acquittal, one surgeon famously jested, 'Now it is hoped that in the interests of science she will tell us how she did it!'

Another of those who many felt escaped justice was a former soldier and schoolteacher who was brought to trial for the murder of Bella Wright. The dead body of the 21-year-old factory worker had been found, by a local farmer, at about 9.20 p.m. on 5 July 1919. Bella was lying on a minor road close to the village of Little Stretton, Leicestershire, and beside her was her bike. A doctor said she had died from a fall, but a diligent police officer re-examined her bloodied face and found a bullet wound – she had, in fact, been shot through the head. A spent .45 bullet was subsequently found at the scene, but no weapon. Bella had last been seen in the company of a man in his thirties, when she had cycled away from her uncle's cottage in Gaulby at 8.50 p.m. However, despite posters asking for information about the mystery man – who had been riding a green bicycle – the months passed with no clue as to his identity.

Then, on 23 February 1920, came an unexpected breakthrough. A coal barge on the River Soar dragged a dismembered green bicycle out of the mud, and it was handed to police. One of the serial numbers on the frame had been filed off, but an expert was able to locate another, making out the faint number 103648. It allowed them to trace the sale of the bike to Ronald Light, who had just taken a job as a maths teacher at a Cheltenham school. A few days later a holster and some .45 calibre bullets, matching the one found at the murder scene, were also found in the Soar.

Light would eventually admit that the bike was his and that he'd kept it in a cupboard for months before dismantling and disposing of it in the river. The holster was his too, he said, confessing to having once owned a matching army revolver. Yet Light vehemently denied murdering Bella, saying that he had not come forward sooner because he was worried of upsetting his mother, who had a weak heart.

At his trial in Leicester, two girls testified that they had been chased on their bicycles by Light on the same day as the murder. There was also no doubt that Light already had a history of sexual misdemeanour. The prosecution's case was that Bella had refused Light's advances before fleeing, but that Light had cycled ahead by another route, then hidden behind a gate and shot Bella as she passed, from a range of about 6ft.

Light had the fortune to be skilfully defended by the brilliant Sir Edward Marshall Hall, who forced the prosecution's ballistics expert to admit that the bullet found near Bella could have come from a rifle as equally as a revolver. Hall suggested that the nature of her injuries indicated she had been shot from further away, perhaps accidentally by a farmer. Light was found not guilty.

Years after the trial, evidence emerged that he may have made a partial confession to a policeman. The officer reported that after the acquittal Light admitted shooting Bella but claimed that his gun had gone off by mistake. One theory had it that Bella was actually killed by a jealous suitor, rather than Light. Both former scenarios involve a complicated and unconvincing re-fashioning of the evidence. Whatever the truth, Light changed his name after the trial and became something of a recluse, dying in Kent aged 89, in 1975.

188,274...

serial number of the gun in the case of Dr Branion

Every gun that is manufactured is stamped with a serial number, which is unique to that firearm. When a gun is used in a crime, and recovered, this information can be used to discover who purchased the weapon, helping to establish the history of the firearm and perhaps to identify the person who fired it. Of course, over the years, criminals have become wise to the fact that guns can be traced. Often, in order to avoid detection, they try to file off the serial numbers or obliterate them in other ways. However, even this doesn't always help them avoid justice, as serial numbers can now be restored thanks to several scientific techniques, such as the use of chemical etching agents and magnetic particle restoration. In the case of Dr John Branion, the serial number of a gun would be central to a murder investigation, even though police didn't have their hands on the actual weapon.

At 11.57 a.m. on 22 December 1967, Branion, a well-respected 41-year-old gynaecologist, phoned police from his home in south Chicago to report the death of his wife, Donna. He said that he'd returned from work to find her lying on the utility room floor and called in a neighbour, Dr Helen Payne, to help. It was she who confirmed that Donna was dead. It turned out that the victim had been shot four times. Investigators found no signs of sexual assault or of forced entry to the property. Nothing appeared to have been stolen.

Ballistics expert Burt Nielson was called in to analyse four bullets and four shell casings retrieved from the scene and Donna's body. He found that the bullets had been fired from a .38 calibre weapon. This, together with markings he found on the casings, led Nielson to determine that the gun used to kill Donna was a Walther PPK. Branion, an avid gun collector, admitted owning a gun that fired .38 calibre bullets and handed officers a Luger – but tests showed it had not been fired. Branion denied ever having owned a Walther PPK.

Initially police struggled to find a motive for Donna's killing. She was not known to have had any enemies; nor did Branion stand to gain financially from his wife's death. But he was behaving oddly for someone whose wife had just been killed. Detectives were surprised at his admission that on discovering the bloody scene he had not, himself, checked his wife for signs of life. Furthermore, just 48 hours after the crime, Branion jetted off for a ski holiday in Colorado. Further enquiries revealed that he and Donna had argued about his infidelity.

On 22 January, detectives returned to the Branion home with a search warrant and, in a cabinet, found a brochure for a Walther PPK. There was also an extra clip and a manufacturer's target. The gun itself was missing, but the manufacturer had stamped the other items with the firearm's serial number, 188274. There was also a box of .38 ammunition. Suspiciously, four shells were missing.

Armed with the serial number, police soon located the dealer who had sold the Walther. It turned out to have been sold to James Hooks, who was a friend of Branion's. Hooks said he had given the gun to Branion as a birthday present. Branion now changed his story, admitting he had owned the gun after all, but said that it must have been taken by the real killer.

Police now suspected Branion was culpable for his wife's murder, but his movements on the morning of the death seemed to provide him with an alibi. He had left the hospital where he worked at 11.30 a.m. Branion said he'd driven straight to a nursery to pick up his 4-year-old son, arriving five minutes later, then briefly called on a friend and been home by 11.57 a.m. Could he have nipped home during this time to kill his wife? When detectives drove the 2.8-mile route, they did it in a maximum of twelve minutes. It was tight, but possible. Additionally, a nursery employee said Branion had not turned up there until at least 11.45 a.m., contradicting the doctor. Also, a neighbour of the Branions reported hearing gunshots at 11.36 a.m.

All the evidence was circumstantial, but on 28 May 1968, after a controversial trial, Branion was found guilty and ordered to spend at least twenty years behind bars. However, he was able to arrange bail while fighting an appeal. When Branion's conviction was eventually upheld in 1971, he fled the United States for Idi Amin's Uganda. The authorities there returned him in 1983. Branion finally began his jail sentence, but he would maintain his innocence until his death in 1990. The Walther PPK never materialised.

383,000...

cubic yards of mud in the 'Piggy's Palace' horror

Police work, particularly for forensic experts, is not for the faint-hearted or those put off by laborious tasks. Officers sifted through 293 tonnes of rubbish from the bins around the home of Joanna Yeates in Bristol when the 25-year-old's body was found dumped 'like a piece of garbage' a few miles away in 2010. They were searching for the packaging from a pizza which she had bought on the evening of her death, in the hope that it would lead them to her killer. He was eventually identified as 32-year-old Dutch engineer Vincent Tabak, who had strangled Joanna. Tabak was found guilty and sentenced to life behind bars in October 2011.

In the case of multiple murderer Robert Pickton, the task facing investigators would be truly mammoth, involving 102 forensic anthropologists and the collection of 600,000 separate exhibits as well as 200,000 DNA samples.

From the early 1980s, women began disappearing from the deprived Downtown-Eastside area of Vancouver, many of them prostitutes and deprived individuals from indigenous communities. The local authorities were slow to act, despite the high number of those who were apparently vanishing – totalling about sixty women over the next twenty years. No bodies were found, but fears grew that a serial killer might be at work.

Pickton was a pig farmer in Port Coquitlam in British Columbia. He had made a mint from selling off some land for development but continued to live in a trailer on the part of the farm he ran with his brother. From the mid-1990s the siblings formed Piggy's Palace Good Times Society, holding wild parties at the property, involving drink, drugs and sex workers. A sign at the entrance read 'This property is protected by a pitbull with AIDS'.

Then, in March 1997, Pickton ended up in custody after he took a prostitute back to the farm and tried to handcuff and stab her. She managed to escape, but a charge of attempted murder against Pickton was dropped as police felt that the woman's drug addiction made her a poor witness.

In 1999, Bill Hiscox, a man employed by Pickton, contacted police about his suspicions that items of personal property seen on the farm might belong to some of the disappeared women.

It was only in February 2002, when another employee reported seeing illegal firearms, that police raided the farm, finding not only the guns but clothes and jewellery that appeared to belong to some of the missing women. Over the next few weeks an asthma inhaler was discovered and linked to Seerena Abotsway, a 29-year-old prostitute last seen in August 2001, while DNA tests on some patches of blood were found to belong to Mona Wilson, a 26-year-old last seen in November of the same year.

Pickton was charged with the two murders, but astonished detectives when, in jail, he suddenly admitted to a cellmate (actually an undercover cop) that he had murdered a total of forty-nine women. He was only sad, he said, that he hadn't been able to make it a round fifty.

Piggy's Palace was soon turned into a 14-acre crime scene, but one that did not readily offer up complete corpses of his other alleged victims. So an operation on an almost industrial scale was launched, with scores of archaeologists and forensic anthropologists drafted in. They would spend the next twenty-one months sifting through 383,000 cubic yards of mud and slurry at the farm, using heavy machinery to dig up to 30ft down. The soil would then be processed for 'finds' using two 50ft conveyer belts.

Along with parts of bodies in a freezer, the team found fragments of human teeth and bone, severed skulls and bloodstained clothing in the dirt, as well as other human remains casually slung into bin bags.

From the items found in the $70 million exercise, the team were able to identify thirty female victims from the DNA samples. Pickton was initially charged with twenty-six murders.

It transpired that he had lured his victims to the farm with the promise of money and drugs, then strangled or shot the women. Most stomach churning of all, he had then put many of their bodies through a wood chipper and fed them to his pigs. When the pigs were later slaughtered, Pickton would sell on the pork.

In the end, the 48-year-old would be convicted of six murders and, in 2007, sentenced to life imprisonment. Pickton may have been both demented and devious, but it was clear that police had ignored tip-offs that could have ended his depravity earlier, and an official inquiry found serious failings in Vancouver Police Department's handling of the grizzly affair.

437,000 ... homicides each year globally

The modern age often feels like a violent one, where murder is commonplace. In 2012 a study by the United Nations Office on Drugs and Crime (UNODC) found that 437,000 people across the world lost their lives in 2012 as a result of intentional homicide. This figure is not solely for murder but 'unlawful death purposefully inflicted on a person by another person'. The UNODC study found a global average homicide rate of 6.2 per 100,000 of the population.

Central and South American countries have the highest homicide rates in the world, with more than a third of the total. Heading the list in 2012 was Honduras at 90.4 homicides per 100,000. In Brazil there are over 50,000 homicides annually and someone is violently killed in the country every nine minutes. Outside this region, Cape Town in South Africa is one of the world's most dangerous cities, with more than 2,500 homicides in any year.

Despite these startling statistics, there is evidence that the homicide rate globally is falling. While the incidence of murder is rising in some parts of the world, in many regions there has been a downward trend in the twenty-first century. For example, the homicide rate rose towards the millennium in England and Wales but declined from 944 homicides per year in 2002 to 571 in 2015–16. In the United States there are around 15,000 homicides annually and some cities have seen their rates increase in recent times. Chicago had 762 murders in 2016, the highest figure in nineteen years. But the overall homicide rate across the country has plummeted since the 1990s and is now back to levels not seen since the 1960s.

Indeed, if you live in Europe, your chances of being murdered are almost certainly much less now than they were in, say, the medieval or even Victorian era. In the late Middle Ages, records suggest that the homicide rate was as high as 40 per 100,000 of the population, compared to only about 1 in 100,000 in modern times. Academics are not sure why the murder rate has declined historically, though better policing and investigation methods are probably factors.

There are differences in how murders are committed in different countries. Globally, firearms are the main murder weapon, while in the UK knives or other sharp instruments are the most common method used to kill, accounting for more than a third of homicides. One statistic, however, remains uniform whichever part of the world you're in – that men commit most murders. They are also most likely to be the victims. People who are murdered are typically young too. Over half of all global homicide victims are under the age of 30.

Until the nineteenth century and the development of modern forensic methods, many murderers could expect to get away with their crimes. Yet even with modern policing methods and developments such as DNA testing, many murders still go unsolved. According to the UNODC report of 2013, just forty-three perpetrators are convicted for every 100 victims of intentional homicide. The clear-up rate is much higher in Europe, but even in Britain many culprits remain at large. Data compiled in 2016, by the *Sunday Times*, from police forces in England and Wales showed that there were a total of 1,583 unsolved killings on their files. Despite the decline in homicide rates, the proportion of unsolved murders has actually increased from 13 per cent in 1995–96 to 23 per cent in 2014–15. Likewise, in the United States, federal statistics reveal that the clear-up rate for homicide plunged from about 90 per cent in 1965 to just 64 per cent in 2012. This phenomenon has largely been put down to a drop in domestic murder, cases of which tend to be more easily solved, while many of those cases that remain tend to be linked to organised crime and are harder to crack.

While murder is shocking, it is thankfully rare. Very rare indeed in the small European state of Lichtenstein, where no murders at all were recorded in 2012. In that year your chances of being a victim of homicide globally were 1 in 16,000. That compares to about 300 million to 1 of being the victim of a shark attack and 10 million to 1 of being killed by a bolt of lightning, but is much less than the chances of being killed in a car accident, which has been put at 8,000 to 1.

525,987 ... number on a gas mask in the case of the 'Blackout Ripper'

In the run-up to the Second World War, the British government thought it inevitable that the enemy would use poisonous gas as a weapon against both the armed forces and the civilian population. It ordered mass production of gas masks and by the outbreak of hostilities 38 million had been manufactured. Initially the authorities insisted that each person should carry their personal gas mask around with them but, as it became apparent that chemical warfare was becoming less of a threat, their use diminished. Thankfully, during the whole six years of conflict, the nation's gas masks were never needed. Yet one respirator, still being diligently carried by its owner in 1942, would help breathe life into one of the biggest murder investigations of the war.

In nineteenth-century London, the infamous Jack the Ripper had been able to murder and mutilate women aided by the poorly lit streets and alleyways of East End London. In February 1942 another maniac was on the loose, attacking women and leaving them with savage injuries. This time the wartime blackout would provide cover for the frenzied killing spree, which was as shocking as anything seen in the spate of murders of prostitutes that had stunned the capital in 1888.

On the morning of 9 February, the body of Evelyn Hamilton was discovered at an air-raid shelter in Marylebone, west London. The 40-year-old pharmacist had been strangled on her way home from a restaurant, but thanks to the blackout, aimed at frustrating German bombers, there were no witnesses to what had happened that night. Her handbag, containing the sum of £80, had been stolen. Though her clothes were in disarray, there was no suggestion of rape and the killing appeared to be a fairly routine case of robbery. The police made a note of the fact that the marks on Evelyn's throat suggested the killer had been left-handed.

Just twenty-four hours later, police were dealing with another murder with more disturbing features. This time the victim was Evelyn Oatley, a 35-year-old former actress and prostitute who had been found dead and half naked in her Soho flat, under a mile away from the first death. Once again the victim had been strangled. But this time her throat had been cut and her sexual organs attacked with a tin opener. Fingerprint analysis of the utensil could not reveal the identity of the perpetrator, but it was clear that whoever had wielded it was left-handed. Police strongly suspected that the two murders were linked and that a dangerous, sexually motivated killer was now at large.

The police did not have much time to act. On Wednesday morning they were called to a flat off Tottenham Court Road where prostitute Margaret Lowe lived. There police were confronted by the body of the 43-year-old, who had been strangled with a silk stocking. Margaret had also been attacked with a razor blade and candlestick.

Leading detective Ted Greeno had barely had time to examine this corpse when news came in that another body had been found. It was of prostitute Doris Jouannet, found at an address in the West End. Once again, she had been strangled and her body ripped open, suffering the kind of graphic injuries that were rapidly becoming the savage signature of the killer.

By that weekend the press were gripped by the speed and ferocity of the wave of killings that had swept the capital, dubbing the unknown perpetrator as the 'Blackout Ripper', since his methods seemed to bear chilling echoes of the madman who had butchered at least five prostitutes, seemingly at random, half a century earlier. That killer, of course, had never been identified. So, as the death toll rose, the pressure was growing on the police for a breakthrough.

Fortunately they had already been handed a slice of luck. In the same week as the other attacks, a woman called Greta Heywood had encountered a dashing man in RAF uniform on a night out in Piccadilly, but had been attacked in a doorway when she refused his advances. He had run off into the night when a delivery boy happened upon them. Police had been alerted and, at the scene, they found what would turn out to be a vital piece of evidence – an airman's gas mask bearing the RAF service number 525,987. The culprit had dropped it in his haste to get away. The respirator number soon led police directly to left-handed aircraftsman Gordon Cummins, who had been stationed in London for training. He was arrested within days and his short, but ferocious campaign of murder brought to an end. Cummins' fingerprints were found to match those at the murder scenes and he was hanged on 24 June 1942.

700,000... pounds paid in compensation to the family of Mahmood Mattan

At his trial in 1836, Thomas Oliver was found guilty of the murder of Jonathan May. Then, as he was being sentenced to death, Oliver suddenly interrupted the judge to plead not for his own life but for that of the man alongside him in the dock, Edmund Galley. Oliver declared that Galley, also convicted of killing May, had not been his accomplice on the night of the murder and was innocent. Despite this sensational statement, both men were sent down to await execution. The robbery and fatal assault on May had occurred on 16 July 1835, as the farmer returned home from a fair at Moretonhampstead in Devon. Galley had been arrested in London for the killing, based on little more than the fact that he was a known ruffian who shared a nickname with a man wanted in connection with the murder. Yet Galley claimed never to have been to Devon.

Oliver was hanged, but Galley was handed a reprieve when new evidence emerged that he had actually been in Dartford, Kent, some 200 miles away, at the time May met his end. Galley's conviction was not overturned – instead he was transported to Australia. It took campaigners until 1879 to achieve a pardon for Galley. He was awarded £1,000 in compensation, one of the first payments of its kind.

From the late nineteenth century there was a growing feeling that when a person was later found to be innocent of a crime like murder they should receive some sort of financial recompense – assuming they were still alive. William Habron spent three hard years in prison for his supposed involvement in the shooting of policeman Nicholas Cock in Manchester in August 1876. It was said that Habron had previously threatened the officer. But when the notorious Charles Peace was sentenced to death for another murder, he confessed that he had also been Cock's real killer. Habron was exonerated and given £800.

One of the most famous wrongful convictions in Britain was that of Oscar Slater. In December 1908, an elderly spinster, Marion Gilchrist, was beaten over the head and left for dead at her home in Glasgow during a robbery. The case against Slater, a German Jew, was thin, relying on a pawn ticket he had tried to sell for a brooch, some unreliable witness statements and the fact that he'd fled to the United States days after the killing. However, Slater voluntarily returned to clear his name and the pawn ticket turned out to be a red herring. Nevertheless Slater was convicted and only saved from hanging following a petition signed by 20,000 people. Sherlock Holmes author Sir Arthur Conan Doyle was influential in getting Slater's conviction quashed entirely in 1928. Slater was freed and received £6,000.

Towards the end of the twentieth century, developments in DNA evidence meant that the number of convictions found to be unsafe increased, as did the size of payouts to those falsely accused. In 1992 Rachel Nickell was stabbed forty-nine times on Wimbledon Common. Colin Stagg, initially charged with her murder, was eventually cleared, but the stain on his character was not properly expunged until another man, Robert Napper, was proven to have been Rachel's real killer thanks to DNA. Stagg received £706,000 for his distress.

The payment was of a similar value to the £700,000 settlement eventually awarded in the case of Mahmood Hussein Mattan. But Mattan would not, himself, benefit. For the Somali seaman had already been hanged. Mattan had been convicted of murdering Cardiff shopkeeper Lily Volvert, 42, whose throat had been cut on 6 March 1952. Mattan was picked up shortly after the killing and police found a broken razor and some shoes with specks of blood on them at his home.

Mattan's trial was a racist farce, relying upon the testimony of Harold Cover, a shady character who stated that he'd seen Mattan leaving the shop. It later emerged that Cover had earlier named a different Somalian, Taher Gass, as the man he'd spotted. Also ignored was the evidence of a 12-year-old girl who told police that Mattan definitely wasn't the man she'd seen acting suspiciously at the scene. There was no forensic evidence to prove that the blood on Mattan's second-hand shoes was from the victim.

Two years after Mattan was hanged, Taher Gass would be convicted of a different murder and declared insane. It would take forty-six years of campaigning before the Court of Appeal found that the case against Mattan had been flawed and quashed his conviction. It was the first time that the relatives of a person hanged in Britain for a crime they did not commit would be awarded compensation.

740,000...

capsules tested for cyanide in a fiendish poison plot

The Nazis knew all about the lethal power of cyanide. It was the basis of Zyklon B, used to gas victims of the Holocaust in the concentration camps of the Second World War. Cyanide, which stops the cells of the body from being able to use oxygen, is capable of killing almost instantly, even in small amounts; hence it was also the choice of poison when the likes of Hermann Goering and Heinrich Himmler decided to take their own lives. Adolf Hitler's propaganda minister, Joseph Goebbels, murdered his six children by administering cyanide capsules to them too.

The use of cyanide by the Third Reich was nothing new. It comes in several different forms and can be distilled from natural sources. As such, it has been used as an agent for murder since at least the time of the Roman emperor Nero, believed to have murdered his brother Britannicus using cyanide. Associated with the distinctive scent of bitter almonds, cyanide has been a favourite poison of crime writers. Agatha Christie made it central to the plot of her novel *Sparkling Cyanide*. In the book, potassium cyanide, which has the appearance of table salt, is dropped into the champagne glasses of both victims.

In the 1980s a series of real-life murder mysteries involving potassium cyanide unfolded in the Chicago area of the United States. In 1982, bottles of painkiller capsules called Tylenol were intentionally tampered with and seven people died after taking the pills – all poisoned by cyanide. No one was ever brought to justice for the seemingly random killings. Just four years later, fear again gripped the nation with the news that another cyanide killer appeared to be on the loose.

On 11 June 1986, 40-year-old bank manager Sue Snow, from Auburn in Washington State, died shortly after taking two pills for a headache. At her autopsy the pathologist was surprised to notice the tell-tale odour of almonds. Tests soon showed that cyanide had been the cause of death, with the source traced to the bottle of Extra-Strength Excedrin capsules Sue had ingested. Several of the remaining pills contained traces of cyanide, and when more were found in two other bottles, in nearby stores, the manufacturer immediately sent out a product recall.

A day later the police got a call from a woman called Stella Nickell, also from Auburn. She was concerned that her husband, Bruce, 52, might also have been killed by cyanide, as he'd died suddenly, on 6 June, after taking some Extra Strength Excedrin pills. Bruce's death had been put down to emphysema. But, following her call, tests on his blood showed that there was indeed cyanide in his body. Sure enough, two bottles of Excedrin found at the Nickell home were found to contain it.

Contamination at the factory where Excedrin was made was soon ruled out. The authorities went on to pull in 740,000 pills from four states for analysis, but found that cyanide was only present in the five bottles already recovered. Police concluded that someone locally must have purposely tampered with them. Yet there seemed to be no connection between the victims that could provide a lead.

FBI agents thought it unlikely that two out of the five contaminated bottles had ended up at the Nickells' home by chance, especially since Stella said she'd purchased them at different locations at different times. There was something else. Investigators had also found tiny green particles from an algae killer in the Excedrin bottles, of a type often used in home aquariums. Stella, a grandmother and security guard who lived in a trailer, happened to own a fish tank. Digging into Stella's background, police discovered that several life insurance policies had been taken out on Bruce's life and she stood to gain $176,000 if his death was found to be accidental.

It turned out that Stella had tampered with the bottles herself in an audacious attempt to make it look like Bruce had been the victim of a random cyanide poisoning, as in the earlier cases. If someone else, like Sue Snow, died as a result of her plot to cash in, then so be it. Frustrated when Bruce's death was put down to natural causes, Stella had contacted the police, knowing that Bruce's cause of death would be re-examined. But it proved her undoing. The police focused their suspicions on Stella, who failed a lie detector test. Then her daughter tipped off detectives that her mother had consulted a library book on toxins. Stella's fingerprints were found on the pages relating to cyanide. In May 1988 Stella Nickell was convicted of product tampering and sentenced to more than ninety years behind bars for causing the two deaths.

1 million ... pounds demanded as ransom for kidnapped Muriel McKay

'We have your wife ... you will need a million pounds by Wednesday or we will kill her.' These were the chilling words from the other end of the line, as kidnappers attempted to extort big sums of money through an abduction in the UK for the first time. Muriel McKay had been kidnapped on 29 December 1970. The culprits had intended to spirit away the wife of media tycoon Rupert Murdoch and get rich by ransoming her. Unwittingly, they had grabbed the spouse of his deputy, Alick McKay. She had been borrowing the boss's car. After putting down the phone to the abductors, McKay called the police. Soon the mysterious kidnappers were calling with demands about how the ransom money should be delivered and sending desperate letters from Muriel to prove they had her.

An initial delivery of the ransom was abortive when the kidnappers spotted police in the area. Then, on 6 February another drop was organised, with police officers posing as McKay and his daughter. Suitcases containing the money were left, as requested, near a garage at Bishop's Stortford, Hertfordshire, as police lay in wait. But suspicious locals reported the suitcases to local police, who collected them, knowing nothing about the operation.

However, a blue Volvo had been noticed passing the garage several times and an officer had noted down the registration number. It led police to a farm in nearby Stocking Pelham, owned by Arthur and Nizamodeen Hosein. Fingerprints found on an exercise book at the farm matched those on the ransom notes and belonged to Arthur Hosein. However, there appeared to be no trace of Muriel. That September both men were convicted of kidnapping and blackmail along with Muriel's murder. Her body was never found, with a suspicion that she had been fed to the farm pigs in an echo of the Stanislaw Sykut case (see page 12).

The crime of kidnapping has been around for centuries, but the issuing of big ransom demands for the return of those abducted is a relatively modern phenomenon. Sadly the cases have often ended in murder through the bungling of those behind the crimes. One of the first cases to receive widespread publicity was the kidnapping of 4-year-old Charley Ross on 1 July 1874 from the front yard of his family home in Philadelphia. Despite ransom demands for $20,000, the suspected men died in a shooting in an unrelated attempted robbery and, although one of them confessed as he died, Charley was never found.

Half a century later, the kidnapping of the son of Charles Lindbergh, the famous aviator, would leave America agog. Twenty-month-old Charles Augustus Lindbergh Jr disappeared from his cot in the Lindbergh family mansion in Hopewell, New Jersey, on the evening of 1 March 1932, a ladder having been used to gain entry to his room. A note demanding $50,000 for the child's return was found and ransom money was eventually paid through an intermediary. Cleverly, however, detectives had recorded the serial numbers on the notes. The man who accepted the cash said the boy could be found on a boat called *Nelly* off the coast of Massachusetts, but when a search was made, there was no sign of such a craft or Charles.

On 12 May a grim discovery was made – the body of the missing toddler lying just 4 miles from his home. It turned out that he had been killed by a blow to the head, probably on the night of the kidnapping itself. Meanwhile, the trail of those responsible went cold until, two years later,

Bruno Hauptman. (Courtesy of the FBI)

Bruno Hauptmann paid at a petrol station in New York using one of the recorded bills. Police discovered $14,000 of the ransom money at his property as well as part of a ladder that appeared to match the one used to enter the Lindbergh home. His handwriting also seemed to match that on the ransom notes. Still protesting his innocence, Hauptmann went to the electric chair for the murder on 3 April 1936.

Since Hauptmann's execution there have been wild theories put about that he was indeed innocent and even the victim of a cover-up involving Lindbergh himself. Another more recent murder case involving a ransom note has led to equal controversy. When child beauty pageant queen JonBenét Patricia Ramsey was found dead in the basement of her Colorado home in 1996, a ransom note asking for $118,000 was discovered at the house too. There were suggestions that her mother, Patsy, now dead, had penned it herself, but just who was responsible for hitting the 6-year-old child over the head and strangling her is still in question.

2.2 million ... 'wanted' posters that caught the Oregon railway killers

In the pages of crime fiction, detectives such as Sherlock Holmes use tiny clues to help them identify people of interest. In one tale, for example, Holmes determines that a man must be lame because he puts less weight on his right foot than his left. In another instance, he is able to give a complete description of a person simply through analysing his hat.

In real life there have been characters with skills that easily match those of Arthur Conan Doyle's imaginary sleuth. Indeed, the character of Holmes was partly based on Dr Joseph Bell, a Scottish surgeon and pioneer of forensic science. He helped police in a number of criminal cases, including the murder of Elizabeth Chantrelle, committed on 1 January 1878. Initially it appeared that the 26-year-old had died from gas poisoning at her Edinburgh home, caused by a damaged pipe. However, her husband, Eugene, had recently taken out a £1,000 insurance policy on her life in the event of accidental death. Bell helped the authorities prove not only that the gas pipe in her room had been tampered with but that there were suspect traces of opium in the vomit stains on his wife's nightdress. Eugene Chantrelle was convicted of Elizabeth's murder and went to the gallows on 31 May 1878.

There was another real forensic scientist who well deserved his nickname as the 'American Sherlock Holmes'. In a forty-five-year career as a criminologist and chemist, Edward Heinrich would help police solve 2,000 different crimes. It was his ability to identify the culprits from just a few clues, ones often missed during the regular police investigation, that came to be his trademark.

Heinrich's most celebrated triumph came after he was called in to help with the pursuit of the mystery men responsible for the murder of four railway workers. On 11 October 1923, three would-be robbers had held up the Southern Pacific Express train as it emerged from Tunnel 13 in the Siskiyou Mountains of Oregon. Their intention was to rob the train's mail coach, which was carrying around $40,000. But they botched the job, blowing up the whole mail van with dynamite as well as the unfortunate clerk inside. The explosion made it impossible to steal the contents and the men fled into the mountains, but not before shooting the train's fireman, brakeman and engineer in order not to leave any witnesses. With most of the train in the tunnel, passengers were unable to give usable descriptions of the fugitives.

Among the few items left behind by the robbers were a sawn-off .45 calibre revolver and a pair of greasy green overalls. With few clues on which to base their pursuit, the police investigation soon ran into the sand, and Heinrich was called in to help. After a few days analysing the recovered evidence, he amazed officers by telling them that the man who had owned the overalls was a 165lb Caucasian in his early 20s, had light brown hair and was 5ft 8in tall. Furthermore, Heinrich deduced that he was probably a left-handed lumberjack from the Pacific north-west of the country.

Heinrich had estimated the height and build by simply measuring the overalls, but he had also found hair clinging to a button, which helped him ascertain a rough age and skin colour. On analysis with a microscope, the grease, which police thought had come from a car, turned out to be pitch from fir trees usually found in the north-west. Wear on the overalls suggested a man leaning against a tree with an axe, using his left hand.

There was more. Inside a pocket Heinrich found a tiny fragment of a mail receipt and used chemicals on it to recover the mark 236-L. He also found a hidden serial number on the revolver that the user had failed to destroy.

Armed with Heinrich's information, police renewed their efforts to track down the killers. The mail receipt was linked to Roy D'Autremont, who had sent $50 to his brother Ray. The twins had another brother, Hugh. Police confirmed that left-handed Roy matched Heinrich's description and had worked as a lumberjack. The gun was traced to a sale in Seattle, where handwriting tests showed it had been purchased by Roy.

The police finally had their suspects and launched a huge manhunt, distributing 2,265,000 'wanted' posters of the brothers across the globe. For four more years the D'Autremont brothers eluded capture, until finally, in 1927, a soldier recognised the face of Hugh D'Autremont on one of the posters. He had been using a false name and was serving with the army in the Philippines. He was extradited back to the United States and the release of new posters led to the arrest of Roy and Ray in Ohio, where they were living under new names. All three were convicted of murder and given life sentences.

5.2million... car number plates checked in the hunt for the Yorkshire Ripper

The scale of the search for the man dubbed the 'Yorkshire Ripper' would end up being truly epic. In the late 1970s the police were becoming increasingly desperate to find the perpetrator of a string of savage murders in the north of England and, in the course of a massive manhunt, interviewed 250,000 people and took 32,000 witness statements. When it became clear that many of the killer's victims were prostitutes, some 5.2 million car number plates would end up being recorded as detectives logged vehicles at red-light districts. The operation cost a massive £4 million, but for all their efforts, police were left swamped with evidence and unable to bring the culprit to justice for six long years.

The Ripper had already seriously assaulted a number of women before he killed mother-of-four Wilma McCann in Leeds on 30 October 1975, picking up the 28-year-old as she hitched a lift. He struck her with a hammer on the back of the head, then stabbed his victim fifteen times. Yet it was not until several more attacks and murders across West Yorkshire exhibiting a similar modus operandi that police realised that they were dealing with a serial killer. With the death of 16-year-old shop assistant Jayne Macdonald, stabbed and then dumped on waste ground in June 1977, it appeared that the mystery slayer was not only killing prostitutes but might target any young woman. The public began to panic, but the police still had few strong leads. Then, on 1 October, a Manchester prostitute called Jean Jordan became the murderer's sixth victim. This time the killer had made a mistake, leaving a £5 note with the body. It was the first real clue for the police. They traced it to a particular bank and interviewed thousands of men who could have received it in their pay packet. One of these was lorry driver Peter Sutcliffe, but detectives were satisfied with the alibis he gave and discounted him as a suspect. The killings went on. In all, thirteen women would end up murdered, many sexually assaulted and mutilated, their bodies callously discarded.

As the investigation continued, it became sidetracked by an elaborate hoax and, in an age before computerisation of records, mired in 4 tonnes of paperwork. It was in this context that the fact that Peter Sutcliffe had been interviewed by the police in the course of their enquiries on nine separate occasions went unnoticed. It would later emerge that his car had also been logged at red-light districts a total of sixty times, yet the link was not made.

In the end it would be a number plate that gave Sutcliffe away, but only by chance. On 2 January 1981, Peter Sutcliffe was stopped in a car by police in Sheffield in the company of a prostitute. The officers ran checks on the vehicle and discovered that the plates were false. It was only when he was arrested and further investigations turned up a hammer and two knives that police quizzed Sutcliffe over his connection to the murders. He soon confessed to being the Ripper. Jailed for life in 1981, Sutcliffe remains behind bars for the crimes.

In August 1966 the logging of a number plate also helped catch the killers of three plain-clothes policemen who were shot dead after they stopped a suspicious, rusting Standard Vanguard estate in west London, near Wormwood Scrubs Prison. Unarmed Detective Sergeant Christopher Head, Temporary Detective Constable David Wombwell and their driver Constable Geoffrey Fox were all gunned down by the career criminals inside the blue van, who were planning an armed robbery. Harry Roberts, John Duddy and Jack Witney then sped away, but the van's registration, PGT 726, was taken down by a quick-thinking young couple who saw it leave the scene.

Before long, detectives were on the hunt for the men behind what would become known as the Braybrook Street massacre. The van was quickly connected to Witney, who was arrested at his home, while Duddy was tracked down to Glasgow. Roberts evaded capture for three months, but by December 1966 he and his accomplices had been sentenced to life at the Old Bailey.

With advances in technology, police can now use automatic number plate recognition to follow vehicles of interest. The first murder case in which its use led to a conviction was on the same turf as the Yorkshire Ripper had operated. On 18 November 2005, PC Sharon Beshenivsky was shot dead after responding to a robbery in Bradford. Her killers were tracked down and convicted after the car they had driven away in was followed on CCTV.

20 million ... years old – the pollen used to catch a killer

When a man holidaying on the River Danube disappeared in 1959, Austrian police believed he had been murdered, and the business partner of the missing man was brought in for questioning. He claimed to be innocent, and with no body detectives were struggling to link their suspect to the crime. However, his muddy boots had been taken into evidence. The boots were sent off to Wilhelm Klaus, an expert in studying pollen at the University of Vienna. The scientist was able to identify several types of pollen on the footwear, including that from spruce, willow and alder trees. He also found fossilised hickory pollen – known to be 20 million years old. While hickory no longer grew in Austria, there was one place where this unusual combination of grains could have come from – a Miocene sediment outcrop on the river about 12 miles north of Vienna. When police confronted their suspect with this information, he was so shocked by its accuracy that he immediately confessed to the killing. He then took officers to the place where he had buried the victim – at the very location identified by Klaus.

The world has some 380,000 plant species and the pollen from each has its own unique characteristics. It also has a knack of getting caught in things like clothing, hair and nostrils, making it useful evidence. The science of using pollen to crack criminal cases is known as forensic palynology and it has been increasingly utilised since the landmark Austrian case. Pollen can be collected from suspects and compared with that found at a crime scene. It can also be taken from a victim's body, helping police to ascertain when they died and whether the corpse was moved after a murder – and, if so, where it came from. In another case from 1959, scientists suggested that a murdered

Swedish woman had not been killed in the place where her body was found dumped because the dirt on her clothing did not contain pollen from the grasses common at the location.

The techniques used in palynology have come a long way since those early days and it has cropped up in increasingly high-profile murder cases. In August 2002, two 10-year-old schoolgirls, Holly Wells and Jessica Chapman, were found dead, their bodies callously dumped in a ditch in the Suffolk countryside. Ian Huntley, a caretaker, was arrested when the girls' clothing was found in the grounds of their school, where he worked. Police discovered that he had a false alibi for the time that the girls had disappeared. Crucial to linking him to the girls' deaths was the work of Dr Patricia Wiltshire, an expert in palynology. She was able to match soil samples at the ditch where their bodies had been found with those taken from Huntley's car and clothes, proving that he'd been there. Huntley was jailed for life in 2003.

Wiltshire's skills were demonstrated again two years later when 22-year-old Joanne Nelson from Hull went missing. Paul Dyson soon confessed to strangling his fiancée, but he was unable to tell police where he had disposed of the body, other than that it was in woodland. Wiltshire was given soil samples from the car used to transport Joanne's body and the garden fork that Dyson had used to bury her. Under powerful microscopes these were found to contain a combination of pollen from a type of fern as well as silver birch, hornbeam and western hemlock trees. This allowed police to narrow down their search to a specific area of Yorkshire and Joanne's body was successfully retrieved.

Pollen would also help solve Humberside's oldest unsolved murder case in 2012, when Wiltshire's work would be fundamental in proving who had killed Christopher Laverack. The 9-year-old's body was found weighted down in a canal near the town of Beverley in March 1984, having suffered savage injuries. He had also been sexually assaulted. Police had a suspect with no alibi who appeared to match the profile of the killer, but they lacked forensic evidence to take their case against him to court. It wasn't until more than two decades later, when they asked Wiltshire to review the case, that a breakthrough was made. Taking pollen collected from Christopher's body, she was able to match the set of spores to the garden of his uncle Mervyn Read. The brick that had been used to weigh down the bag containing his nephew was found to come from the same garden. Read, already in prison for other sex offences, died behind bars in 2008 before he could be made to answer for Christopher's killing, but the authorities were satisfied that the culprit had finally been found.

26 million ... pounds in a heist that led to a murderous curse

Robbery and murder have always gone hand in hand. Yet some of the biggest and most infamous heists of all time have been executed without loss of life at the scene. The Great Train Robbery of 1963, in which £2.6 million was taken from a mail service in Buckinghamshire, resulted in no deaths, although locomotive driver Jack Mills was left badly injured. The Securitas depot robbery, which took place in Kent in 2006, was the largest cash robbery in British history and saw the perpetrators make off with £53 million. Several people were abducted and threatened; others were tied up, but thankfully no one died. What became known as the Brink's Mat Robbery in 1983 certainly involved some violence, but again there were no immediate fatalities, and those responsible made off with £26 million of gold bullion in what was labelled 'the crime of the century'. For many of those linked to the raid, however, there would not be a happy ending. In fact, thanks to a trail of bloodshed over the following years, talk grew of a 'Brink's Mat curse'.

It was at 6.30 a.m. on 26 November 1983 that six men wearing balaclavas arrived at a trading estate near London's Heathrow Airport and gained access to the Brink's Mat warehouse, thanks to insider knowledge from security guard Anthony Black, who purposely 'overslept' that day. The robbers were aiming to steal £3 million in cash that they knew was being kept on the premises.

Led by Brian Robinson and Mickey McAvoy, the gang poured petrol on some of the other guards and threatened to burn them alive if they didn't reveal the combination numbers to the vaults where the money was kept. Once opened, the robbers were astonished to find that, along with the cash, they contained nearly 6,800 gleaming gold bars, not to mention £100,000 worth of diamonds. It took the gang two hours to load the van, before making their getaway with the vehicle groaning under the weight of 3 tonnes of loot.

The gang soon realised that they did not have the expertise to turn the gold into ready cash, and a huge criminal network become embroiled in laundering the proceeds. Much of the gold would end up smelted down and as much as 70 per cent would never be traced.

Police soon identified that Black was the mole, as his sister had been living with Robinson, and once arrested he gave up the gang's ringleaders. Black would be given six years in jail for his part in the heist, with Robinson and McAvoy receiving sentences of twenty-five years.

Kenneth Noye, who had been brought in to help smelt the gold, was placed under police surveillance. In 1985 he stabbed DC John Fordham eleven times when he found him in his garden – the first gruesome killing that would be associated with the heist. Incredibly, Noye was acquitted on the grounds of self-defence, but a few months later he was found guilty of handling the Brink's Mat gold when some of the original bars were found at his home. He went to prison for seven years, but would end up back inside, serving life, after murdering a motorist in 1996.

Many of the other Brink's Mat robbers and conspirators would continue to evade justice, yet the sheer amount of money and number of individuals involved would lead to a web of suspicion and revenge among them that would see the criminal fraternity exacting their own forms of retribution.

Jeweller Solly Nahome, alleged to have fenced some of the gold, was gunned down on the doorstep of his north London home in 1998. Taxi firm boss Brian Perry did go to jail for handling some of it in 1992. But amid rumours of missing millions, he was shot dead outside his office in 2001, receiving three bullets in the back of the head. In 2003 George Francis, also thought to have been involved in laundering the Brink's Mat haul, was shot as he leaned into a car in south London. And, in 2015, John 'Goldfinger' Palmer, who had been sensationally acquitted of laundering some of the gold in 1987, was shot in the chest at his home in Essex, in what police described as a 'professional hit'.

In all, more than twenty people connected to the heist went to an early grave. Ironically, one of the earliest to perish was Charlie Wilson, who had formerly been convicted for his role as the 'treasurer' in the Great Train Robbery. After being released from prison, Wilson had gone to live in Spain and it was there that he was shot, apparently over £3 million of the Brink's Mat money that had gone missing in a drugs deal.

73 million... to 1 – the flawed statistic that convicted Sally Clark of double murder

'There are three kinds of lies: lies, damned lies, and statistics,' said the author Mark Twain. The statement was never more apt than in the history of criminal prosecutions for murder. While mathematical probabilities have proved useful in helping to highlight the probable guilt of killers, the limitations and misuse of such figures as evidence have also led to some shocking miscarriages of justice.

An early example that showed the danger of relying religiously on statistical analysis in criminology followed the introduction of the anthropometric system invented by French policeman Alphonse Bertillon. Himself the son of a statistician, Bertillon began working on his system in 1879. Bertillon's idea was to devise an identification system that relied on more than the logging of names or photographs. Based on research that showed no two human bodies were likely to be identical, he devised a new system involving the recording of different body measurements. As well as height he included such elements as the length of ears, feet and fingers in his basic set of eleven measurements that should be recorded. He estimated that the probability of two persons having an identical set was more than 4 million to 1.

Bertillon's system was soon taken up in France and the United States, with suspects and inmates measured according to his rules. 'Bertillonage', as it was known, soon proved its worth, helping to catch a string of repeat offenders. However, it wasn't as foolproof as Bertillon had imagined. In 1901 Will West was sent to prison in Leavenworth, Kansas, to serve a life sentence for murder. Two years later another man called Will West arrived at the same prison convicted of a different crime. When his measurements were taken by officials at the jail, they were found to be identical to those of the first Will West. The two were not related, but photographs showed that they bore an uncanny resemblance. It brought into question Bertillon's original calculations and also showed that, even if there was a small probability of a match occurring, that didn't mean that there was no chance, potentially leading to errors that could cost a person their liberty or life. At the very least, better odds were needed. When the fingerprints of both Wests were taken, they were found to be different and it was this more reliable science that spelled the end of Bertillon's system.

When experts testify in court that something has an extremely high or low probability of occurring, a jury is likely to take this evidence at face value. The figures can often be startling and help sway the verdict. Yet it's vital, especially when a charge of murder is levelled, that the mathematical reasoning behind these assertions is correct. Sadly this hasn't always been so, as in the case of Sally Clark. She was a 35-year-old solicitor, convicted in 1999 of killing her two babies by smothering and shaking them. They had died, suddenly, in separate incidents, but Clark maintained that she had not been to blame. At the trial, the issue of whether the children could have both been the victims of sudden infant death syndrome was central. Professor Sir Roy Meadow testified that the chances of a middle-class, non-smoking family like the Clarks suffering one cot death was 1 in 8,543. The probability of two occurring in the same family was roughly 1 in 73 million. It was similar, he asserted, to the chances of backing an 80 to 1 horse in the Grand National four years in a row and winning on each occasion.

It was persuasive testimony but Meadow's numbers were wrong. In October 2001, with Clark serving life in prison for murder, the Royal Statistical Society issued a statement in which it demolished Meadow's calculations. First, it pointed out, Meadow had not taken into account medical considerations that meant some families might be more predisposed to suffer cot deaths. Nor was the court given the separate probability of a double infant murder occurring, in such a family, for comparison. This was also a highly unlikely event. It was later pointed out that Meadow had failed to take into account other factors, such as the fact that both Clark's babies were boys, which increased the chances of cot death. The real probability of Clark being to blame must be much lower than the jury had been led to believe.

In 2003, thanks to the emergence of supressed medical evidence that indicated death by natural causes, as well as concerns about the veracity of Meadow's statistics, Sally Clark was released from prison. The stress had, however, taken a toll on her health and she died in 2007.

262 million... murdered by their own governments

It has been estimated that up to 1 billion people in the whole history of humanity have been killed in wars or armed conflict. Of course, war is killing with intent that is legally sanctioned and not, technically, murder. The *Oxford Dictionary* defines murder as 'the unlawful and deliberate killing of one person by another', but many would argue that the line has often become blurred, especially where the deaths of civilians are concerned.

As we have seen in this book, incidents of mass murder can sometimes be carried out by individuals, potentially with scores of victims. Terrorist organisations also kill on a grand scale. In 2014 a total of 32,658 people fell victim to terrorist attacks, one of the highest totals so far recorded by the Global Terrorism Index. The numbers involved in mass murder by governments, however, can be even more eye watering.

The term 'genocide' was first coined in 1944 by Raphael Lemkin, a lawyer of Jewish–Polish descent, who combined the Greek word *genos*, meaning 'race or tribe', with the Latin word *cide*, meaning 'to kill'. Lemkin was responding to the murderous policies being pursued by the Nazis across Europe. The Holocaust saw an estimated 6 million Jews exterminated by the regime during the 1940s. The killing was on an industrial scale, with many victims perishing in concentration camps and specially built gas chambers. Lemkin himself would lose forty-nine relatives in the course of the Holocaust. In total, some 15 million civilians may have been specifically targeted and murdered by the Nazis, including groups such as the Romany and the Slavs as well as the mentally and physically disabled. A total of sixteen leading Nazis would be found guilty of 'crimes against humanity' at their trials in Nuremberg following the end of the Second World War.

In 1948 the United Nations would go on to define genocide as 'acts committed with intent to destroy, in whole or in part, a national, ethnic, racial or religious group', though there would be much debate about which episodes of mass killing could be classed as genocide under this somewhat narrow definition.

Beyond the Holocaust, one of the most horrific examples of mass murder which many commentators have branded genocide is the killing of 1.5 million Armenians by Ottoman Turks between 1915 and 1920. While the Turkish government has long refused to accept the term 'genocide' to describe these events, there's little doubt that Turkey's former rulers connived to systematically massacre the country's own citizens.

In Cambodia, 2 million people are thought to have died through execution, disease or starvation thanks to the terror meted out by Pol Pot's vicious Khmer Rouge between 1975 and 1979. This passage of violence has also been called genocide.

The killing of 800,000 Tutsis and moderate Hutus in 1994 in Rwanda was undoubtedly genocide, and a number of people have since been convicted for their part in the horrors perpetrated in the African nation.

Belsen concentration camp victims. (Courtesy of Wellcome Library, London)

In Bosnia, the 1995 massacre of more than 7,000 Bosnian Muslim men and boys at the town of Srebrenica was ruled to be genocide by the International Criminal Tribunal for the former Yugoslavia. In March 2016, Radovan Karadžic was found guilty of genocide and other crimes against humanity and sentenced to forty years' imprisonment for his role in the episode.

One estimate is that more than 50 million people have been the victims of genocide in forty-three separate incidents since 1956. However, in recent years another term, 'democide', has been used to encompass other examples of mass murder by states that have not hitherto been seen to fall into the genocide category. Democide has been defined by the political scientist R.J. Rummel as the 'murder of any person or people by a government including genocide, politicide and mass murder'. This would cover those who died in Great Purges in the Soviet Union in the 1930s, and from famine during the 1950s and 1960s in China at the hands of the Communist regime. For the years 1900–99, Rummel calculated a total of 262 million victims from democide, reckoning that this was six times the number that died in combat during the same period. This concept, and the staggering statistics that go with it, certainly gives a different and alarming perspective to what we think of as the crime of murder.

1 billion... to 1 chance in the Stephen Lawrence murder

Fingerprinting, comparison microscopes, toxicology tests, ballistics, examination of blood samples and spatter, hair and teeth, and even the work of maggots on a corpse – developments in all these areas have transformed the ability of criminal investigators to identify murder suspects and make a case against them. Police have also utilised other advances in technology to help them in cases of homicide, whether it's analysing data from mobile phone records, computer files or CCTV cameras. But in the last half-century it is advances in DNA technology (see page 167) and its application to forensics that has undoubtedly provided the biggest leap forward when it comes to catching killers.

Forensic scientists can now identify DNA samples from hair, bone, skin and tissue, blood and other body fluids, while new techniques can amplify them and provide the ability to retrieve vital information from those who may have lain dormant for decades.

Gary Ridgway was one of the most prolific serial killers in the United States, murdering at least forty-eight women and girls in the 1980s and 1990s, and dumping many of his strangled victims in the Green River, near Seattle, Washington. Ridgway became a suspect as early as 1987 when a saliva sample was taken from him. However, the semen samples left on the victims were too small to make a DNA match at the time and he remained free.

In 2001, thanks to the advent of polymerase chain reaction (PCR) testing, scientists were able to replicate the old samples, making them easier to analyse. This time they were able to make a DNA match with Ridgway. He pleaded guilty and was sentenced to life without parole, later admitting, 'What got me caught was technology.'

Of course, DNA evidence is not foolproof and samples can be contaminated, but it has become some of the most trusted evidence that can be presented in court and its reliability has led to convictions in some of the most high-profile and contentious of murder cases.

Take, for instance, the case of Roy Whiting, convicted of murdering 8-year-old Sarah Payne. Whiting, a known paedophile, was a chief suspect in the case, and his alibi for the time of Sarah's disappearance from a country lane in West Sussex on 1 July 2000 was found to be false. Initially there was little evidence to connect him to the murdered girl, whose body was found on 17 July. But when one of her shoes was also recovered, 350 fibres were discovered on the Velcro fastening. Five of them were found to have come from Whiting's van. Most damning was a single 9in-long blonde hair found on a sweatshirt seized from the vehicle. Forensic experts were able to extract a full DNA profile from it and announce in court that the chances of it not being Sarah's were 'in the order of 1 billion to 1'. The 42-year-old received a life sentence.

The murder of Stephen Lawrence was probably the most infamous case of racial killing ever committed in Britain. The facts of the murder were straightforward. On the evening of 22 April 1993, a gang of youths stabbed the 18-year-old to death as he waited at a bus stop in Eltham, south-east London. Five suspects were soon identified; however, the badly flawed police investigation would be anything but routine and, despite court proceedings, no convictions could be made due to a lack of sufficient evidence.

In 2005 the double jeopardy law was repealed, which meant people could be tried again for the same offence if it could be shown that there was new evidence. Following this, a cold case review of the Lawrence murder was undertaken. All the forensic evidence was reviewed. This time a 0.5 x 0.25mm speck of blood was found on a grey bomber jacket belonging to Gary Dobson, one of the original suspects who had been acquitted in 1996. The DNA proved to be a match for Stephen's. Dobson was re-tried in 2011 and, again, the jury heard the same statistic as the one in the Whiting case – the forensic expert gave his opinion that there was a 'billion-to-1' chance that the blood on the jacket was not Stephen's. The stain had been fresh when it was made, placing Dobson at the scene. Hair strands matching Stephen's DNA and fibres from the victim's clothes were linked to the jeans and sweatshirt of another suspect, David Norris. Dobson, then 36, and Norris, 35, were convicted of Stephen Lawrence's murder in January 2012, bringing a measure of justice for his family at long last.

Just as DNA evidence now routinely solves criminal cases, future developments in forensic science, such as virtual autopsies and 3D imaging, are destined to provide even more tools for those investigating homicide, ensuring that it becomes even harder to commit a murder and get away with it.

SELECT BIBLIOGRAPHY

Bardens, Dennis, *The Ladykiller: The Crimes of Landru, the French Bluebeard* (Peter Davies Ltd, 1972)

Begg, Paul, Fido, Martin, and Skinner, Keith, *The Jack the Ripper A–Z* (Headline, 1992)

Brandon, Craig, *The Electric Chair: An Unnatural American History* (McFarland & Co., 2009)

Brook, Timothy, *Death by a Thousand Cuts* (Harvard University Press, 2008)

Brunelle, Gayle K., and Finley-Croswhite, Annette, *Murder in the Metro* (Louisiana State University Press, 2012)

Buckingham, John, *Bitter Nemesis* (CRC Press, 2007)

Cleckley, Hervey, *The Mask of Sanity* (Martino Fine Books, 2015)

Colquhoun, Kate, *Mr Briggs' Hat: A Sensational Account of Britain's First Railway Murder* (Abacus, 2012)

Colquhoun, Kate, *Did She Kill Him? A Victorian Tale of Deception, Adultery, and Arsenic* (Little, Brown, 2014)

Dash, Mike, *Thug: The True Story of India's Murderous Cult* (Granta, 2006)

D'Enno, Douglas, *Foul Deeds and Suspicious Deaths around Brighton* (Wharncliffe, 2003)

Donkin, Andrew, *Dead Giveaways* (Element, 1998)

Donnelley, Paul, *Essex Murders* (Wharncliffe Books, 2007)

Durston, Gregory J., *Fields, Fens and Felonies* (Waterside Press, 2017)

Emsley, John, *The Elements of Murder: A History of Poison* (Oxford University Press, 2006)

Emsley, John, *Molecules of Murder* (Royal Society of Chemistry, 2008)

Erzinclioglu, Zakariah, *Illustrated Guide to Forensics: True Crime Scene Investigations* (Carlton, 2004)

Evans, Colin, *The Casebook of Forensic Detection* (John Wiley & Sons, 1998)

Evans, Colin, *Murder Two: The Second Casebook of Forensic Detection* (John Wiley & Sons, 2004)

Fabian, Robert, *Fabian of the Yard* (Naldrett Press, 1950)

Fulton, Laura, *The Crimes that Shocked Britain* (New Holland, 2016)

SELECT BIBLIOGRAPHY

Gannon, John, *The Killing of Julia Wallace: Liverpool's Most Enigmatic and Brutal Murder* (Amberley, 2012)

Gristwood, Sarah, *Elizabeth and Leicester* (Bantam, 2007)

Guy, John, *Thomas Becket* (Viking, 2012)

Harding, Luke, *A Very Expensive Poison* (Guardian Faber, 2016)

Harkup, Kathryn, *A is for Arsenic: The Poisons of Agatha Christie* (Bloomsbury Sigma, 2015)

Harrison, Fred, *Brady and Hindley: Genesis of the Moors Murders* (Grafton, 1987)

Hickey, Eric W., *Encyclopedia of Murder and Violent Crime* (Sage, 2003)

Hostettler, John, *Famous Cases: Nine Trials that Changed the Law* (Waterside Press, 2012)

Houck, Max, and Seigel, Jay, *Fundamentals of Forensic Science* (Academic Press, 2010)

Innes, Brian, *Bodies of Evidence* (Amber, 2012)

Jones, Nigel, *Tower* (Windmill Books, 2012)

Kellermann, Arthur L., and Mercy, James, 'Men, Women and Murder' (*Journal of Trauma-Injury Infection and Critical Care*, July 1992)

Kershaw, Ian, *Hitler* (Penguin, 2009)

King, David, *Death in the City of Life* (Sphere, 2012)

Lee, Carol Ann, *One of Your Own: The Life and Death of Myra Hindley* (Mainstream, 2011)

Lee, Carol Ann, *A Fine Day for a Hanging: The Real Ruth Ellis Story* (Mainstream, 2013)

Liston, Robert, *Great Detectives* (Platt & Munk, 1966)

Lyle, D.P., *Forensics: A Guide for Writers* (Writer's Digest Books, 2008)

McLynn, Frank, *Famous Trials: Cases that Made History* (Crux, 2016)

McCrery, Nigel, *Silent Witnesses: The Story of Forensic Science* (Arrow, 2014)

McDermid, V., *Forensics: The Anatomy of Crime* (Profile, 2015)

McLaren, Angus, *A Prescription for Murder* (University of Chicago Press, 1995)

Marks, Vincent, *Insulin Murders* (Royal Society of Medicine Press, 2007)

Milner, E.R., *The Lives and Times of Bonnie and Clyde* (Southern Illinois University Press, 2003)

Morris, Jim, *The Who's Who of British Crime* (Amberley, 2015)

Morson, Maurice, *Norwich Murders* (Wharncliffe, 2006)

Murphy, Paul Thomas, *Shooting Victoria* (Pegasus, 2013)

Murray, Raymond C., and Tedrow, John C.F., *Forensic Geology* (Prentice Hall, 1992)

Nash, Jay Robert, *Nash's Crime Chronology: A Worldwide Record, 1900–1983* (Facts on File, 1984)

O'Connor, Sean, *Handsome Brute: The True Story of a Ladykiller* (Simon & Schuster, 2014)

Odell, Robin, *Medical Detectives* (The History Press, 2015)

Oleson, James C., *Criminal Genius: A Portrait of High-IQ Offenders* (University of California Press, 2016)

Parascandola, John, *King of Poisons: A History of Arsenic* (Potomac Books, 2012)

Petrocelli, Daniel, and Knobler, Peter, *Triumph of Justice: Closing the Book on the O.J. Simpson Saga* (Graymalkin Media, 2016)

Pierrepoint, Albert, *Executioner: Pierrepoint* (Harrap, 1974)

Pratt, Fletcher, *Detective No. 1: Case Histories of Ellis Parker, American Detective* (Methuen, 1936)

Preest, David (translator), *The Chronicle of Geoffrey le Baker* (Boydell & Brewer, 2012)

Putkowski, Julian, and Dunning, Mark, *Murderous Tommies* (Pen & Sword Military, 2012)

Putkowski, Julian, and Sykes, Julian, *Shot at Dawn* (Pen & Sword, 1998)

Ranson, Roy, *Looking for Lucan: The Final Verdict* (Smith Gryphon, 1994)

Robins, Jane, *The Magnificent Spilsbury and the Case of the Brides in the Bath* (John Murray, 2011)

Root, Neil, *Frenzy! Heath, Haigh and Christie* (Arrow, 2011)

Rumbelow, Donald, *Complete Jack the Ripper* (Virgin, 2013)

Rummel, Rudolph J., *Democide: Nazi Genocide and Mass Murder* (Transaction, 1991)

Russell-Pavier, Nick, *The Shepherd's Bush Murders* (Century, 2016)

Schneider, Paul, *Bonnie and Clyde* (St Martin's Griffin, 2010)

Simpson, Keith, *Forty Years of Murder* (Harper Collins, 2008)

Skidmore, Chris, *Death and the Virgin* (Weidenfeld & Nicolson, 2011)

Smith, Douglas, *Rasputin* (Macmillan, 2016)

Song, Ci, and McKnight, Brian E., *The Washing Away of Wrongs* (University of Michigan, 1981)

Strauss, Barry, *The Death of Caesar: The Story of History's Most Famous Assassination* (Simon & Schuster, 2015)

Vale, Allison, *The Woman Who Murdered Babies for Money: The Story of Amelia Dyer* (André Deutsch, 2011)

Vronsky, Peter, *Serial Killers: The Method and Madness of Monsters* (Berkley, 2004)

Warner, Kathryn, *Edward II* (Amberley, 2015)

Watson, Katherine D., *Poisoned Lives: English Poisoners and Their Victims* (Hambledon Continuum, 2006)

Whittle, Brian, *Harold Shipman: Prescription for Murder* (Time Warner, 2005)

Wileman, Julie, *Past Crimes* (Pen & Sword, 2015)

Wilkes, Roger, *The Mammoth Book of CSI* (Robinson, 2007)

Wilson, Colin, *A Criminal History of Mankind* (Mercury, 2006)

INDEX

MURDER BY NUMBERS

The History Press

The destination for history
www.thehistorypress.co.uk